The Naked Roommate:

Sixth Edition

And 107 Other Issues You Might Run Into in College

Harlan Cohen

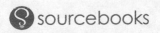

Published by Sourcebooks, Inc.
P.O. Box 4410, Naperville, Illinois 60567-4410
(630) 961-3900
Fax: (630) 961-2168
www.sourcebooks.com

Library of Congress Cataloging-in-Publication Data is on file with the publisher.

Printed and bound in the United States of America.
VP 10 9 8 7 6 5 4 3 2 1

Other Books By Harlan Cohen:

- *The Naked Roommate: For Parents Only*

- *The Naked Roommate's First Year Survival Workbook*

- *Getting Naked: Five Steps to Finding the Love of Your Life (While Fully Clothed and Totally Sober)*

- *Dad's Expecting Too!*

Follow Harlan on Twitter: @HarlanCohen

Follow Harlan on Facebook: /HelpMeHarlan

Follow Harlan on Instagram: HarlanCohen

For Stephanie,
my higher education in love and in life

Acknowledgments

To my wife, Stephanie (my lifelong naked roommate), thank you again for all of your love and support throughout this entire process—pieces, pieces. To Eva Kaye, Harrison, and Asher, the best roommates in the world! To my parents, Eugene and Shirlee—thank you for opening the door to college life and always offering all the opportunities and love a child could ever want or need. Thank you to my brothers, Victor and Michael, and my sister-in-law, Irene, for loving me, guiding me, and always being there for me (and to Phoebe and Rae, too). Thank you to Marvin, Francine, Daniel, Rozi, Ethan, and Hannah for all of your love and support.

Thank you to my agent, Eliot Ephraim, for your endless commitment and continued support on this amazing journey. Thank you to my original Naked editor, Peter Lynch, and the entire team at Sourcebooks for pouring so much passion, wit, and wisdom into this project. Thank you to my newest brilliant Naked editor, Michelle Lecuyer. A special thank-you to Pete Vanaria, Becca Sage, and Chris Norton. Thank you to Glenn Mott and the entire team at King Features Syndicate for helping to make Help Mc, Harlan! one of the most well-read advice columns in the country. A special thank-you to all the newspaper editors that run Help Me, Harlan! and to all those people who read it and write to me with questions, comments, and suggestions (even the ones who write about my ears).

A heartfelt thank-you goes out to all the students, professionals, and contributors who offered information for this book! Thank you for being so open, honest, and candid about your lives. Your stories will impact millions of students. I couldn't write without you. Thank you to all the high schools, colleges, organizations, and associations that have hosted my speaking events over the years and enabled me to conduct such detailed research.

A special note of gratitude is extended to Cynthia Jenkins, the BACCHUS Network, Linda Sax, John Pryor, and the Higher Education Research Institute at UCLA, the *Indiana Daily Student*, Michael Evans and the Indiana University School of Journalism, NSSE, the Associated Collegiate Press, the National Orientation Directors Association, the NACA, NASPA, ACPA, ACUHO-I, AFA, ACHA-NCHA Alpha Epsilon Pi fraternity, Krishnan Anantharaman, Larry Rout, the *Wall Street Journal Classroom Edition*, and all the people who have been in my corner during this journey over the years. I can't thank you enough for all of your kindness and support.

A special word of thanks is extended to Dr. David Adams and his family—Dave, your memory and legacy are ever-present in the lives of students you've mentored and in the lives of all those we touch. Thank you for everything.

Contents

Chapter 3
Roommates: Good Ones, Bad Ones, and
Everything in Between

Chapter 4
Finding Friends:
Your Social or Antisocial College Life

Chapter 5
Getting Involved on Campus:
An All-You-Can-Do Buffet......................143

Chapter 6:
Greek Life: Behind the Doors, Windows, and Walls of
Fraternity and Sorority Life 169

Chapter 7
Life Inside the Classroom:
Assuming You Wake Up and Go to Class 191

Chapter 8
Dating and Relationships: Your Higher
Education in Lust, Love, and Loss 247

Chapter 9
Sex: Having It, Not Having It, Hearing
Other People Having It

Chapter 10
Drinking on Campus: Tapping the Keg of Truth

Chapter 11
Drugs on Campus: The Smoking, Snorting,
and Pill-Popping Truth 379

Chapter 12
Money, Laundry, and Cheap Eats: Assuming You
Have Enough Money to Eat and Do Laundry 409

Chapter 13
Things Not Mentioned in the College Brochure:
What They Don't Tell You 447

Chapter 14
College: A Higher Education:
It's Almost Time to Say Good-bye. 503

Book Orientation

The Stuff before the Tips

Welcome Students

Welcome to the sixth edition of *The Naked Roommate*. Yes, this is the sixth edition (not a typo, the typos come later in the book). This is the very best edition ever as opposed to the worst edition ever. Welcome to page one. I'm Harlan. I'll be your Naked author and host throughout this book. I've included a picture of myself on the back of the book (fully clothed) so you can see what I look like. And yes, I've actually been wearing that same outfit while writing this entire book (but I have gained about five pounds). As your host and author, I'd like to offer you something to eat or drink (nonalcoholic), but I don't know where to find you or if you can eat or drink where you are. If you're reading this at a place where they're serving food or drinks, please get yourself something. I can't pay for it, but if I were there, I would. I just want to make sure that you're comfortable. So please, slip off your shoes, unbutton the top button on your pants if they're snug, find a comfortable place to sit if you're standing. Do whatever it takes for you to get comfortable, as long as what you need to do to get comfortable isn't prohibited by any indecency laws. If getting comfortable means breaking the law, take this book home with you. I'm not trying to get you to buy it (well, maybe I am a little), but what is more important than your owning this book is that you are as comfortable as possible while reading it. Because when it comes down to it, that's what this whole book is all about—and it's really what the college experience is about. It's about helping you to get comfortable for what can be an uncomfortable (at times) journey ahead. Now, I'll give you a break to get comfortable. And please, feel free to browse through the book after you settle in.

— A Break in the Book —

Welcome Back

Hi, Harlan here again, your author and host. From browsing through this book, you are probably expecting a lot of tips. When it comes to "tips," there are many different kinds in the world. There are good tips, bad tips, informative tips, tips that touch the surface, tips that give you something to think about, tips you leave on a table after eating at a restaurant, rib tips, fingertips, tiptoes, and various other miscellaneous tips. This is a tip book unlike any other tip book. It's a book that goes far beyond the tip and leaves you with something to think about, and when applicable, even offers you places to go for help on and off campus. I'd like to go so far as to say that this is the best tip book in the history of tip books. (Minus the 1762 classic, *Ten Tips for Settlers to the New Country*. I do love that book.)

This might come to you as a surprise, but I wasn't a fan of "tip books"—that is, until I wrote this book. I don't just like this one because I wrote it (although that is part of the reason). It's because this book is genuinely different. It's based on what today's college students are honestly thinking, feeling, and doing on today's college campuses. It's their voices sharing their stories and experiences that will expose the uncensored truth about what's really going on in college. Not only will you get page after page of telling tips from students on over one hundred college campuses across North America, you'll also get the latest facts, stats, resources, support services having to do with college life, and some advice from me—someone who has been a freshman twice, has visited over four hundred college campuses, and has interviewed over a thousand students.

About the student-offered tips—one thing that I've discovered while writing my syndicated Help Me, Harlan! advice column and interviewing students over the years is that it's the rest of the story, the story of how someone came up with his or her tip or advice, that is the most telling. And that's exactly what you'll find here—the tips and the stories behind them. That's just not something you see all the time.

Speaking of time, I appreciate yours. I promise not to waste it. This book will be helpful. At the very least, it can always be used as a doorstop, a coaster, or a way to level out a shaky table. The actual information written on the pages of your new doorstop/coaster/level will also prove helpful. Whether you're commuting to a college down the street or living on a campus across the country, this book has something for you. Whether you're headed to college as the star of your high school or you're one of those students who blended into the cement block walls in the back of your classroom, this book has something for you. And that includes all those people who fall somewhere in between blending into the cement blocks and being a star. Whether you're attending a two-year school, a four-year school, or a virtual school, *The Naked Roommate* is written with you in mind. Whether you're the first person in your family going to college or the last, this book is for you. Whether you're from the United States, Canada, Spain, Australia, Austria, India, China, or a country I haven't mentioned, this book is for you too.

(P.S. If you are a commuter, a community college student, a first-generation student, a Canadian student, an international student, or a nontraditional student, head to www.NakedRoommate.com for special notes written just for you. While the tips in this book are relevant for all students, you may have unique circumstances or challenges to deal with, so I want to make sure you feel welcome too.)

The Naked Roommate is the book that I only wish someone had written for me when I went to college. I'm so happy that you finally have it in your hands. I hope you will keep this close to you through your college career. You might not need everything on the pages to follow today, but you'll use different parts of the book during different times throughout your college career. When you do need it, it's here. I know it will help.

Please note—you probably won't encounter every single issue and obstacle discussed in this book (and if you do, you should write your own book). That said, you will encounter many of them, if not in your own life, then in the lives of your friends. When that happens, you can share this book or get them their own copies. One thing I should mention before continuing: I promised many of the college students who offered advice for this book not to just talk about the bad parts of college; they didn't want this book to scare you, because the truth is that most of life in college is great. It's just once in a while it's not great. And that's what this book is here for. To help make it great even in the not so great times. And with that, I've fulfilled my promise.

As you read this book and live out your own college experience, please send in your thoughts, tips, and stories. Make sure to check out www.NakedRoommate.com (the world's nicest community for students) to connect with other college students and share your experiences. You can also find me at www.HarlanCohen.com. Then there's Facebook: www.Facebook.com/NakedRoommate and www.Facebook.com/HelpMeHarlan. Oh, and there's also Instagram (@HarlanCohen) and Twitter (I tweet, do you tweet?): @NakedRoommate and @HarlanCohen.

As your author and host, please let me know if there is ever anything I can do to help you along your college journey. I know you have a choice when it comes to books about college life, and I appreciate your choosing this one. Thank you.

My Reason for Writing This Book

I never thought college would be like this. No one ever told me. I expected it to be how it looked on the websites and in the brochures. I have two older brothers, and both went to college (one is five years older, the other eight years older). They were jealous of me when it was my turn to go. They graduated and wanted to go back. I went to a big high school and an even bigger university (University of Wisconsin–Madison, 30,000+). I expected everything in college to just fall into place. But instead, I only felt out of place.

While life in high school did a great job of preparing me to handle the academic transition, once I arrived on campus, I was socially and emotionally lost. There was so much I didn't know. So much no one told me. My roommate wasn't my best friend, I didn't get into the fraternity I wanted, and my long-distance girlfriend dumped me (her father compared our relationship to a dying puppy, urging her to shoot the puppy). It took almost two semesters and transferring from UW–Madison to Indiana University in Bloomington, Indiana, to figure it all out. What I discovered is that life in college can be uncomfortable at times. College is a huge transition. And transitions are naturally uncomfortable at times. Fighting uncomfortable just creates more discomfort. But facing it and working through is how we get comfortable with the uncomfortable. Working through it means finding PEOPLE, PLACES, and PATIENCE. It's asking yourself the questions, "Who are my five people? Where are my three places? How patient am I willing to be to get there?" This book is filled with people, places, and the true story about life in college that will help you find the patience to get wherever you want to go. It's the book I wish someone had written for me.

This book is about everything no one ever tells you about life in college, and the things that will make college easier and more manageable. If you come to college understanding and appreciating what it takes to get comfortable with the uncomfortable, when the uncomfortable pops up (and it will), it won't be so hard to handle. You won't hate. You won't hide. You'll look inward, look outward, and move forward with confidence. While we are all unique, our problems are universal. They connect us. I hope this book will help you create the best college experience inside and outside the classroom. I look forward to hearing your tips and stories for future editions of the book! Send them to Harlan@helpmeharlan.com, subject: Seventh Edition.

How This Book Was Written

The Naked Roommate was compiled while visiting over four hundred college campuses, interviewing countless college professionals, and participating in conventions and conferences. Like previous editions, this updated edition combines the voices of students and college professionals with the latest trends, facts, and stats. Also included are resources, support services, recent data, the latest government information, hotlines, websites, and places for students to find answers to their questions.

The tips and stories behind the tips were compiled during face-to-face and phone interviews, via written request forms, and collected through my websites (www.HelpMeHarlan.com and www.NakedRoommate.com), and via email, Facebook, and professional organizations that requested students forward their stories and tips. Some of the quotations cited in *The Naked Roommate* were excerpted from articles I've written for the *Wall Street Journal Classroom Edition*.

The latest facts, figures, and information were provided by the Higher Education Research Institute at UCLA using the CIRP Freshman Survey and Your First College Year data (2003, 2005, 2006, 2007, 2008, 2009, 2011, 2012, 2013, and 2014), the National Survey of Student Engagement (NSSE) (2006, 2007, 2008, 2009, 2011, 2012, 2013, and 2014), the BACCHUS Network, the ACHA/NCHA II survey (2008, 2009, 2010, 2012, 2013, and 2014), and various U.S. government websites. I also contacted the offices of the National Orientation Directors Association, the National Resource Center for the First-Year Experience, the National Association of College and University Residence Halls, the National Panhellenic Conference, the North American Interfraternity Conference, and member schools of the National Association of College activities while gathering materials for this book project.

My goal continues to be to create the most complete and fact-based look at college life ever presented. I'd like to think of *The Naked Roommate* as an encyclopedia of what may or may not happen to students in college. It's a tool to help ease students' anxiety while helping them take the necessary steps to find their places on campus and create a world of options.

Please keep in mind: the tips on the following pages are in no way a fair and accurate representation of the entire student population at each institution or of the institutions themselves. Due to the sensitive nature of some tips, and to protect free-flowing information from students, proper names could not be used. If a student had strong concerns, his or her year in school was changed (but not the name of the school). The tips and the stories behind them are not direct quotes but are as accurate as possible.

The Sixth Edition: Toned, Leaner, and Fitter

If you're reading this book (and you must be, unless someone is reading it to you), then you are reading the most updated version of this book. Think of *The Naked Roommate* getting a six pack (of abs, not beer). In this latest edition you'll find updated stats and facts, some new websites, Facebook links, Twitter feeds, and more voices from more students.

You'll also notice bonus content. I've added new info about sexual consent, depression, bystander intervention, sexual health, online safety, transition, roommate advice, and additional tips and stories from students. Online, I've been doing a tremendous amount of work to support students. Please visit and become a "Naked" member of www .NakedRoommate.com.

Additional Resources

The Naked Roommate has proven so helpful over the years that it's now being used as required reading, as a textbook, and as a training guide for student leaders on campus. In addition, there's a *Naked Roommate's First Year Survival Workbook* and an online instructor's guide to go along with the book. There's even a book for parents to help them support students throughout their college experience—*The Naked Roommate: For Parents Only*.

Check out my new Naked Roommate College Boot Camp for Students and Parents online courses. Visit www.NakedRoommateBootCamp.com for sample lessons. There's a track for students and a track for parents. Enter coupon code "NAKED6E" for a special discount just for readers of this book.

In addition to my books and online courses, visit www.NakedRoommate.com. Here you'll discover college news, blogs, the Naked Roommate forums (for students and parents), and advice from my Help Me, Harlan! syndicated advice column and speaking programs and tour. You can also find me on Facebook (www.Facebook.com/NakedRoommate) and Twitter (www.Twitter.com/NakedRoommate).

If you're interested in my events, keynotes, and workshops for students, parents, and professionals, visit www.HarlanCohen.com. You can read advice, ask me questions, and sign up for my newsletter. My continued goal is to help students get comfortable with the uncomfortable while providing resources, support services, and information that will help them to thrive during the transition to college life and beyond.

A Note to Parents

Hi, parents. This is Harlan. Welcome! Thank you for picking up this book and reading this note. It's a pleasure to meet you!

There's something no one has told you about college planning. There's search and selection, but there's a third part—it's the most crucial. It's called TRANSITION, and it's the time from when your child commits to a school to the end of the first year. It's emotional, high stakes, and intense. It's when a student thrives, survives, or struggles. It's what this book is about. The college transition consists of five parts: Social, Emotional, Physical, Financial, and Academic. *The Naked Roommate* will help your child navigate them all.

Twenty years ago, parents of a student living away from home were lucky to get a call from their kid once a week. Now, with the help of cell phones, texting, Twitter, Facebook, FaceTime, and Skyping, a student can communicate problems to parents when they happen in real time. Never before have parents been so connected to their children's college experiences moment by moment as they unfold. Many parents are literally pulled onto campus. This can be a good thing, but also a not-so-good thing.

First, the good. Being so connected means that you can offer more support than ever. Now the not-so-good: while you may be accessible, you may not always know how to respond. This book and *The Naked Roommate: For Parents Only* can be helpful resources. If you know what to expect and how to help your child navigate through it all—you can be the best resource. Once you know what's normal and natural, you can guide your children through the normal obstacles that are part of college life. When a problem arises, instead of wanting to fix it (which may only heighten it), you can step back, listen, and point your child in the right direction to get help. It's the difference between overpowering and empowering.

One suggestion to help you point your child in the right

direction: visit your son's or daughter's college website to see specific resources and support services on campus. When visiting campus, introduce yourself to the people who will help your child. Know the people and places online (and on campus) that are available so that you will be prepared to guide your child to them. My hope is that you pick up a copy of this book for your son or daughter and page through it yourself. Then pick up a copy of *The Naked Roommate: For Parents Only*. Keep it close by, and when a problem comes up, use it as a tool (or if a door needs to be held open, it's a great doorstop). Both these books can be your study guide/cheat sheet for college life.

Thank you for reading *The Naked Roommate*.

A Note to Educators

It's a pleasure to have you here! I wanted to take a moment to visit with you—specifically.

College planning is all about search and selection. But there's a third part and it's called transition. Now more than ever, incoming first-year students lack an understanding of transition. According to ACT, Inc., roughly one in four students doesn't return to the same campus for their sophomore year (the number is higher at many institutions). Less than two-thirds of students who start college will finish with a degree (percentages vary by type of college). Then there are the social and emotional challenges that throw students. This book is a tool to help students navigate the social, emotional, physical, financial, and academic transition.

In addition to the book, please check out my webinar on college planning and my newest online program for students and parents. My online resources, free mini-courses, and college boot camp for students and parents are all available to help you guide, support, and prepare your students for life in college.

Since the first edition of the book, *The Naked Roommate* has established itself as the #1 book on college life and is being used as a required text in college classrooms across the country and as a part of staff training and development. In addition to the book, there is now *The Naked Roommate's First Year Survival Workbook* and an online instructor's guide, both coauthored by Cynthia Jenkins, PhD, for use in college and high school classrooms. In fact, it's an entire Naked Roommate First Year Experience Program. The goal of this program is to provide a student-friendly program to help students make the social, emotional, physical, financial, and academic transition to life in college. The program is designed for students, residence life staff, campus leaders, peer educators, orientation staff, and any student or professional working with students in transition. It can be used in training as well as in the classroom. The workbook makes it easy to pull out relevant exercises and activities. The online instructor's guide takes the best of the book and workbook and makes it efficient and easy for instructors, professionals, and student leaders to use both resources.

A new resource to help in the classroom is The Naked Roommate College Boot Camp for Students and Parents. This new online course contains self-contained lessons to bring different aspects of the book to life. The program can be used as a guidance resource, summer program, or compliment to first year courses. Visit: www .NakedRoommateBootCamp.com for information.

One last note: if you're using the book, workbook, or online course in the classroom and want to connect with other instructors, feel free to send me an email and I will be more than happy to introduce you. There is a passionate and friendly community of "Naked" instructors who would love to share tips and ideas. It's wonderful to be a partner with you.

Thank you and enjoy the nakedness.

A Final Note to All Readers

The Naked Roommate is an ongoing experience. This is the sixth of what will be many editions of this book. Please send me your feedback, suggestions, and insight while reading through these tips and stories. If you have a story, advice, or a tip that could help other students, just send it my way. Send feedback and new tips via email to harlan@ helpmeharlan.com. Please include "Seventh Edition of Naked Roommate" in the subject line. Thank you.

WARNING!!!

THE TIPS ON THE FOLLOWING PAGES ARE IN NO WAY A FAIR OR COMPLETE REPRESENTATION OF THE ENTIRE STUDENT POPULATION AT EACH INSTITUTION OR OF THE INSTITUTIONS THEMSELVES

not even close to it

no way, not at all

that means no

no, no, no, no

seriously, no

again, no!

last time

no, no,

no

wow, you have really great vision if you can read this

First Page, First Tip, and First Days of College

Welcome to the first page, the first day of college, and my first tip.

There are a lot of firsts happening here—first time possibly away from home, first time possibly living with a stranger, first college class, first college professors, first college hookup, first love, first loss, first time possibly having sex (or not having it, or just hearing other people have it), maybe your first pregnancy scare, first sexually transmitted infection (also called sexually transmitted disease), first time seeing people use drugs, first time borrowing thousands of dollars and first time spending thousands of dollars, first time having to make choices on your own, first time staying out all night, first time having to make a new life for yourself, and the first time when you can do as much as you want or as little as you want and have no one to answer to but you (assuming you don't answer your phone).

Naturally, the first time you do something, it's normal to not be completely comfortable doing it. Comfort takes time. So understand that it will take time to find your comfortable places in college. Be who you are, not who people want you to be (or who you think people want you to be). Focus on what you want, not on being wanted. Work to find what you love to do inside and outside the classroom. Create a world filled with options—socially, academically, and spiritually. Don't wait for people to give you your college experience. Create it. Make it happen. And along the way, appreciate that no matter what happens, no matter what you're feeling, no matter what obstacles you encounter—you are never alone. You are surrounded by people who can listen, support, and guide you. As someone who has lived it, seen it, and heard about it in my advice column and from students on college campuses around the world, I can tell you: it's a fact. You are never alone in college.

As one resident director and recent graduate said to me, "They always say that college students deal with the same issues, but until I was a resident director, I never realized it was true. So many people are going through the same things, but don't know it." Each day is unpredictable. You never know what's going to come your way. That's part of the wild ride. In the words of an advisor I interviewed, "In college, you can have the best day of your life and the worst day of your life—and all within the same hour."

Welcome to your college experience.

Arriving on Campus

So Real You Can Smell It, Touch It, and Taste It

Dear Harlan,
How much of a change is college from high school life? Is it a hard change to make?
—Curious about College

Dear Curious,
If you grew up sharing a room with a total stranger, eating breakfast in a cafeteria-style kitchen, going to classes with hundreds of people, coming home whenever you want, staying out as late as you want, bringing random guys or girls back to your room, wearing shower shoes, and being accountable to no one but yourself twenty-four hours a day, college life should be little if any different than life in high school. If you are not doing these things—it's different, very different.

The biggest difference between high school and college life is that you're in control. What you do in college is your choice. Who you want to do it with is your choice. When you want to do it is your choice. It's adult life, but with a safety net. Some people move too fast, some people move slowly, but no matter the speed you choose to go, if you find yourself losing your footing or heading out of control, you are surrounded by people who will help and support you.

As for change, I have a hard time with it. The only things I felt comfortable changing in college were my socks and underwear, assuming they were clean (a rare occurrence). The secret is to know yourself well enough to know what to expect. For example, if you're someone who has a history of having a hard time with change, expect college to be a challenging transition and get support in place before you need it. If you can handle change well, expect fewer problems, but be prepared for the unexpected. Experiencing so many firsts so fast can be unpredictable. But once you find your people and places in college, you'll probably *never* want to leave! College can be the best four, five, or six years of your life—hope it doesn't last six or more.

Tip #1
Expect the Unexpected

The Tip
Don't create too many expectations. You might think that you know what will happen in college, but really, you don't.

The Story
I left for college expecting my high school boyfriend and I to stay together forever. Well, we ended up breaking up in December of my freshman year. I had always gotten As in high school classes. It was easy for me. I left for college expecting to do the same amount of work in college as I did in high school (not all that much) and to get the same grades. In reality, I've never had to work harder and no longer always get the A. I thought my friendships in college would be the same as they were in high school. But I soon learned that it takes time to develop those same kinds of friendships. Once I

Expectations versus Reality

68.5 percent of students expected to make at least a B average.

79.3 percent of students actually did.

(But this book will help you to get an A average.)

48.8 percent of students expected to participate in student clubs or groups.

59 percent of students actually did.

(But this book will help make it easier than ever to get involved.)

10.9 percent of students expected to seek personal counseling.

16.7 percent actually did. (But this book will make it easier than ever to get help along the way.)

—Higher Education Research Institute at UCLA

stopped expecting so much and started expecting the unexpected, college got so much better.

—freshman, Northwestern University

* * *

I know, you didn't expect the unexpected to be the first tip.

Welcome to your college experience. Right now, you're on that upward climb, preparing for a wild ride. It's like a roller coaster moments away from running at top speed down the tracks, and unless you're able to handle the unexpected twists and turns ahead of you, you risk running off the tracks or just getting sick to your stomach. Not good.

While it's unnatural to leave for college with NO expectations, try leaving with flexible but BIG expectations. If your expectations are too rigid, when the unexpected pops its head up (and it will), you'll snap or possibly break. If you begin college with flexible expectations and can move with the unexpected twists and turns, the ride ahead will take you to places you never imagined.

"Attend summer pre-orientation. I went to a summer camp with 300 of my future classmates and spent four days playing games, singing songs, and basically laughing and celebrating."
—grad, University of New Hampshire

And make sure to dream big. You'll be surprised where you might end up if you plant the seed early. (I ended up as an intern at *The Tonight Show*, a syndicated advice columnist, and *New York Times* bestselling author—nothing I had ever imagined.)

If you and I were close enough that I could grab you by

your shoulders and talk to you, I'd tell you exactly what I wish I could have told myself before heading to college.

Relax.

Have fun.

Enjoy every minute.

Your job is simple:

Be your personal best,

Meet lots of people,

Make new friends,

Make smart decisions,

Possibly find a career,

Possibly find love,

And take risk after risk after risk so that you can figure out what you love and what you don't love. Expect that all the risks you take will not always go as planned. Many will, but not all. When a risk doesn't go as planned, don't go on the attack, don't give up and hide—look inward, look outward, and move forward. Do this again and again and you'll leave college with more than a degree. You'll leave knowing what it takes for you to be happy. And really, what more could you possibly want out of your life in college?

Bottom Line
When you expect the unexpected, everything is an adventure.

Tip #2
Patience, Patience, and More Patience

The Tip
Don't expect everything to happen at once. It takes time.

The Story
Freshman year, I came to college expecting everyone to be friends right away and for it all to be great, because that's the way they built it up in high school. They made us think college was going to be a perfect place. I got here and expected to wake up in the morning and love my classes, love my roommate, and love my friends, but I didn't—everything was not perfect. It took me a while to realize that it takes time. It took me a while to find friends—and I mean real friends, not just acquaintances. One of my friends lived in my hall, another one was in my classes, and another one was in theater crew. There was a defining moment our sophomore year when we realized we were such close friends. It happened on Valentine's Day; we were having dinner because none

Impatient or Out of Place?

45.1 percent of students attending a public two-year community college do not return their sophomore year.

35.7 percent of students attending a private two-year community college do not return their sophomore year.

35.8 percent of students attending a public four-year college do not return their sophomore year.

30.2 percent of students attending a private four-year college do not return their sophomore year.

—ACT Institutional Data File, 2014

of us had a boyfriend. That's when we realized how close we had become. It still took a while before we could have screaming fights and know that it would be all right. Now, they are like family. It all took time. It also took me until junior year to realize what I wanted to do with my life. It might sound stupid, but I had to learn to chill out. I had to relax and let it all happen.

—junior, Brandeis University

* * *

I put this tip at the beginning of the book for you impatient people. I know you're contemplating skipping ahead to the dating, drugs, sex, relationships, managing your checking account...Wait.

Rename the first year THE UNCOMFORTABLE YEAR. Then, you can be more patient. I know, you want it all NOW. Google the word "patience" and you'll get 40 million results in less than .45 seconds. Texting, Tinder, Snapchat—it's all instant gratifcation. But college is different.

I know, you want friends, grades, and the good life as soon as possible. While you might want it right away, appreciate that it doesn't always happen that way. New takes time. Like breaking in a

"The first year is a strange time for everyone. Let things roll off you."
—senior, Webster University

new pair of shoes, a new pair of jeans, a crisp textbook, or a firm mattress fitted with extra-long twin sheets, it takes time for it all to feel right.

Don't give it two weeks or even two months. Give it two semesters, or two years. I know—two years sounds like a ridiculous amount of time, but it can take two revolutions around the sun to find your people and places on campus. Comfortable takes time. When you get to college and begin discovering that everything doesn't feel comfortable immediately, know that it's normal. Things like finding your way around campus, finding your classes, finding professors you like, finding a major that keeps you awake in class, finding great friends (or good ones), finding a roommate you actually like being around, and finding the cheapest wings, best breadsticks, and fastest pizza delivery takes time.

If you're looking to speed up the process, leave for college with a plan. The plan should include three parts: Places, People, and Patience. Having patience will give you time to get comfortable with the uncomfortable that's part of the normal college experience. Having places (campus clubs, organizations, athletics, spiritual groups, etc.) will give you things to do once you arrive on campus. Having people in your corner (at least five) will give you a support system at all times. With places, people, and patience, you'll be ready to create your own college experience and handle anything that comes your way. Use what you loved doing in high school to guide you to the right people and places. There's more about this in Tip #3.5. It took me three semesters, two campuses, and *two* freshman years to figure it out. I was totally impatient. I either tried way too hard or just stopped trying. Had I only known, I could have been so much more patient and kinder to myself.

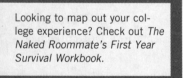
Looking to map out your college experience? Check out *The Naked Roommate's First Year Survival Workbook*.

Bottom Line
Take good shoes, a favorite pillow, and lots of patience with you to college. You'll need them all to get comfortable with the uncomfortable.

Tip #3
Finding Your Three Places on Campus

The Tip
Get involved, join something, and meet as many new people as possible.

The Story
My senior year of high school was amazing. I was the prom king, president of my senior class, and King of the Year. I was dating a beautiful runner who was a state champion, I received more scholarships than I could count, and I set a school record in backstroke—as the first student from my school to go to state in years. Needless to say, I was feeling good! Yet, immediately when I went to college, everything tottered and fell apart. No one knew me, not many of my friends went here, and my girlfriend broke up with me within two weeks.

"Try not to allow your fear to consume you. If you follow what's in your heart, then you're on the right track. Just don't hold back."

—junior, St. Peters College

I wandered around pining and depressed for weeks, trying to figure out what had gone wrong. The moment I got involved with freshman orientation, a student organization on campus, everything turned around. I had new friends, a sense of purpose, and found my place at a huge university. Get involved with something that feels right and make as many new contacts as possible. It opens up a world of opportunity and creates strong new friendships. College went from a scary and foreboding realm to a place that I can call home.

—junior,
Indiana University

* * *

Given that this is only the third tip, it's not a good idea for me to call this the most important tip of the book—then you might decide not to read the rest, throw the book away, burn it (why so angry?), or just return it. I'll just mention that this tip is extremely important.

Finding your places is so important—because if you have no place, you'll end up lost, and if you're lost with no place, there isn't anywhere to go, and that's when you will want to go home.

Notice I wrote "places," not just one place. This is not a typo ("plazess" would be a typo). If you only have one place to go and the people in that place turn out to be complete morons, you'll either become a moron or hate this place. That's why you always need three places. If people in one place do something that makes you feel uncomfortable (examples: drinking, hazing, smoking crack), you can go someplace else. If you don't have other places to go, you might start doing things that surprise you. Find at least three places on campus to find connections and avoid doing crack.

In high school, everything seemed to just kind of fall into place. You might have found your places by participating in athletics, the student council, plays, debate, a student newspaper, academic clubs, or some kind of other activity. Your parents might have pushed you in a particular direction, or maybe it was a friend or older sibling who helped you get involved. But in college, you have to work to be the one to help yourself find your place. Without as many friends around and without as much structure to your day, it doesn't all just happen right away.

Start with what you love doing and go from there. Seek out the places where you were your best and most comfortable in high school. If you're athletic, figure out how you can get involved with club sports and intramurals (see Tip #31). If you're into academics, figure out how to get involved with academic clubs and organizations (see Tips #30 and #32). Having places creates a world of options. The more options you have, the easier it will be to make choices that fit your personality. Then you can say what you think and do what you feel without worrying about other people.

"I'm in a sports team, involved in student organizations, and I live on campus. If you're stuck in one group with people who don't share your goal or ideas about life, you have nowhere else to go."
—freshman, Kenyon College

Leave for college with a plan in mind for where you'll find your three places. Visit your campus's website, ask your advisors, talk to your RA, talk to the staff in the student activities office, ask a counselor in the counseling office. Talk to student ambassadors, grads from your high school, and students in leadership positions. Don't expect your college experience to magically come to you. You have to be the one to get up, get out, and get involved. You need to be the one to make it happen.

Bottom Line
Attending college is like attending a live event that has general seating. The ticket gets you inside the venue. You have to be the one to put yourself in the center of all the action.

A Naked Pause

Here's the naked truth about college planning: Students are rarely told the truth. I'm not saying students are told lies; you're just not told about the natural, normal, and everyday challenges that are part of college life. This part isn't advertised. The truth is that college is 90 percent amazing and 10 percent difficult (or a bunch of BS). The problem is that the 10 percent BS can take up 100 percent of your time if you're not expecting it. It can take a good year, or two, or three, for expectations to meet reality.

For most new students, expectations are high when entering college. But once they arrive and settle in, reality can be lower. When reality doesn't meet expectations, we get uncomfortable and panic. And this is when one of two things happens: you try too hard to fit in and make poor choices or you become totally withdrawn and give up (can you say transfer or drop out?). The problem is that most students don't start college with realistic expectations and thus are set up for problems.

When you come to college with realistic expectations you can be patient, create a world of options, and be more forgiving of yourself and others. You can be imperfect and allow yourself time to figure out what you love and don't love. You can reach out to people, places, and resources. You can put yourself in rooms with people who share common interests. If you can learn to embrace and face the 10 percent difficult, life will get better faster. If you fight it, trust that the uncomfortable will be all-consuming and long lingering. When you have your places, people, and patience, life in college is happier, healthier, and far easier to manage.

The First Year Thong

In all new roles we play in life it is as if we are wearing a tight thong. When wearing a tight thong, we do not want to be noticed. Being noticed means being judged. The more uncomfortable we are in our thongs, the harder it is to interact and react. We are always hiding, defending, and distracting. We can't say what we think or do what we feel. When someone tells us something sensitive or makes us uncomfortable, our reaction is to attack or hide.

Give yourself time to get comfortable in your first-year thong. Accept that change can be uncomfortable at times. Give yourself permission for the first year to be uncomfortable at times. Appreciate that most of the people around you are also uncomfortable in their thongs. The people attacking, distracting, and doing stupid things are covering something up. Appreciate that you are not alone in this experience and draw strength knowing that we are all in this together. Take comfort in the group discomfort. Surround yourself with people who can support, guide, and help you along the way. Find people who are paid to help, who volunteer to help, or who you can ask for help. Also, turn to professors, support staff, and professionals. And don't forget about family and positive friends.

Wear your first-year thong with pride (and wash it regularly). The more comfortable you can be with the uncomfortable, the easier it will be to take the emotional and social risks that will help you find your places on campus. And the sooner you find your places on campus and get the right people in your corner, the sooner reality will meet and exceed expectations.

Tip #3.5:
The Five People in Your Corner

The Tip
Find people on campus who will support you and love you for who you are. Never give up.

The Story
My entire life I knew I was different. I also knew that I would not be able to count on my parents. My father has called gay people names such as fag, stool stuffer, queer,

and so many derogatory and hurtful names. He once got in a verbal altercation with a man who showed interest in him. My mother, on the other hand, is highly religious and will never say something bad about a person to their face, but when she sees somebody that she perceives to be gay, she'll whisper how disgusting that it is and how it goes against what the Bible says. When something comes on the television about a person being gay, my parents make some type of rude comment before changing the channel. This is only a small part of what I go through on a day-to-day basis when I am at home. I could not wait to leave—just so I can try and find someplace in this world where I can truly be who I was meant to be. I came to terms with who I was and the potential that I had when I was in my senior year in High School. I was scared of what was going to happen and what people were going to think about me, but when I went on a college visit, I found out the university that I wanted to attend had a Gay-Straight Alliance. I knew immediately this was a place where I could find connections. Now, almost four years have passed. I'm Vice President of the Gay-Straight Alliance, a member of the Diversity Council, and so much more. I've spoken to the freshman classes about human sexuality and sexual orientation, given a presentation for our Emerging Leaders program, and regularly copresent to every Education major on campus whenever they have their Education Conference in November. I will admit that my family situation has not changed much but I have found a better place away from home where people accept and love me for who I am. Never give up.

—junior, University of Mount Union

Who are the five people in your corner? For every problem, question, or concern, you'll need FIVE people on campus who can help you. There are people who are paid to help you, people who volunteer to help you, and people you can enlist or ask to help you. Like a boxer who enters the ring, you need people in your corner. College can be emotionally grueling at times. You are surrounded by people who can support, guide, and help you 24–7. If you don't have people in your corner, it's easier to get lonely, get scared, panic, feel desperate, and do things you regret. Everyone should have at least five people in their corner on campus. You can start finding these people before ever heading off to campus.

Where do you find the people in your corner? EVERYWHERE! These people can be orientation leaders, campus guides, admissions counselors, financial aid advisors, therapists, counselors, professors, teaching assistants, tutors, coaches, support staff, grads from your high school, advisors of clubs and organizations, spiritual leaders, friends, family, upperclassmen, doctors, psychiatrists, authors, professionals, deans, grad students, other students on different campuses (www.NakedRoommate .com), and a long list of other people I didn't include here. They are in their offices, online, and on campus waiting for you.

How do you ask people to be in your corner? Introduce yourself. Send them an email. Follow them on Twitter. Make an appointment with them. Find them on the campus website. Ask the admissions department. Go to meetings on campus where you can get to know them. Ask them for advice. Let them know that you need help. Most people will LOVE to help you. What's so cool—eventually, you will become someone who can be in other people's corner.

WARNING: Make sure you have the right people in your corner. Make sure they aren't threatened by your happiness. Too many times, certain friends and family members can be toxic people in your corner. You need people in your corner who are going to tell you what you need to hear—not just what you want to hear. If someone tells you the truth and it hurts, you need to know that it's coming from a loving place. Oh, people who tell you that you're stupid, ugly, or not good enough are NOT people you need in your corner. Distance yourself from the haters and surround yourself with the lovers.

Need Help? Get People in Your Corner

- Academic problem? Turn to a professor, teaching assistant, academic advisor, upperclassman, tutor, or department chair.

- Roommate problem? Turn to a residence assistant, counselor, therapist, orientation leader, peer advisor, upperclassman, or campus security officer.

- Relationship problem? Turn to an advisor, an administrative assistant, counselors, a therapist, a first-year experience class instructor, the police, or campus security.

Bottom Line

I'm in your corner. People on campus are in your corner. Find me at www.HarlanCohen.com and on Twitter @HarlanCohen.

Tip #4
When Lost or Confused, Ask

The Tip
Ask questions when you get confused. You'll be surprised at what you learn.

The Story
I came to campus not knowing very many people. It's easy to get lost. When I did get lost, I'd ask anyone who I thought could give me an answer. I'd ask my questions and the answers would lead to even more answers. When I got lost on campus, I'd ask for directions and find new places I didn't expect to find. People would give me their maps if they had an extra or direct me to a website. When I got tired of eating at my residence hall, I didn't know where to find other places to eat. So, I asked, and some guy told me about other places that I didn't know were part of my meal plan. When it came to preparing for classes, I asked people who had already taken the class in my major how to get through a class and how to study for certain professors. I asked questions and found answers.

—freshman, Ohio State University

* * *

Please note. For this tip you'll need a map of your campus. Refer to your school's website and print out a map. Once you have it in your hand, staple or glue the map to this page (punch staple here: _____).

Whether you leave with a plan for college or not, you'll need some help getting around. You might need directions to a location on campus, directions for getting involved in a club or organization, directions for finding new friends, or directions for rushing a fraternity or sorority (see Tip #35). You might need directions for how to find the best defense attorney or bail bondsman (that would be bad). If you get to college and find that you need directions on how to find your place on campus, do not hesitate. Ask for directions. Most people will stop and help. Most won't steer you wrong. And I'm not just talking directions from point A to point B. Directions can include helping you answer any questions on your mind.

> "Moving to a new city my first year of college at age seventeen was a huge challenge. I had to overcome financial and social challenges on my own. The strength these events contributed to my character is overwhelming and undeniable—something every college student should experience."
>
> —senior, Cal State University–Fullerton

If you want to get somewhere in life, ask for directions. Talk to all the support staff on campus to help you map out a course, and then check in with the same people while on your journey. The people you reach out to when asking for directions can become the people in your corner.

> "Stay true to yourself and don't do what other people want you to do just because you want to fit in."
>
> —sophomore, Allegheny College

When doing your mapping, check out your campus's website before starting life on campus. Contact students on campus doing the things you want to via Facebook (you'll be surprised how cool they can be). These people and places will guide you. And again, when you find yourself getting lost or confused, turn to people who look like they know where they're going (hint: they tend not to be people also looking at maps).

Turn to your academic advisor for an educational map. Turn to professors to help you travel through each class. Talk to your resident assistant or an older friend on campus to help guide you socially. Turn to a religious club or organization to guide you spiritually. Don't be afraid to ask questions when you get lost—the people waiting to guide you want to help you.

Bottom Line
If someone gives you wrong directions on purpose, don't feel like an idiot. Find the person again and thank them. Say, "Thanks, GREAT directions! Awesome shortcut!" Then walk away before he or she can speak. This way, they'll either waste time trying to find the "shortcut" or feel stupid for actually having helped you.

Tip #5
Be Yourself: Not Me, Not Him, Not Her

The Tip
Relax! Be yourself.

The Story

I was a freshman in college and knew virtually no one at my university. So, I decided that the best way to fit in was to fit in with a bunch of different groups and act like them when I was around them. Well, what I didn't count on was the fact that a few people from each of the groups knew each other and started talking about me. It turned out that in the process of trying to fit in, I ended up with no friends and I didn't know who I was anymore. After that, I was just myself and people liked me a lot better that way. Now I have tons of friends and am happy with the "myself" I found in the process.

—graduate student, Eastern New Mexico University

* * *

A little story on this tip. It was a late addition to *The Naked Roommate*. It happened after most of this book was already written. After interviewing more than a thousand college students, researching hundreds of hours, and putting together all the ingredients that make up this book, one theme came through again and again. It's simple, but it's important—just be yourself. Don't be me. Don't be that guy sitting across from you. Don't be the girl over there.

While there's nothing wrong with wanting to redefine yourself once you get to college, don't lose yourself. Start with who you are now and go from there. Take small steps in new directions. Make life about what you want, NOT ABOUT BEING WANTED. Avoid the idiots you couldn't avoid in high school and surround yourself with good people who want you to be your best. Forget fitting in and focus on what fits you.

Whatever you do, avoid becoming the person you think people want you to be just so they will accept you. It's exhausting. Focus on what you like, rather than being liked. When you change to be liked by other people, you end up doing stupid, regrettable things that lead you to bad places and bad relationships (examples: getting into drugs, sleeping around, and crawling through dumpsters late at night while drunk looking for old hamburgers). Relax, and be true to yourself. If you don't know yourself, be patient, take smart risks, and figure it out. You've got time to find you.

> "Don't be afraid to do things that interest you even though other people don't think they're cool. This isn't the same as high school. There are enough people in college who do things that are uncool to make them 'cool.'"
>
> —junior, University of Pittsburgh

Bottom Line
Try too hard to please the world and you end up pleasing no one.

Tip #6
About Your Parents...

The Tip
Work out a plan for when you're going to talk to your parents once you get to school. If you don't, plan on having problems.

The Story

I'm the older of two daughters. When I left for college, my parents and I didn't talk about when I would call or when they would call. I moved about five hours away. From the first day, they called me *every single night*. I'm not kidding. Please, we sent email and instant messages every day! They wanted to know what I was up to. They would ask me the same annoying questions night after night after night. There were questions about how specific classes were and about every single detail of my whole day. After a few nights there was nothing new to talk about. Still, they kept calling. A month or so into the semester, I started getting upset. It had built and built up. I didn't tell them sooner because, me being the oldest, and being five hours away, I was being nice to them. I didn't want to hurt their feelings.

One night, I lost it. I just kind of blew up at them. After getting in trouble for giving them so much attitude, they asked me, "Do you want us to call every night?" I was like, "No, I'll call you when I'm free." They were fine with that. It shocked me, but they're pretty understanding parents. A semester later, things are much better. We talk two to three times a week—and we regularly text and send email and instant messages.

—freshman, Texas A&M Commerce

***

Parents, parents, parents…These people love you, but some of them are a little freaked out. Can you blame them? Your parents will fall into three categories: (1) parents who never leave you alone, (2) parents who occasionally leave you alone, and (3) parents who always leave you alone (Mom? Dad? Where are you? Hellloooo). Some parents will think of you as thirteen forever. Other parents try to control their kids by using guilt, money, or hypnosis (although hypnotist parents are rare). And other parents will give you all the room in the world. They'll wait for you to send the first text or make the first call (call at least once a week). All parents will have their own approaches, but whatever the approach, it's all out of love (and not a love of making you miserable). They miss you. They love you. They want to hear from you (some more than others). Appreciate that this whole college thing is also a transition for them. Appreciate what they're dealing with—debt, aging, lack of control, fear, and for the first time, you possibly not living at home.

You might not realize it, but you have a lot of control over the relationship you have with your parents—more than either of you can grasp. Following the third edition of this book, I wrote and researched a new book for parents of college students. It's *The Naked Roommate: For Parents Only*. I would have called it *The Naked Parent*, but no one wants to see that on the cover. The reason I wrote this book is because parents are first responders, but most of them don't know how to respond. I wanted to help YOU by helping them to chill out. And most of the time, it's you who is texting, calling, video chatting, Facebooking, and talking to them as your problems unfold. Then they're involved. By the time you've moved onto the next problem, they're still solving the previous problem. But now that you have *The Naked Roommate*, you can hold off on asking your parents to solve your problems because you can manage them yourself. Instead of asking your parents to fix it all, you can. If you find that parents are overly involved or you feel that they need help with this transition, suggest *The Naked Roommate: For Parents Only* (check it out at the library if you don't want to pay for it). Whatever you do, appreciate that this is a huge transition for them too. The more comfortable they can get with the uncomfortable, the better equipped they'll be to support and empower you—not control and overpower you. When life gets uncomfortable they don't have to blame you, the school, your friends, or themselves—they can blame the college experience. When you get ready to start life in college, pull them aside and tell them, "Mom and Dad, it's not letting go, it's just about changing the grip. This means I need to loosen the grip and you do, too." This will be the moment they'll realize you're not thirteen.

No matter what category your parent(s) fall into, use this three-step approach to dealing with all parents.

1. Listen to them.
2. Appreciate them (and tell them that you do).
3. Do what makes you happy.

Please note—this approach only works if you're being reasonable. If you're skipping classes, selling drugs, and drinking to the point of blacking out, they have a good reason to interfere. You need help.

Helicopter Parents

You've heard the term. Helicopter parents get overly involved in your life whether you like it or not. When something goes wrong, they're right there. Instead of encouraging you to fix your own problems, they make the calls, make the trip, and attempt to make everything better. Sometimes you ask for help; other times they take it upon themselves to help. A lot of times they can't help themselves. New research says involved parents can actually be helpful. How involved is the question. Do not let them fix your problems. If you need help finding answers, ask them to point you in the direction of the people, places, and resources on campus that can help—but do not let them solve your problems. Professors don't enjoy calls from parents, residence life professionals don't look forward to calls from parents, and your friends don't appreciate calls from parents.

When you talk to your parents about a problem, let them know if you want them to listen or if you're looking for advice. If they offer to intervene on your behalf, thank them for wanting to help and then do it yourself. Considering 13 percent of parents frequently intervene and another 25 percent occasionally intervene (source: NSSE), talk to them before they intervene. This is your life—it's your job, and it's your responsibility.

A Quick Parent Checklist

○ Set a general time and day of the week to check in (make sure the time is loose so that you can move it around based on your schedule).

○ Decide on a method to keep in touch (texting, phone calls, video calls).

○ Appreciate that if you involve them in every decision you make, you will never learn how to make your own decisions. Use your parents as a resource, but don't abuse them.

○ If living on campus, plan when your parents will visit you, and plan when you'll come home. If you're close to home or living at home, set up some parameters on when they'll visit and how important it is for you to stay on campus.

○ When you're venting, tell them. Unless you make it clear that you're venting, they might try to solve the problem and start offering advice.

○ When getting advice—wanted or unwanted—ask yourself if what they're saying is right for you. If they don't agree with your choices (and you're sober, healthy, and not in an abusive relationship), make sure you have a strong support system on campus to support you.

○ If your parents don't agree with your choices, make sure you understand why they don't agree without getting defensive or angry.

○ Send them a thank-you card or letter. Mailing a card to your parents will make them very excited (see the Bottom Line).

○ Check out *The Naked Roommate: For Parents Only*

and highlight sections that will help them to understand your experience. Also, encourage them to get
feedback on the Facebook page for parents: www
.Facebook.com/NakedRoommateForParents.

Bottom Line
If you want to surprise, shock, and floor your
parents, send them a handwritten thank-you
card. They eat that card thing up (not literally).
Note: avoid saying thank you and asking for
money in the same card.

Tip #7
Homesickness: Breathe Deep, It's in the Air

The Tip
First semester is not the easiest or happiest. It's normal to
get homesick.

The Story
The brochures never mentioned grabbing meals and sitting on my own in the cafeteria and then not going out on
the weekends because I didn't have good friends to hang
out with. No one mentioned that I could get depression (see
Tip #100). No one told me that it was normal to get homesick. After Thanksgiving, I started hanging out with new
friends in the dorms. Sometimes it can take longer. This
isn't something that just happens here, it's everywhere. All
my friends said the same thing. This is my second college

this year, and it's been the same experience at both schools. Knowing that it's normal and what to expect makes it easier to handle.

—freshman, George Washington University

✳ ✳ ✳

College brochures and websites are filled with shiny, happy pictures of smiling students appearing to have the time of their lives. It's giggles and good times with images of cheerleaders cheering, students studying, and everyone smiling in picturesque spots on campus, arm in arm in a multicultural snapshot with everyone donning their officially licensed college logo-branded clothes. Coincidentally, it never rains, never snows, and always appears sunny on campus.

> "I had a friend who was really homesick and down. She was thinking of transferring out. One of her main problems was that she never got out of her room. She was upset that she hadn't met anyone, but I was like—you can't meet people if you're in your room."
>
> —freshman, Salve Regina University

The not-so-shiny part of college is something you don't see or hear about. The truth is that life in college can also be difficult, lonely, and sad at times (and it does rain, snow, and get cloudy). The emotional pendulum swings both ways. And when you're swinging in the other direction, and you start yearning for the things that you once had at home, just know that it's totally normal.

Homesickness: Who's Catching It?

66.6 percent of surveyed freshmen "frequently" or "occasionally" felt lonely or homesick.

—Higher Education Research Institute at UCLA

I'll say it again: getting homesick is normal. It happens to **most** students. In fact, 66.6 percent of surveyed freshmen "frequently" or "occasionally" felt lonely or homesick. If you're not getting homesick, you're not the norm. It usually hits midfall—after the newness fades to normal. You miss your bed, friends, pets, home cooking, and walking to the bathroom without having to wear flip-flops (and for God's sake, always wear flip-flops in the bathrooms—I can't stress this enough).

"It hit me in late October. A lot of work was coming down on me, and I missed hanging out, riffing with my friends from home. I have an older brother who went to a different college and went through the same thing. Had my brother not prepared me for what would happen, I think it all would have been so much harder."
—sophomore, Carnegie Mellon University

Now that you know it's normal, when it happens, you can think. "YES! I remember this was going to happen!" The cure to homesickness is NOT at home. It's to make your new home more comfortable. This is when patience, places, and people will make all the difference (see Tips #2 and #3 for a reminder). When homesick, try to remember that comfortable takes time. The knee-jerk reaction is to run back to the familiar when you get uncomfortable. There's nothing wrong with visiting home once in a while,

"The best advice for finding male friends is to learn how to play any EA sports game. It's an obsession for some people, but don't play too much. I have a friend who failed out because he skipped classes to master the game."
—freshman, George Washington University

texting and talking with friends, visiting a friend at another campus, or bringing home-cooking back to school with you.

But do it in moderation. Avoid hiding from your feelings. Don't bury yourself in technology (see the next tip, Technology: The Fifth Wall, for more on this). Avoid using bad relationships, drinking, drugs, and things that can get you arrested to cope.

The cure to homesickness is to make your new home a place that will make you sick to leave in the future. This takes time, work, and the tips in this book. If you do it right, by the time you graduate college, you'll be homesick again—only this time you'll be sick because you don't want to leave.

> "I never felt more homesick than the day I had a stomach virus and had to hang out in my room wishing my mom was there to take care of me."
> —freshman, Dartmouth College

Bottom Line
Going home to cure homesickness is like giving someone with a chocolate addiction a candy bar. It will just make you sicker.

Tip #8
Technology: The Fifth Wall

The Tip
Don't stay in your room and live online. It's hard enough to explore on your own without having the Internet, online dating, instant messenger, video games, and all the other electronic gadgets that make being alone much more tolerable. You'll miss out on so much.

The Story

I hated the first college I attended and the community around it. I didn't exactly help myself make it work. The campus was in a very urban place and I didn't know anyone on campus. I wasn't the most outward person, which didn't help.

I'd literally spend some of my weekend nights at home online. I'd have a couple of beers, open instant messenger, and download umpteen punk rock classics online—for me that was quite a good night. I kept talking to people I previously knew from high school instead of getting out of my room and making an effort to meet more people. I was quite apathetic. It's just so easy to get lost in it. I'd hear the "ding" or "door opening" sound and then have to see who was online. And now people have these elaborate Facebook profiles, YouTube, and blogs. Be careful not to live your life online.

—senior, Emerson College

* * *

Like pop-up ads that won't go away, there's a big issue that came up again and again during research for this book. Before I introduce you to The Fifth Wall of Technology, appreciate just how powerful media has become in the lives of college students. There are now more than 1.35 billion people on Facebook. There are more than 500 million tweets and 2.1 billion queries on Twitter per day. The average teen receives 60 text messages a day. And college students spend an average of 12 hours each day engaged with some type of media. By the time you read this, these numbers will be even higher. You might even be reading this on your phone, tablet, or some kind of digital device right now. It's amazing, it's incredible, it's almost incomprehensible what's happened in the last ten years. I can't even imagine what it will be like when it's time to write the next edition of this book.

There are five walls in your room when you arrive in college. No, The Fifth Wall is not a wall of dirty clothes (that would be the sixth wall). This wall is invisible. It's the wall I call technology. This includes the Internet, Facebook, video chatting, instant messenger, email, cell phones, video games, and anything that takes an electric current to play. Getting caught behind The Fifth Wall happens when you least expect it. It's when you are physically on campus, but socially and emotionally connected to people off campus. It works like this—college is naturally an unfamiliar and uncomfortable place. When in an unfamiliar place, your urge is to spend time in your comfort zone. This includes talking to friends from home, hanging out on Facebook, tweeting, Snapchatting, talking to a long-distance boyfriend or girlfriend, dating online, texting, blogging, Skyping, emailing, or playing video games with people halfway across the world (or across the hall). The Fifth Wall is easy to get stuck behind without even realizing it.

The risk is that you end up missing out on the moment. You risk missing out on meeting people face to face. You risk not getting involved with clubs, activities, and organizations because you're running back to your room to jump online or have your head buried in your cell phone (look up and stretch that neck every once in a while). You risk not knowing your professors because you just email or send them a Facebook message when an issue comes up rather than talking to them (they know your username or email address, but not your face). You risk depending on your parents for everything because you're in constant contact with them every moment via technology. You risk not being as patient or as flexible when twists and turns come up (because instead of figuring out the answers yourself, you hide out online or complain to anyone who will listen). You risk getting homesick more easily because you're still so deeply rooted in everything that is part of your old life at home. You risk not making new friends because all you do is connect with old ones. And should these old friends at other colleges have a better time than you, there's a decent chance you might start thinking about transferring to be with them (see the note about Facebook Headlines at the end of this tip). If the five people in your corner are all off campus and your three places require a Wi-Fi connection, you're stuck behind The Fifth Wall.

I'm not saying that you should avoid technology, sending emails, instant messaging, calling friends, and playing video games—that's not it at all. Just be careful not to overuse technology (some people get addicted). Use it, but don't abuse it. Never before has it been easier to be in one place physically and in another emotionally. Watch out for The Fifth Wall—don't get stuck behind it.

Facing The Fifth Wall: Facebook, Texting, Twitter, YouTube, Snapchat, Tumblr...

I don't know how to say it, so I'll just come out and say it. Like me. Be my friend. I need you to like and friend me. I want your likeship. Give me your damn friendship too...

Hold on. Wait. So sorry about that outburst. I should never talk to you that way. Forgive me? Please? Thank you...I appreciate that. Don't worry about being my personal friend. You can just follow me on Twitter at @HarlanCohen and on Instagram @HarlanCohen. You can check out *The Naked Roommate* Facebook page at: www.Facebook .com/NakedRoommate and my author page at www .Facebook.com/HelpMeHarlan.

So, what's in it for you?

As a Facebook, Twitter, and Instagram follower you can look at pictures of me on the road. You can keep tabs on my mood swings. You can also keep up to date on my relationship status. At times, I will let you know what I'm eating for breakfast, lunch, and dinner. I'll also show you pictures of airports (oooh fun). Once in a while, I will post updates regarding competitive eating contests (I make those up). Last fall I provided regular updates on a candy corn eating contest sponsored by the Milwaukee Chamber of Commerce. I finished second with 54,543 corns in twenty-four hours (again, just a joke). Best of all, as a Facebook "liker" or Twitter follower, you have a place to stay when you are traveling through Chicago (not with me, but I know a lot of hotels and city parks). I would like to hear from you during your college experience, to help you and share your stories with other students who are dealing with similar issues. You can find all these links and a "Naked" forum at www.NakedRoommate.com and www.HarlanCohen.com. Just make sure you don't spend too much time following me and watching what I ate for breakfast, lunch, and dinner. That would be getting trapped behind The Fifth Wall of Technology.

The Good, Not So Good, and Really Not So Good about Facebook, Social Networking, and Technology

The Good

It feels good to be liked, to tweet, and to check in. It's nice to read the writing on the wall or posts on the profile page. There are so many ways to find out so much about people you would never talk to in real life without ever opening your mouth. You can find out personal interests, academic interests, and social interests. You can even find out what people are doing, where they're doing it, and who they're doing it with. Not only do you get to read about

> "As my advisor once said, if you wouldn't show it to your grandmother, then don't post the picture on Facebook."
> —freshman, Carnegie Mellon University

it, but there are pictures as well (I love pictures). You can see the people and the people in their lives. On top of that you can join interest groups, send out invitations to events on campus, and communicate via email.

For someone who is looking at college or is new to college, online networks are a window into the world of college life that has never been visible before. And it's totally acceptable and not weird at all to send a note to someone on Facebook, via Twitter, LinkedIn, or through some other social network. You can reach out to the president of a club or organization, a member or coach of a team sport, or a professional who can help you find answers and mentor you. These are all good things. Never before has it be easier to connect with people who interest you and can ultimately help you.

The Not So Good

Three letters—TMI (too much Internet). The problem is that some people use texting, technology, and the Internet as a substitute for actually approaching someone (shy people, strangers, stalkers). Facebook, texting, and social networking should NEVER be a complete substitute for a face-to-face conversation. It should only be a first step. There's nothing wrong with doing a little "creeping" to see if someone is in a relationship or to peruse pictures. BUT this shouldn't prevent you from getting to know this person, regardless of his or her relationship status. Some people make up their relationship statuses or don't include them to avoid creepers.

You can't trust the information you read in a profile. It tells only the smallest part of a long story. Too many people assume too much based on these profiles. NEVER BEFORE HAS IT BEEN EASIER TO JUDGE SOMEONE BEFORE EVER MEETING THEM. It happens with friends, roommates, coworkers, and members of organizations. Be careful what you assume and be careful what other people assume. Use technology as a way to meet people and get information, not to fantasize about or secretly follow people (a.k.a. stalking).

The Really Not So Good

Don't be stupid. Be careful what you post. Posting a picture of yourself drinking is stupid—especially if you're underage, a student leader, or looking for a job. Sending a naked picture of yourself is stupid—and sending a naked picture of someone else who happens to be underage is especially stupid (and illegal—it can get you arrested for distributing child porn and put on a sex offender list). And expect "private" videos to become public porn. Once it's posted, it's forever. Snapchat isn't even safe. Students have been expelled, arrested, and fired for social media posts. If you're doing something illegal, don't post yourself doing it (better yet, don't do it). If you're a pageant contestant, don't post pictures of you flashing your thong at a bar. Potential employers, professors, friends, stalkers, and family have access to your information. Expect EVERYONE you don't want to view your pictures to view them. Make sure to set your privacy settings. If you want to know more about these privacy settings and the rights you're giving up, check out the documentary *Terms and Conditions Apply*. I watched it on Netflix. Shocking and scary come to mind.

Another thing to keep in mind: now that you have the option of posting your physical location via social networks using GPS, think about what you're posting and who has access to it. When you reveal your location, people know you're not home (the perfect time to steal your stuff) and know where to find you (the perfect time to follow you). If you're posting or tweeting that you're all alone, people who want to hang out with you might come calling or knocking at your door. And not all these people will be the type of people you want to come a-knocking. Think about this before letting the world know too much information.

One more not-so-good part—Facebook, texting, and technology can become addictive. Did you know that teenagers send an average of more than 3,000 texts a month? That's craziness. College life shouldn't mean spending hours on your computer or living with your head buried in your cell phone. With all the changes that come with college, the Internet can become a substitute for real-life communities. Use your online relationships to initiate real relationships. And one last thing before I'm done with this one—don't get caught up in status updates from friends on other campuses. Facebook is a headline culture. We mostly hear the good and NOT the bad. People will talk about the party, but they won't talk about the hangover. They'll talk about getting an A but not a D. They'll talk about the good, but keep the bad a secret. Don't be fooled by the headline culture. Appreciate that you're only getting the very best part of the story. No one tweets or posts "Just got the results, I have herpes!"

Bottom Line

Send me your questions at www.HarlanCohen .com/Ask, but please don't sit around for hours in front of your computer or staring at your phone waiting for a reply. Get out. Go for a walk. Just do something.

Harlan's Tip Sheet

Naked People, Places, and Resources

- *College website:* Spend a few hours getting familiar with all the different parts of campus. You'll be surprised at what you'll find on the campus website. The more you know about your campus, the more comfortable you will become once you're there. Do this and you'll be totally prepared. If you don't do anything else on this Tip Sheet, do this.
- *Twitter feed:* Almost all colleges will have Twitter accounts. You can follow college and university presidents, deans, professors, student affairs professionals, campus departments, clubs, and organizations.
- *Student Activities Office:* Visit in person or online. The Student Activities Office is similar to the student activities office in high school—it's where you'll find lists of student organizations, activities, and clubs. Pick organizations that you want to get involved with before you even get to campus.
- *Recent grads:* Get in touch with former graduates from your high school who are attending the college that you'll be attending. Don't hesitate to find them on Facebook (or other social networks) and send them a message (it's not weird). Ask them any questions you have. They've been there and done that. Don't hesitate to call. Then you will know someone on campus.

- *Me:* Connect with me on Facebook and Twitter. Please use my network of friends to connect with other students on campus. I'm more than happy to make introductions and connect you to people in my network. Find me @HarlanCohen, www.Facebook.com /HelpMeHarlan, and www.HarlanCohen.com.

- *Orientation events (summer/fall):* Whatever type of orientation program your school has, absolutely go to it. It helps. It's a way to meet students and professionals on campus and become familiar with the place that you'll call home for the next four (or more) years.

- *Campus tours:* Visit your campus before classes begin. Take advantage of the campus tours organized through the college. At the least, take a trip there with a few friends.

- *Counseling office:* Visit the counseling office (in most cases therapy is free). If you're a little uncomfortable before going to college or uncomfortable once you get to college, it's helpful to have a contact on campus who can help you. If you're going to school with a medical condition, make sure that you identify people who can help you and a plan should you need medical attention.

- *Campus newspaper:* Read your college's campus newspaper before you get to campus. In most cases, you can find it online. If you don't have a great newspaper on campus, check out the local newspaper. This will give you a feel for what's happening on campus and in the community, and an idea of how you can participate.

- *Privacy settings:* Use the privacy settings on your social media accounts. You never know who's checking you out.
- *www.NakedRoommate.com:* This website offers you a chance to connect with other students. You can also post questions and offer answers in *The Naked Roommate* forums.

Residence Halls

2

Living, Eating, and Bathing with Hundreds of Strangers

*Commuter students: feel free to flip ahead to Tip #24, and be sure to read Tip #104. I just wanted you to know that I'm constantly thinking about you and your college experience.

Dear Harlan,

I can't decide on where I want to live in college. The problem is, I have a two-year-old puppy that I love very much and I want to take her with me. However, many people have told me that if I don't live in a dorm I won't make friends that easily. I am a very shy person, so it would be beneficial to me to be around people my own age in a dorm. On the other hand, if I could choose between sharing a bathroom with twenty girls or having my own bathroom and own apartment (money is no problem), I would choose the apartment. Plus, I would get to bring my puppy.

What should I do?

—Dilemma

Dear Dilemma,

If your puppy went to college and she were given the choice to either live in a residence hall for a year, where she could meet different breeds of puppies from around the world, or live off campus in a cage far away from everyone else, what would she do? While all the other puppies are eating together, walking to classes together, playing together, and sniffing each other, your puppy would be isolated, away from the activity, sniffing herself. Sure, your puppy could visit, but being a shy puppy makes it more difficult.

The best choice is to live with all the other puppies. Sure, the living conditions might not be as comfortable at times, but the positive side of life far outweighs the negative—at least for a year. Residential life helps freshmen with the college transition. In addition to being with all the other new students, there are RAs (resident assistants) who live in the residence halls to help answer questions and address issues and obstacles. There are floor activities, flyers on the walls to recruit new students for new activities, and plenty of people to hang out with. There are sometimes even classrooms in the residence halls. Living in an apartment is the perfect way to isolate you and your puppy from the college experience, making you both sad puppies.

Tip #9
Residence Halls:
A Cruise without the Water

The Tip
At all costs, live in the dorm your freshman year!

The Story
The words "girls' dorm" not only sent chills up my spine, but made me want to puke as well. So when I found out I had no choice but to live in the dorm, I wanted to shoot myself in the foot. I have never been what you call a "girly girl." When naming my friends, I would almost always name more guy friends than girls. I had no desire to live in a building with a bunch of giddy girls. Boy, was I wrong. The girls on my hall have truly been one of the highlights of college life, much to my astonishment. They always have a willing ear to listen when I need to talk, and we have made some wonderful memories such as doing cartwheels down the hall, having midnight ice cream parties in our rooms, and representing our dorm in intramural volleyball. (Go North Russell Rockers!) As corny and cheesy as it may sound, they are no longer the giddy girls that I had stereotyped in my mind; they have become more like my sisters whom I have grown to love and cherish. So if you are considering not living in the dorm your freshman year, consider it no longer. Live in the dorm. It is only for a year, and you will be surprised at how many fantastic people you will have the opportunity to get to know.
—freshman, Baylor University

* * *

Residence halls, dormitories, dorms, campus housing—whatever you call it, these are the places most new students who live on campus call home. They are long halls filled with hundreds of mostly clueless people on a common journey. It's like a cruise, but without the swimming pools, room service, spa, casino, alcoholic drinks, ports of call, free midnight buffets, fine dining, all the water, and the boat. See, exactly like a cruise.

Living in a residence hall is a once-in-a-lifetime experience, so you should experience it at least once in a lifetime (more if you enjoy it). Living in campus housing is so important the first year that some campuses require new students to do it. It's required because not living on campus means missing out on so much. The logic is to put all new students in a place where everyone is equally clueless, naïve, lost, and seeking to find their own place in one place.

Bonus Tip

ALWAYS wear flip-flops in the showers. If the floors could talk, they wouldn't speak, they'd just scream!

There's an electricity that buzzes in first-year residence halls (if the buzz is too loud, call maintenance, but don't expect them to come right away). And if that doesn't excite you, appreciate that it's just easier living. There is enough going on during your first year of college to not have to deal with things like paying bills, paying rent, setting up utilities, dealing with landlords, getting cable, getting groceries, finding a place to live, getting to classes, and setting up Internet connections.

Yes, it's true that living with so many people can get annoying, irritating, and disgusting, but the alternatives do not compare to what you do get. If you're a commuter student, look into living on campus. At the very least, work to make friends with people living on campus. Between the cost of traveling, the inconveniences of driving, and the challenges of feeling connected to campus life, you might be better off living on campus. Talk to a financial aid advisor and see if you have any options. But everyone should do it at least once.

Perks of Residence Life

- Meet people without even trying.
- Possible amenities include cable, high-speed Internet, heat, bathroom suites, a gym close by, air conditioning, coed floors, study suites, libraries, on-site counseling, free tutors, twenty-four-hour computer access, mini food marts, and dining options.
- Help, support, and answers to your questions are just a few doors away.
- Living and learning communities—live, eat, and learn with people who share the same major. Who knows, you might even have your professor as a neighbor down the hall.
- Great location—usually near classrooms, campus, and transportation.
- Floor activities on the weekends (and often on week-nights) and opportunities to participate in residence life student government.

- Flyers, notes, and general information flows on bulletin boards, on walls on the way to the cafeteria, and in any common area.
- Reasonable cost (in most cases).

Bottom line

Live in a residence hall and feel the pulse of campus life (and occasional banging noises coming through the wall next door).

Tip #10
Meet People without Even Trying

The Tip

Always leave your door open. Close it only if you're sleeping or not at home.

The Story

I was the kind of person who, unless I knew someone or was comfortable around them, I wouldn't be around them. At first, when I got to college, I was like, I'm keeping my door shut, because I didn't know anyone. The second day after keeping my door shut, I started to hear people outside my room. It happened all the time. I felt like I was missing out on college life. That day when I opened my door I literally started to meet people. People would just come in and say hi. They just stopped in. I lived in a six-floor high-rise and it was coed by room. Keeping my door open helped me make so many friends (a lot of them athletes who lived on my floor). The friendships

I formed those first few weeks on campus have lasted throughout my college life. I made a group of friends that all lived in the same hallway. Four years later, a few of them transferred, some moved off campus, but we're all still in touch, even today.

—senior, University of Akron

* * *

Living in campus housing makes meeting people as simple as waking up, eating lunch in the cafeteria, going to classes, coming home, eating dinner in the cafeteria, and going out at night. It's easy because most first-year students come to college without close friends (or any friends) at the same school. Considering that most people need friends, meeting people and making friends becomes pretty easy. Even if you're shy or antisocial, you'll meet people while living in a residence hall who will become part of your life (to the antisocial people—sorry).

It all starts with being forced to meet your roommate(s). Then there are all those friends of your roommate(s) you'll meet. Then there are the people in your hall. Then there are people in your classes who live in student housing (you can walk

> "Participate in all 'floor/residence hall bonding' activities. These activities helped me make friends and meet people."
> —freshman, University of Delaware

back to your room together and study for exams together in the study lounges). Then there are all the people in the dining hall that you see again and again, many of whom you'll eat with. Then there are people at parties who look familiar from seeing them in the residence halls. Then there are opportunities like floor events, hall events, and all campus events. Familiar people from the residence halls will become the people with whom you become friends. And another perk worth mentioning—with coed dorms and even coed floors, you can find more than friends by living in student housing.

The opposite of on-campus housing is off-campus housing or private housing. And yes, living in an apartment off campus, living with a boyfriend or girlfriend, or living in a place other than a residence hall means missing out on an opportunity to meet people in most cases (some schools have communities for first-year students).

Quick note to transfer and commuter students: try to live on campus your first year. Even if you end up with first-year students, it's worth it. If you just can't live on campus, find friends who do live on campus. It will give you a place to crash and a way to meet other new friends. This can give you the best of both worlds.

Bottom Line
It's hard not to make friends while living in the residence halls (but if you really want to avoid making new friends, it's possible. For help on not making friends, see Tip #8).

Tip #11
Resident Assistants:
Your Personal Assistant

The Tip
Don't be afraid to talk to someone else's RA. If you don't mesh with your RA, find another one who can help.

The Story

When I first moved into the residence hall freshman year, my roommate and I didn't get along very well. I went to the RA on my floor and she wasn't supportive at all. She didn't listen to me and didn't help very much. It was extremely frustrating. That's when I started spending more time on my friend's floor. She lived below me. I mentioned my problems to the RA on my friend's floor. She not only listened, she helped me find ways to deal with my impossible roommate, and kind of took me under her wing. She adopted me as one of her own residents. It made life so much better. One time she called me to invite me to a floor program she was running. They were making homemade lip balm and she called me up. She said, "You should really join us because you practically live here." Second semester, after moving out of the room with my roommate from hell, my surrogate RA from the floor below continued to check in to make sure I was happy with my new living situation. She turned a hostile situation into one that was livable. She made living in the residence halls a lot more enjoyable. This year, I got lucky enough to get on her floor. Now she's my RA for real!

—sophomore, University of Miami–Coral Gables

*** * ***

Some people call them Resident Assistants. I've heard them called CAs, and I've also heard them called other names (but I can't publish those). For this tip, I'm going to call them RAs, but you can change the RA if you get confused—grab some Wite-Out, cover up RA, and fill in the appropriate initials that represent your RA.

Your RA is typically a student employee who lives, eats, and showers in the residence halls with the students (no, he or she shouldn't actually shower with you). Your RA's job (and it's often a paid job) is to make sure those living in the residence halls are comfortable in their homes and following the rules. It's a best friend–worst enemy relationship—best friend if you follow the rules, worst enemy if you break them.

Most RAs are there for the right reasons: to make your life comfortable. If you have a question or concern, talk to your RA. Should you need help dealing with a difficult roommate, talk to your RA. Should you need to find a new roommate, talk to your RA. Talk to your RA if you need directions to class, suggestions for a place to order in food, help dealing with dropping or adding classes, help adjusting to college life—the list goes on. If your RA doesn't have an answer, he or she can direct you to the people who can help you. If your RA is too busy or apathetic to help you with your problems, try an RA on another floor, your residence hall staff, the resident director, and the office of residence life.

> "When I was a freshman, I needed something to anchor me to the university. I decided to be an RA. I got to know so many people and made friends so quickly. I've been an RA for two years and plan on becoming a Hall Director."
> —sophomore, Eastern Oregon University

If your RA is a miserable lump and ignores you and your floor's needs—don't let it go. Report him or her. Every RA has a supervisor, and those supervisors have supervisors. Don't stop until you get answers. Should you find that your link to campus is an RA looking for a free ride, don't hesitate to make noise.

I spend a lot of time working with residence life staff, and they are some of the most passionate and supportive people on campus. Make your RA one of the five people in your corner. If you ever think you're alone, think again and reach out to your residence life staff. They can only help you if they know you need help. Don't be shy about letting them know you need something. They love to help! At least most of them.

Bottom Line
Resident Assistants are paid people in your corner (although they can bust you if you break the rules). Take advantage of them, but don't let them take advantage of you (no dating your RA).

Tip #12
Not All Residence Halls Are Created Equal

The Tip
Figure out what your campus has to offer in the way of student housing before getting to campus, and get your housing application in as soon as possible. When it comes to housing, it is often first come, first served.

The Story
As a senior resident assistant, I've seen a lot. I had one student who came down to school and was the last one to move into the student housing. She realized she was going to get the bed that was up high and also the smaller

closet. She ended up moving to another housing unit and then came back to the original one. If she had investigated the student housing, she would have known what she was getting into. Some of our students live in eight-person townhouses, and we also have four-person campus views with doubles and singles. What living arrangement you get also depends on pricing and when you sign up. This is pretty much standard at most campuses where I have friends. Another suggestion to new students is to get there early. A lot of students will come the night before and stay in a hotel. It helps to get there early if they want to get the good closet, the right bed, the desk near the window, and the dresser on the right side of the room. Also, if you get there earlier, there's a better chance of changing your room. Whoever gets there first gets to put their stuff all over the room.

—senior, Shawnee State University

* * *

This tip is pretty self-explanatory, but I'll explain it anyway.

Each residence hall has its own look, feel, and personality. Shop around. For example: dorm rooms come in singles, doubles, or triples (the most I've heard is four in a room). Bathrooms are community, suites (two or more rooms sharing one common bathroom), or private. Some residence halls are all men or all women. Some are coed by floor or by room (that's every other room, although some schools are considering coed rooms for couples). Some halls have visiting hours and/or quiet hours. There are ones with dining halls, ones with no dining halls, ones with little mini-marts inside, and ones with only vending machines.

Ones with dining halls might offer different dining options (like fast food franchises as opposed to just fast food) and different dining hours (some are closed on the weekend). Some halls are gigantic and others are tiny. Some are close to campus, others are far away. Some are newer, others are older. There are ones filled mostly with freshmen, ones with sophomores, and ones with upperclassmen. Some allow alcohol, but most don't. There can be parking or no

> "Living in a freshmen building turned out to be the best decision I made. The first week I made friends with people in my freshmen building that would become my second family. Eight years later, the bond is still as strong."
> —recent grad, University of Massachusetts–Amherst

parking. There may be classrooms or no classrooms inside the buildings, big study lounges or no study lounges, computer labs or no computer labs, RAs on every floor, RAs on every other floor, or just one RA per building. Some are more liberal and others are more conservative. Some are filled with athletes, some with international students, some with students in living and learning communities (programs where students attend class together and live together). Some are more diverse. Some lack total diversity. Some are less expensive and others more expensive. You get the idea.

Clearly, not all residence halls are created equal. To get the inside info, talk to the people already living in the places you want to live. You can do this during a campus visit. Just hang out near the residence hall that interests you and ask people questions when they walk by you. If you're not going to be on campus or feel like a freak stopping people, don't. You can also find students to contact via Facebook or the Residence Hall Association website (RHA is the student-run government for the campus's residence halls). Just send the student leaders listed on the page a note.

Surprisingly, the newest and nicest residence halls might not be the best. They can be filled with upperclassmen. While they might have more space and better water pressure, it can be better to live with first-year students in an older building. Each campus has different types of residence halls and different rules on when and how you can switch rooms, but you can usually work something out. Once you get to campus, you'll get a better sense of what the right fit means for you.

Bottom Line

The best place to live on paper might not be the best on campus—talk to upperclassmen or get in touch with current students via the admissions office, orientation office, and housing office and find the best places to live.

Tip #13
The Ugly Side of Residential Life

The Tip

I don't care where the dorm is or who lives there—always lock your door and your window when you're not in the room.

The Story

The old not-locking slapped me twice my freshman and sophomore years, at two different dorms. My roommate and I used to forget to lock our room's door—we knew our suitemates a little, so maybe the fear wasn't there. I woke up one October morning and saw the door wide open, a pile of weird sweats and tube socks on the floor. Turns out a drunken suitemate had disrobed in our room, thinking it was his, and later passed out naked in the right room. The lock was checked by each of us every night thereafter.

The next year our room was broken into, along with a dozen others, over Thanksgiving break. The guys were never caught, and they went through all the rooms with unlocked windows. Apparently the screen wasn't enough security. Weirdly, they left the TV, my roommate's computer, all of my CDs (I was offended), and my PlayStation, taking only my roommate's old Super Nintendo and games. Completing a collection, no doubt. But they also searched through my underwear drawer, a deep violation I'll never shake. The moral? Whoever you live with, no matter where, check the locks. Often. It's a dog-eat-Super Nintendo world out there.

—sophomore, University of
North Carolina at Chapel Hill

* * *

Most of the time, the ugliness is minimal, but any living situation can present problems.

Narrow-minded, selfish, stupid, arrogant, ignorant, and uncomfortable people who steal, vomit in the bathroom sink, cut their hair and/or nails in the bathroom, leave trimmings on the floor, don't flush, take four-legged showers, shout in the hallways, make noise, leave floaters on the bathroom shower floors, emit odd odors, leave garbage in the hall, smoke, pull fire alarms (yes, always evacuate), create absurd rules, have strange lifestyles, and think they're on a new reality show can be a serious nuisance. Should you have problems (and moving is not possible), instead of ignoring the problem or idly bitching and moaning, talk to the people on campus who can make things better (no, do not let your parents fix the problems—you do it). If the people who are supposed to fix the problem become a new problem, then talk to the residence hall director. If that doesn't work, then talk to the director of residence life. Get names. Document your journey through what can be a bureaucratic mountain of manure. Keep going until you reach the college president's office. And if that fails, blog about it, tweet about it, and get the media involved as a last resort—the campus newspaper, the local newspaper, the local TV news. The last thing a college wants is for parents, future students, and alumni to hear about how terrible life is on your campus—that's bad PR. Do not get pushed around.

And be smart with your stuff—while it's important to keep your door open to make friends, keep your doors and windows locked at all times when you're not around. Even if you're leaving for five minutes to shower, lock your door. Also, consider getting a footlocker to keep your expensive electronics, games, and other valuables (keep it locked). People who want what you have will work fast to get it. Put your name and ID on your personal items (I engraved my license number into digital equipment).

Keep your electronic passwords protected and change them frequently. Don't leave jewelry, cash, checks, credit cards, or bank statements sitting out. Keep valuables hidden in a small locked box in your closet or buried in a drawer.

Bottom Line

Appreciate the ugly side of residential life for all its beauty. It's all part of what makes this a once-in-a-lifetime experience. In ten years it will all be hilarious. Or maybe, twenty years.

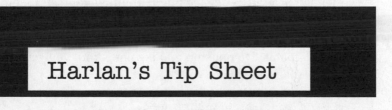

Harlan's Tip Sheet

Naked People, Places, and Resources

- *Start with the office of residence life.* This is the place where the director of the residence halls works. If you have issues that need to be resolved, this is the place to go. If your residence hall has an information desk, you can talk to your hall director.
- *Visit the office of the dean of students.* The dean of students or president's office is where you can find the people running the college. If you can't get answers to your question, concern, or problem in the office of residence life, head to the higher-ups.

- *Check out the residence hall student government.* The residence hall government is a great way to get involved and make new friends.
- *Go to floor activities/hall activities.* Attend these events. At least check them out. Go alone so other people who go alone can meet you and not be alone.
- *Get your housing application in early.* The sooner you apply, the better your chances of living where you want.
- *Find out how to change residence halls.* Every college has a different policy. If you're really unhappy, talk to your RA, the director of your residence hall, and then the head of residence life. If you find yourself in the wrong residence hall for whatever reason, talk to someone immediately. There are often waiting lists to change rooms. Do not stop making noise until you get results that will ensure your comfort.
- *Know all your dining options.* Different residence halls often offer different dining hours and food options. Some residence halls have fast food options in different dining halls. What you have at your hall isn't necessarily what's being served in other halls. Ask your RA.
- *Put your name on everything.* Engrave your electronics using an engraving gun. Put an ID number or your name on it. It makes it easier to identify it should it get stolen. Also, record serial numbers (there's got to be an app for that).
- *Regard the rules and regulations.* If you follow the rules, there's no problem. Most RAs are cool about things. Most of them follow the motto: "We just don't

want to see it, hear it, or smell it," because they don't want to have to deal with it.

- *Limit what you bring.* Don't bring everything. Leave your "maybe" pile at home. You can have it sent to you or you can get it on a quick trip home. For example, don't bring all your winter clothes in fall. As for CDs (if you still use them), burn them into MP3s. People love to steal music. As for jewelry and irreplaceables, leave them at home if possible.
- *Think twice about pets.* Start off with a plant. Keep it living for a semester, then move onto fish. Check out rules about pets, but college isn't the best atmosphere for pets that you want to live long and healthy lives.
- *Do NOT let your parents pick your residence hall or your roommate.* There is a line and that's crossing it.

3

Roommates

Good Ones, Bad Ones, and Everything in Between

Dear Harlan,

My roommate and her boyfriend are driving me crazy. They fight constantly and then they have make-up sex every day. I try to keep my nose out of it and ignore them, but they are constantly in our room. They never go to his place because she doesn't like his roommate. If I'm in our room alone watching TV or studying, they come in and take over the whole place. They'll change the channel or be loud and wrestle while I'm working. If I leave the room for even a second, they put up our "signal" on the door, which means they're having sex, so I can't come back in. I've tried talking to her, but she just laughs and denies being rude. I'm at my wit's end. What do I do?

—Ready to Move Out in Wisconsin

Dear Ready to Move Out,

A roommate who denies being rude is stuck in rude denial, one of the rudest forms of roommate rudeness. The question is, how can you get her out of rude denial? You can try being equally rude, but then she'll just think you're being rude and then have a reason to be rude on purpose, which will probably be far ruder than the way she's acting now, considering she doesn't think she's rude.

Try this approach—tell her that you want to talk, but don't accuse her of anything. Explain that you want to get along and hope you can be friends, but something has been making you uncomfortable. Then explain what has been happening. Pick out specific examples of when this has been a problem. Then ask her, what would she do if she were you? Ask what the best way to approach you would be. The hope is that she will begin to see the problem from your perspective and come out of rude denial. Then she can even help come up with solutions to the problem.

You might want to then add in a few of your own ideas. Ask her to keep the "signal" to a maximum number of times a week. Also, consider creating another "signal" that means you need time to yourself. If she's still unresponsive and rude, then talk to your resident assistant. Have him or her help you find a way out. If your roommate wants to get along, your roommate will find a way to get along. But first, she needs to come out of rude denial. Then you'll find out if she wants to get along.

The Tip
Respect each other's differences and make rules before you need rules.

The Story
My roommate was totally different from me in more ways than I can ever even explain, but we always had college in common. That was enough to help us get along. We respected our differences and wanted to get along. We created room rules together to avoid uncomfortable situations that could become big problems in the future—things like smoking in the room, overnight guests, sharing food, and cleaning needed rules to avoid big problems. Lastly, I knew coming into this that not all personalities mesh. You can be great roommates and not be great friends. As it happens, we turned out to be great friends.

—sophomore, Bay Path College

* * *

Assuming you've never spent time in prison and don't intend on spending time in prison, this could be the only time in your life that you'll spend a year or more living with a complete and total stranger. Until you've experienced living in an eight-by-eight-foot room (dimensions may vary) with someone you've never met before, it's hard to understand what it takes to get along. Even if you're living with someone you know extremely well (this tip applies to college students of all ages), even the most compatible roommates will have disagreements. Living together and having disagreements is as

> **"If you have a conflict, you need to work it out as soon as possible."**
> —senior, Bentley College

normal as living together and having to smell your roommate's gas on occasion. It's part of the experience (especially if your roommate has a high-fiber diet). Disagreements are normal. No couple, no friends, and no roommates will get along 100 percent of the time. Yet for some reason roommates think they're supposed to get along 100 percent of the time. Not true. Whether it's in a residence hall, an apartment, a fraternity or sorority house, or even at home, disagreements are unavoidable. How you and your roommate deal with the disagreements can be the difference between having a spirited conversation and an ugly confrontation.

Are you the roommate from hell? Yes, YOU? Want to be a great roommate and have a great roommate? Agree to follow these three rules before moving in together. RULE #1: Roommates who want to get along will find a way to get along. You don't have to like your roommate (think countries that hate each other). You just have to want to get along. RULE #2: Roommates are not automatic friends. Friendship is a bonus. Living with someone is about saving money and

How Much Trouble Are Roommates?

48.9 percent of students surveyed reported "frequently" or "occasionally" having difficulty getting along with roommate(s)/housemate(s).

—Higher Education Research Institute at UCLA

making college life affordable. Everyone living together needs to agree that they don't need to be best friends, they just need to be roommates and respect each other's stuff. Find your friends in other places. RULE #3: All roommates must agree to follow The Uncomfortable Rule. This Uncomfortable Rule states that if something makes any roommate uncomfortable, that roommate must talk about the problem within 24 to 48 hours or never talk about it all. NOT sharing the truth means breaking the rules. Most roommates will tell everyone on the planet when something is wrong BUT their roommate—and that's just wrong.

> "Someone didn't pick up this little candy wrapper that was sitting out...it was there for four days and then the dam broke. That's when they had a blowout."
> —sophomore, Thomas College

Have a conversation early in the roommate relationship and make it clear that you want to get along. Then ask your roommate to let you know when you do something that makes him or her uncomfortable. Then ask if it's cool for you to do the same. This will give all roommates permission to talk about uncomfortable situations. In fact, not talking about it turns into the wrong thing to do. Then, when a problem comes up, instead of a confrontation, you can have a conversation. If the issue is too uncomfortable and you live in a residence hall, see if your RA can help you figure out the best approach. If you want to get along and your roommate wants to get along, you'll get along. If not—welcome to roommate hell.

> Want more advice? Search "Roommate" on www.Naked Roommate.com and find more questions and answers. Search "Pop-Tart Roommate" for one of my favorites.

Remember, *roommates who want to get along find a way to get along*. You don't need to be best friends (this is why it's so important to have people, places, and patience to make other friends). Appreciate that your roommate doesn't need to want to get along for you to get along. My roommate my first year gave me the silent treatment. I just kept talking to him. He turned out to be a great listener.

As for the getting-along part of this, see if your roommate wants to get along before moving in together. For example, when you talk on the phone for the first time during the summer, mention a minor concern that you might have. It could be people smoking in the room (blame it on allergies), strange people spending the night in the room (blame it on your parents), or concern over getting to sleep for your 7:30 a.m. classes (blame it on not wanting to fail). Casually mention The Uncomfortable Rule and one thing that concerns you most. Do not go through a list of every single small issue on your mind. Just test the waters. If you sense that your roommate neither cares nor wants to get along with you, be concerned. Responding to you with, "Too bad. Sounds like your problem, not mine," is a bad sign. Try having another conversation or two and give your future roomie another chance. If he or she doesn't have a better attitude when you arrive on campus, consider finding a new roommate.

"After weeks of being teamed up on 3–1, I finally sat down with my roommates to discuss the issue. They told me what I did wrong and I told them what they did wrong. The tension after our talks lasted for about two weeks, but it subsided. I have never been happier with my decision."

—freshman, Michigan State University

If you find you and your roommate just don't click—that's fine. You just need to respect each other's space. If you arrive on campus with a plan of how you'll find friends outside your room, you won't arrive depending on your roommate to be your best friend. Oh, one more thing. If you contact your roommate via Facebook, do it to get essential information for moving in (like what stuff to bring and basic background info). Avoid having too deep of a friendship. This can leave you with little to talk about when you move in together. If your roommate should be slow to respond or accept your friend request, chill out. A lot of people travel abroad, work a lot of hours, or don't want to deal with college life until they have to. Don't take it personally. Ninety-nine percent of the time it has nothing to do with you.

> ### Are You the Shy Roommate?
>
> Shy roommates keep their feelings a secret, hate conflict, and blame their roommates for things that roommates have no idea they're doing. If you are keeping a secret because you are shy, you are the roommate from hell. Apologize to your roommate and share the truth. The roommate contract will help you get comfortable with the uncomfortable.

Bottom Line

Are you the roommate from hell? Use the roommate contract to guide you. Find a link at www.NakedRoommate.com/contract.

Tip #15
The Random Roommate

The Tip
Avoid judging your roommate based on first impressions.

The Story
The summer before I entered college, I remember getting really excited about who I was going to live with, who my "random rooming person" would be. The day finally came when I got her name and contact information in an envelope. I was so excited. I ran straight inside and called her. She didn't seem as enthused as I was, and it didn't seem like we had anything in common. We talked a few times before school, and still there was no real connection, so I was scared. On move-in day, her stuff was already in the room, so I looked at her shoe and movie/music collection to try to get a feel for the type of person she was. I got mixed messages from the dozen Disney movies and the Metallica albums in her music library. We were different and I didn't know if we would be friends. As the days went on, we got along fine, respected each other, and had fun. It's funny, because we don't know when exactly it was that we clicked, but we became friends—best friends,

> "Don't spend all your time freshman year with your roommate that you just met. I did everything with my roommate my first year only to realize that I had no other friends. As I found out more about her, I didn't want to spend time with her."
>
> —junior, UC–Davis

even. We joke around that we'd never have been friends in high school. We have different interests, but we connected on the same level. After freshman year, I had to transfer to a school that was in-state because of financial reasons (and then I was ten hours away from her). Leaving her and my hall of friends that I had grown to know and love was so hard. It has been three years since I lived with her, but we talk at least two times every single day, and I've been to visit a few times each year. She is still my best friend.

—senior, George Mason University

✳ ✳ ✳

For your entire life, you're told to avoid complete strangers; then you're thrown into a room with one (sometimes more than one). It's a strange phenomenon. It's the ultimate reality show—only this time it's real and no cameras are rolling (you hope). For some roommates, all you'll find that you have in common is college, breathing, and the same clothing (until you realize your similar taste in clothing is actually your roommate stealing your clothes). No matter what kind of roommate you find living in your room with you, remember this—strangers are only strange until you get to know them better. Then they're just weird.

> "I liked to stay up late every night and she was in bed by ten. She was into music, drama, and theater, and I was into sports and dancing. She was from a small private school, and I was used to my large public high school. It could have been a disaster, but when we got to school, it was perfect!"
>
> —sophomore,
> University of Wisconsin–Madison

It's normal to pass judgment on a new roommate when you first meet, or BEFORE you first meet. Chances are that your roommate will do the same thing. With social media and Google, it's easier than ever to pass judgment on a new roommate without ever meeting. You might decide not to get along before even seeing each other in person (don't do that). The user profile doesn't tell the story. There's the heavy metal roommate who turned out to be the clean, kind, and sober roommate; the pretty cheerleader roommate who turned out to be anything but the self-indulged popular girl her roommate expected her to be; and the roommate who thought he was a cool guy, but turned out to be anything but cool. It works both ways. It can take months to honestly know your roommate. Give him or her a chance before slapping on a label. Different = a good thing.

That said, not all roommates will become best friends. Some just tolerate each other. If you and your roommate appreciate that a roommate isn't required to be a friend, you can make this work. Not loving your roommates doesn't have to ruin your experience. Just make an effort to find close friends outside of your room.

Bottom Line

Don't judge your roommate until you live together for a couple months. Then judge your roommate and invite your roommate to judge you. When judging, it's sometimes more fun to actually dress up like a judge. Then your roommate knows that it's judgment time.

Tip #16
The Naked Roommate

The Tip
Realize that all people have different comfort levels with themselves and their bodies.

The Story
My first roommate in college was a very nice and interesting girl. Then, out of nowhere, she began to walk around without her shirt on. Not just in my room, either! She would walk in the halls, other people's rooms, boys' floors, and even in the office area of our dorm. To say the least, everyone has seen the girl in her bra. At first, it kind of bothered me, but after a few months, I have realized that it's just how she is. Plus, it could be worse—I mean, at least she wasn't walking around completely naked.

> "My sorority sister walked in early and her roommate was sprawled out on the futon, totally naked. The next week the naked roommate moved out. I guess she needed her own space."
> —junior, University of Georgia

—sophomore, Loyola University–Chicago

* * *

Nudity is like the cafeteria food served in the residence halls; everyone reacts differently to it. Some get completely disgusted, others delight in the experience. The bad experiences can spoil your appetite. The good can leave you hungry for more. Nakedness in a room is unavoidable—we are all naked at some point. Some of you might be naked right now (please, put something on). While researching the naked roommate tip, I came across three forms of roommate nakedness.

Category I:
The "I'm Naked, Look at Me" Roommate

This roommate loves being nude. He or she works in the nude, orders take-out food in the nude, plays video games in the nude, chats online in the nude, and lounges on your furniture in the nude. When someone says something to the naked roommate about his or her nudity, this roommate tends to be surprised. These roommates can be considered borderline or all-out nudists. Nakedness is freedom.

> "My roommate likes to change when the door is open. She doesn't seem to care that boys from other floors are walking by—come to think, that's probably why they're always walking by our room."
> —freshman, University of Georgia

Should you live in this environment, make it clear that it's not about his or her body, it's just that you're not quite comfortable with this level of nakedness. If you have to come to a compromise, perhaps your roommate can wear boxers, or a thong. Should you find yourself in this situation, take the top bunk and put plastic on the furniture.

Category II:
The "I'm Naked, Do Not Look at Me" Roommate

This naked roommate doesn't like being nude. He or she doesn't like to be looked at by others. This roommate is highly sensitive to any shape or form of nakedness (including his or her own). This roommate often exhibits behavior such as dressing in the closet, performing the "underwear under" maneuver (putting on his or her underwear while still covered by the towel), making an announcement such as "I'm changing, turn around," or directing your attention elsewhere by pointing out the window ("Wow! Look! A rainbow! A double rainbow!"). If you're afraid of nudity, the best approach is to get comfortable with your own nudity. If you're living with someone who can't handle nakedness in any shape or form, don't force them to change—let them change where, when, and how they want to change.

Category III:
The "I'm Naked, But Didn't Mean for You to See Me (Or Us)" Roommate

Two words—surprise nakedness. It's a shock to the nude and the clothed. It can happen after a shower, while in a sexual situation (with or without a partner), while changing, or while lounging. The best approach is to laugh (but not while pointing at any particular body part) or to apologize and never mention it again. If it happens more than once, say something sooner rather than later. If not, this will evolve into the "I'm Naked, But My Roommate Doesn't Care That I'm (We're) Naked, So I'll (We'll) Continue Being Naked" Roommate.

Whatever the level of nakedness in your room, the more you allow it to happen, the more likely it will become a habit. (And if it makes you uncomfortable, follow the precedent in Tip #14 and address the undress.) As a general rule, someone will be naked at some time. It's the law of roommate living. Address the undress or accept the naked truth.

Bottom Line

When finding yourself living with a naked room-mate, ALWAYS take the top bunk, put towels on the furniture, and request that there be no eating in the nude (for your health and his or her safety—cheese pizza can be hot and dangerous). If you are the naked roommate, then be kind and courteous while naked.

Tip #17
The Best Friend Roommate

The Tip
Do not live with your best friend from high school.

The Story
I made the mistake of living with one of my best friends from high school. We got along, but we got so sick of each other. We just got on each other's nerves. It's not like we ever threw down or anything like that—at the worst it was throwing a plate of French fries at him, but no punches. The biggest problem with living together was that it was harder to meet new people. We were always chilling in the room. It was way too easy to stay inside and do nothing. I did meet some new friends, but we shouldn't have lived together our first year. It could have waited. Honestly, I do feel like I missed out.

—junior, DePaul University

* * *

Living with a best friend in college is like eating ten pounds of chocolate every day for ten months out of the year. What once made you happy can make you sick. (If you don't like chocolate, please substitute ten pounds

> "I got sick of looking at my best friend's face, hearing my best friend's voice, and smelling my best friend's gas."
> —senior, University of Illinois

of your favorite candy.) I know this is a controversial tip. But no matter what you think about rooming with friends, there is definitely more to lose than there is to gain (yes, it can work, but that's not the point of college). Here's why:

1. Best Friends Don't Try as Hard to Get Along

When you've known someone for most of your life, they don't always try as hard to please. A best friend is more likely to leave the room messy, expel gas at will, and abuse your stuff. The more comfortable the relationship, the more complacent the people in the situation tend to become.

> "There is nothing to gain by living with a friend. It's a lose-lose situation."
> —senior, Bentley College

Friends take advantage of the situation—and that leads to resentment. Cleaning, respecting each other's space and things, and following rules become optional. Not that a stranger is guaranteed to respect your space and your things, but at least with a stranger, there isn't much of a loss if you never speak to each other again.

2. College Is about Making NEW Friends

Living with a best friend is *not* what college is all about. Living with a friend is just a security blanket—it can end up suffocating the relationship. Living apart helps you branch out and get to know each other's new roommates (and their friends). Should you or your best friend want to hang out, you can always choose to be together. But it's a choice. Living together means not having a choice and not being motivated to meet others.

3. Living with a Best Friend Means Missing Out

Being forced into a room with someone forces you to learn how to compromise, communicate, deal with conflict, and most important, appreciate another person's culture, lifestyle, and family dynamics. Never again will you have the opportunity to see the inner workings of a stranger's world (and you might never want to see the inner workings again). It's a once-, twice-, three-, four-, five-or-more-times-in-a-lifetime experience, depending how many roommates you have. Living with a best friend means missing out on living with someone you don't know—and that means missing out. No question about it!

> "Don't live with a large group of friends. It sounds like fun but by the end of the year we wanted to kill each other. We constantly talked behind each other's backs and could barely communicate. Since moving out, we've become friends again, but I would never again live with people that close to me."
>
> —senior, UCLA

Bottom Line

If you live with your best friend and hate it, you'll lose a best friend. If you live with a stranger, you'll lose someone you never knew—not a loss.

Tip #18
The Gay, Lesbian, or Bisexual Roommate (pick one)

The Tip
To roommates who aren't gay: listen to other people's stories and try to learn. Everyone is unique. To those roommates who are gay: don't be afraid to be yourself. The people around you will respect you—the ones who don't will lose out.

The Story
When I moved into a dorm freshman year, I swear everyone had a boyfriend. They would talk about them all the time. The pictures overwhelmed their counters and desktops. My pictures were of family and friends. In the bottom drawer of my closet sat a picture of my girlfriend, hidden so no one would find out. After dodging the boyfriend question for a while, I found the courage to put her picture on my desk. Nobody seemed to notice for a long time until my roommate said, "Is that your sister?" After a short pause, I answered in a manner sure not to offend, "That is my girlfriend. We have been dating for about a year." "Oh," was all I got. She was only my roommate for two more weeks.

One thing I want to tell gay/lesbian/bi-questioning people is that it's not that bad. Being yourself is so much better than being the person you think people want you to be. It took me a long time to accept myself and show my true colors. I went from being a freshman who hid the truth to a junior who has a rainbow flag and other icons up in my room. People respect me more now that I am completely open and honest to myself and everyone else. A lot of the time, friends and floormates knock on my door and ask if they can come in and talk to me about my life and what I've dealt with. They want to know what it's like and what offends me. One friend walked into my room and asked how my parents dealt with my homosexuality. After a long discussion, she went home and talked to her parents about it. The interesting part? She wasn't gay, not even bi. She just wanted to tell her parents about me. If you're not gay, talk to people who are and listen, listen, listen. If you are gay, lift the veil and let your true self breathe! Show the world the beauty underneath.

—junior, Bemidji State University

* * *

Some of you will have gay, lesbian, bisexual, transgender, queer, or questioning roommates. Some of you will be the LGBTQ roommate. Assuming that your college doesn't have an all-LGBTQ residence hall, there's a fairly decent chance that you or a friend will end up living with someone who is gay, lesbian, or bisexual. If you are gay or lesbian, whoever lives with you will have a 100 percent chance of living with a gay or lesbian roommate.

If you're not gay, lesbian, or bisexual and find yourself living with a gay, lesbian, or bisexual roommate, there are three ways to react. The first is to have a problem. The second is to create problems by alienating your roommate by verbally or physically attacking him or her (called bullying and assault). The third is to look at this situation as a unique once-in-a-lifetime experience. Unless you're gay, lesbian, or bisexual, this is probably your first opportunity to live with someone who is. And considering the huge number of people in the world who are LGBTQ, this is an opportunity to learn about something totally foreign to you (the situation would be extra foreign if living with a gay, lesbian, or bisexual international student). If you're afraid that living with a gay or lesbian roommate will turn you gay or lesbian, you are probably the Q (queer or questioning) because people don't turn into anything—either you are or you aren't.

Your roommate's sexual orientation is not your right to know. If your roommate is out (signs can include rainbow posters, pictures of gay icons, and wearing T-shirts reading, "Gay, Proud, and Your New Roommate"), feel free to talk to him or her about it. Start with, "I really want to get along, but I've never lived with someone who was gay before. (Note: if you are following The Uncomfortable Rule from Tip #14, this all becomes a lot easier.) Can I ask you a few questions?" If your roommate is cool with that, then ask away. Don't be offended if you express your concern about your roommate possibly making a pass at you and he

> ### Beware of Roommate Bullying
> If you're being bullied because of your sexual orientation, tell the authorities and advocates on campus and get help immediately. You are surrounded by people, places, and resources to help you.
>
> Resource: www.Facebook.com /AntiGayBullying

or she answers with, "It would never happen—I don't find you attractive at all. Besides, I'm already involved."

If you're gay, lesbian, or bisexual and you're living with

a roommate who isn't, only come out when you have support on campus. You need to have your people and places so you can handle any possible reaction. When you're ready, let your roommate know that you're open to answering any questions. You can say something as little as, "You might have guessed from the pictures of my boyfriend/girlfriend that I'm gay. I don't know if you've ever had a gay roommate before or if you have friends at home who are gay, but I don't mind if you ask me any questions…"

Should you find yourself living with a gay, lesbian, heterosexual, or bisexual roommate and find that it's too much for you to handle, move out. But please, be respectful. It's your problem that you can't handle your roommate's sexual orientation, not your roommate's. He or she is just being him- or herself. Attacking your roommate with words or actions like secretly taping him or her in a romantic situation isn't just cruel and insensitive—it can be criminal. For those who are gay, lesbian, or bisexual and are concerned about finding your places on campus, find out if there is an LGBTQ group or organization on campus. If you can't find resources and support services on your campus, look to a nearby campus community and find people in your corner.

For more on LGBTQ issues, see Tip #99.

Bottom Line
If you're afraid living with a gay roommate will turn you gay, you're already gay—you just haven't admitted it.

Tip #19
The Noisy, Naughty, and/or Nasty Roommate

The Tip
Say something to your roommate immediately if there is a problem or it will only get worse and worse. Don't be afraid to speak up!

The Story
My roommate was disgusting. She never put anything away. She left crumbs, pizza stains, and random spots on the furniture. She didn't want to clean, she didn't care to clean, and she didn't know how to clean. We had our own bathroom

> "Every evening at 9:01 p.m. her cell phone rang (free nights and weekends). She would spend hours talking on the phone. She never stopped talking!"
> —freshman, University of Mount Union

attached to the room and she would leave used items wherever they landed (use your imagination). It was so disgusting. I made the mistake of not saying anything until later in the semester. It was too late. I exploded. She stopped talking to me. And we still don't talk. My advice—don't let it get out of control. If it gets bad fast, say something or get out of the living arrangement.

—sophomore, Wheelock College

* * *

Like a growing mold on a half-eaten chicken finger under your roommate's bed, the noisy, naughty, and/or nasty roommate can be hard to spot at first. It can take weeks before becoming a serious problem. The master tip—deal with it before it gets ugly. The longer you let it go, the more out of control the situation will become.

"I was asleep; they were in the next bed having sex."
—sophomore, University of Michigan

Most roommates are reasonable if you deal with the issues right away (and you've set a precedent already for dealing with the uncomfortable).

Deal with the Noise Factor

It's about common courtesy and respect. If you have early classes, let your roommate know what nights need to be early nights for you. If your roommate wants to talk on the phone during late-night hours, suggest he or she talk in the hall or lounge. If your roommate wants to listen to music, suggest headphones. If your roommate wants to watch TV at night, then find a way to work it out without making him or her leave—it's your roommate's room, too. But considerate roommates will minimize the noise.

Avoid Medical Misunderstandings

If you're coming to campus with a diagnosed medical condition, consider telling your roommate. People with ADHD, autism, depression, and other medical conditions can easily be misunderstood.

Deal with the Naughty Factor

Once you discover that you have a naughty roommate, make some rules. Don't just let it go and complain to your friends. Find a system to let each other know if you're "busy." This includes a system for roommates who insist on getting it on while they are alone (yes, it happens). Try to limit the "I'm getting it on" signal to a certain number of nights a week. If having sex while you are in the room is unacceptable, say something the first time it happens. If your roommate ignores you or loses control, talk to your RA (assuming your RA isn't the naughty partner). Oh yes, if your roommate insists on doing things with someone while you're in the room, you DO NOT have to pretend to be invisible. You have every right to stand up

> "Every residence hall I've ever supervised has a smelly roommate situation; it's the roommate that doesn't shower, doesn't clean, and doesn't care. Talk about it when the stink starts—if not, it will only start to smell worse and worse."
> —experienced college professional

and watch. You can even make comments. Shouting, "Wow, that was fast!" is not inappropriate. Inviting friends over to watch can be a quick way to get things to end. But do not Snapchat the action (that's plain wrong).

Deal with the Nasty Factor

By week four, you'll smell it, see it, or step in it. If you follow the rules in Tip #14 you can safely have honest (and uncomfortable) conversations. If your roommate smells funny, suggest deodorant. For bad gas, ask that you at least get fair warning. For the nude or sweaty roommates, ask them to put down a towel on the couch when lounging. Whatever the situation, try and approach the problem the way you would want your roommate to approach you. For super nasty

> "Watch out for the crazy roommate who has a 20,000 volt Taser, eats catnip, and entangles his testicles, causing them to be surgically removed. It happened!"
> —sophomore, Juniata College

roommates, see if your RA can get the roommate to sign a roommate contract that includes a hygiene clause.

Bottom Line
If you have a noisy or nasty roommate, sleep in the top bunk or in a high loft close to the ceiling. Makes you less likely to find new stains (yes, I just crossed the line).

Tip #19.99
The Masturbating Roommate

The Tip
If you wake up to your roommate masturbating, talk about it before it becomes a habit.

The Story
My first year in college, I woke up several times to my weirdo roommate petting the kitty (if you will) and couldn't ever go back to sleep because of it. We had absolutely nothing in common in the first place, but I didn't think she was THAT freakish; I never expected to wake up every other night to the Plain-Jane from Wanaukee doing such a thing, especially while I was in the room sleeping! I didn't have the heart to call her out on her doings or to switch roommates at semester because she was nice and tidy, so I dealt with it for the rest of the year and ended up not spending any time in the dorms like I should have to meet new people!

—recent grad, University of Wisconsin–Milwaukee

***

I know. Why go here? We must. You men and women have grown up with online porn. It's as accessible as bottled water and chewing gum. You might find yourself in a situation where you hear noises coming from across the room (or above or below you), but your roommate is all alone. Or you might open the door and find your roommate sharing an intimate moment—alone. Then again, you might be the one across the room or behind that door who gets caught. However it may happen, nip masturbation in the bud before it becomes a dangerous weed. Remember, silence in a roommate situation is viewed as consent. If you see it or hear it and don't do or say anything about it, your roommate might think you're cool with this. If you've followed the previous tips, you should have set a precedent to be able to talk about things that make either of you uncomfortable. This classifies as uncomfortable for most roommates. Assuming this makes you or your roommate uncomfortable (who knows, you might be comfortable with this), talk about it.

As a rule, wait twelve to twenty-four hours to discuss the situation following the surprise discovery. Don't talk about it while it's happening (awkward). Mention that you know you're supposed to discuss things that make you uncomfortable. Approach it the same way you'd approach walking in on your roommate being intimate with another person (or multiple people). Mention what happened and that you're fine with self-love, just not seeing or hearing it. Then see if you can come up with a system so it doesn't happen again. Create a "sex signal" that can be used to avoid interruption (for example, a sock on the door or a picture of a hand on a white board). This can be the same sign used to indicate that one of you is with a partner. If this is too hard to discuss, have your residence life staff lend a helping hand. But don't just let it go. If you do, you risk unleashing a masturbating monster.

Bottom Line
The perfect, affordable holiday gift for your roommate: a box of tissues.

Tip #20
The Your-Girlfriend/Boyfriend-Doesn't-Live-Here Roommate

The Tip
If your roommate has a girlfriend/boyfriend, discuss up front when the significant other will and will not be allowed in the room. There's nothing worse than having an extra roommate.

The Story
My freshman year in college, I lived with a sophomore. He had a girlfriend that he had been seeing for years. She used to come by all the time. She even had a key. It got so bad that she was there when I left and there when I came home. She was even there by herself. Because I was new at school and he was older, I didn't have the courage to tell him what I felt. I just let it go. It got so bad that I

wouldn't even change in the room because she was always there. She ate my food and smoked cigarettes in the room.

> "Freshman year, I lived in a triple. We had to sit one of our roommates down and tell her that she needed to get our permission to have her boyfriend spend the night."
> —sophomore, Boston University

He did ask if I minded once or twice, but I told him that it was fine, it didn't matter. I didn't want him to get upset. I didn't have the courage to tell him. It all got even worse after that. I ended up moving out after a few weeks, so it never got too heated. I should have told him when I had the chance, but I didn't.

—sophomore, University of Illinois

* * *

There are few things more uncomfortable than finding yourself stuck with an extra roommate—like finding yourself stuck with two, three, or four extra roommates (or catching your roommate in the act of self-love). Typically, it unfolds in one of two ways:

1. Your roommate comes to campus with a significant other. From day one, your roommate thinks that his or her boyfriend or girlfriend can come over and do whatever he or she wants. The significant other even gets his or her own key.

> "My freshman year, my roommate would leave sticky notes on the door that always said he was 'studying.' That was always the tip-off—he never studied."
> —junior, University of Minnesota–Twin Cities

2. Your roommate falls in love during the year. It starts out with a night here and there, and then quickly turns into endless nights *here* and never there. You are the third wheel living in your own home.

Both situations are problematic, but both can be avoided by preemptive planning. For those moving in with a roommate who has a significant other, ask your roommate how often he or she plans on having the significant other spend the night. Mention that it makes you very uncomfortable having someone else hang out in your room alone (assuming it does). If it's a problem, find a way to compromise or find a new roommate.

If you're moving in with a roommate who isn't attached, make sure you have a plan to avoid gaining an extra roommate (or two). Agree not to make a copy of the keys for boyfriends or girlfriends. Insist that a significant other can't be in the room alone. And mention that if it ever gets to be too much, you'll let the other roommate know.

Again, set a precedent early on that if something bothers you or your roommate (I know this is repetitive, but most people do not do this), you'll both talk about the situation. That way, it's not as if either of you is attacking the other and nobody will be put on the defensive. It doesn't have to be a confrontation, it can be a conversation.

One last thing. Some roommates really don't want any significant other of the opposite or same sex hanging out in the room. It can be a cultural thing, a safety thing, or some other thing that you can't begin to understand. Before assuming your roommate is trying to ruin your life, understand that your roommate might be a survivor of sexual assault or have genuine fear that has nothing to do with trying to upset you.

Bottom Line

The only good thing about having an extra roommate—if you get locked out there's someone to let you in.

Tip #21
The Lying, Stealing, Klepto Roommate

The Tip

If your roommate takes, borrows, or steals your stuff, say something—don't just let it go. You might never get it back.

The Story

I had one particular roommate who was extremely hard to live with. Besides being messy (she would smear peanut butter on the couch), she'd steal my stuff and then lie to my face about it. It got so bad that I was forced to put my initials on everything, including food, clothing, iPod, toothpaste, and even tampons. Still, she would take things. I tried to make rules, but it was too late. My biggest mistake was not saying something sooner. One time, I went into her closet and saw a few of my friend's missing

> "One day, I discovered that she had been 'borrowing' my underwear. I moved my underwear to my desk drawer. She stopped sharing, but I sometimes find paper clips and other office supplies in my underwear."
> —sophomore, Bay Path College

sweaters. Later, she lied to us about it, and this was while they were still hanging in her closet. It's important to set

ground rules early when you move in together, like what you'll buy together and what you'll share and what can be borrowed. It's a trust issue, and until you know your roommate, it's hard to trust. Even then, you can't be totally sure that things of yours won't end up in her closet.

—senior, University of Wisconsin–Madison

* * *

You might not realize it, but this book or the device you're reading it on could get stolen (yes, a scary thought). Sadly, some roommates like to steal. Some take clothing, jewelry, money, food, tampons, or condoms (and then sell them to people down the hall at 3 a.m.—the condoms, not the tampons). Know that most roommates will not take your things, but some might—and do. And if it's not your roommate, it could be someone who has had access to your room.

To minimize risks:

- Put your initials on *everything*. Use a permanent marker on clothing labels, food (on the wrapper, not the actual food), toiletries, condoms, and tampons (again, on the outside labels, please). For electronics, consider using an engraving tool and putting your driver's license number or something else that will distinguish it into the actual casing. Take pictures of your stuff on your cell phone (and email the pics to yourself in case your phone gets stolen). Make sure to include the serial number. It makes recovering and identifying stolen stuff easier.

- Do not bring valuables or irreplaceable things to campus. If you're afraid of having something stolen that can't be replaced, leave it at home.
- Keep anything you do not want to get stolen out of sight. If it's in plain view, someone can easily be tempted to take it without you ever noticing.
- Lock your room door (that's double lock) whenever you leave the room (even if it's for 10 seconds). It's easy to open doors with credit cards (I've done it when locked out). It's even easier to get in when the door is unlocked.
- Get a footlocker and keep it in your room (under a bed or in a closet is optimal). With thousands of dollars in electronics, computers, video games, and valuables, a footlocker is one more layer of protection from someone looking to make a quick grab.
- Don't hesitate to tell. Alert your RA or an authority in the residence hall if something is stolen. Mention to your roommate that you think someone is stealing and he should put his stuff away. It's not accusing your roommate, but it's telling him or her that you're aware.

Bottom Line

I'd like to take this opportunity to confess that I still have a CD I "borrowed" from my roommate in college.

The Tip
When you have a roommate who comes in drunk, don't try to deal with it when he or she is drunk and you're sober. It will annoy you, and he or she won't be able to comprehend it. Instead, wait until the morning when he or she sobers up…or build yourself a canopy.

The Story
My roommate loves going out; it doesn't matter what night of the week it is. It's not that she's inconsiderate; she's just not really "there" when she drinks. During the first few weeks of school, almost every night, she would come into the room after I was sleeping and yell something—not a word, just a weird "ohhh-ahhhh." Then she'd turn on the lights, see that I was sleeping, and realize that she'd woken me up. Then she would begin to apologize for waking me, not realizing that she's now keeping me up later. After her nightly apology, she'd stumble all over the room and finally go to sleep. My first approach was to get her a night-light. When that failed, I decided to build a canopy. I went to the fabric store and spent $80 (I got carried away—the whole interior designer part of me). I then suspended the fabric with a little shower curtain connected to a wire hanging across the ceiling. I

> **"He was the nicest guy and most considerate roommate, but he sold drugs."**
> —junior, Indiana University

took matters into my own hands. It works great. She stills come in at night, but she's quieter. Building my customized noise barrier helped her get the hint. People could take a much easier approach by talking to their roommate. I went a different route.

—freshman, University of Georgia

***

If your roommate uses this book as a coaster for beer or uses this page as rolling paper for a joint, you might have a drunk, high, or just incredibly stupid roommate. The ultimate roommate rule holds true with drunk and/or high roommates.

> "My roommate jumped off his bed, opened the middle drawer behind my bed, and started urinating. It went all over me, my bed, and all my pictures from home. I was pissed."
> —recent grad, Ohio State University

roommates who want to get along will find a way to get along. That's assuming your roommate isn't too drunk or high to remember to try to get along.

There are kind and considerate drunk and/or high roommates, and then there are angry and inconsiderate drunk and/or high roommates. For example, the considerate roommate leaves the room to vomit. The inconsiderate roommate lets it fly wherever it lands (hopefully you're not on the bottom bunk). Until you live with your roommate, it's hard to know which one you might encounter. Also worth mentioning: you may not have a drunk or high roommate—he or she might be a completely sober roommate. Imagine that.

Again, make sure to deal with the problems when they come up because issues involving alcohol and drugs tend to get worse as the term progresses. The biggest mistake roommates make is saying nothing. When dealing with a roommate who is under the influence, wait until he or she is sober to discuss the situation. If the roommate vomits, urinates, or defecates in the room, take videos and/or pictures. Your roommate won't remember and might need evidence to help jog his or her memory (here's you drunk, here's you pulling down your pants, here's you pooping in my shoe). Talk about it sooner rather than later. Avoid letting it brew inside you because one day it will boil over. The first time is the best time to deal with it.

> "I'm the kind of roommate who likes to hang out in my room and do my own thing. He was the kind who liked to party and wanted to be popular. Mostly, he took his partying to other places. When he did come home, he was wasted and usually just passed out."
> —sophomore, Loyola University–Chicago

As for problems like using or selling drugs or alcohol in the room, if it's in the room and it's against the rules, then you could be busted, too. If you're uncomfortable with your living situation, talk to your RA. And if you happen to be the one bringing drugs or alcohol or into the room, don't be irritated or surprised when your roommate asks you to keep it out of the room. It has as much to do with him or her as it does with you.

One more thing to keep in mind —if your roommate is ever nonresponsive, unconscious, or

When Getting Peed on

1) Cover your eyes.

2) Get something to absorb the pee.

3) Record it (so when your roommate sobers up you can show videos and photos).

vomiting blood, please *seek medical attention*. If you're not sure if your roommate needs medical attention, this is a sign that your roommate 100 percent needs medical attention. Do not let him or her just "sleep it off." There's always the chance that your roommate might never wake up.

Bottom Line
Your roommate's constant partying will only be a temporary problem—until he or she fails out, passes out, or forgets where he or she lives.

Tip #23
The Roommate in Need

The Tip
When you live with someone, talk to a professional when you see signs that he or she needs help.

The Story
I had a really emotional roommate. We had talked to her parents and tried to get help, but there was only so much they could do. One day, I came home and found that she was trying to commit suicide. It was relationship-related. She was dating someone long distance and he had dumped her a month before college. She just had downhill depression. She wasn't enjoying school. She didn't settle in and make friends. I actually came home and walked in and found her really emotional. She had gone to the bathroom—and I just knew that something

was happening. She had taken pills and was trying to cut herself. We had to call the ambulance. She was pretty angry and violent, but they got her under control and took her to the hospital. My friend and I followed her. She was taken to another hospital. She came home a couple days later. She survived, and she's doing a little better, but she is still having a hard time dealing with everyday life. College is full of emotionally unstable people.

—senior, University of Virginia

* * *

I hate to end this roommate section on such a downer, but you can save lives (see, this isn't such a downer). It's a tough tip, but this could happen. I know, it's not fair that you should be the one to have to get someone you barely know the help he or she needs. When you're a roommate, you see things most people don't see. You see more than family, friends, boyfriends, and girlfriends. You see more than the RAs. You see things you don't want to see, but if you see it, please don't ignore it.

For depression information, see Tip Sheet on page 500.

For alcoholism information, see Tip Sheet on page 375.

For drug risks information, see Tip Sheet on page 405.

For eating disorder information, see Tip Sheet on page 502.

If you think that your roommate is in danger, get other people involved who can help keep him or her from hurting him- or herself. While researching this book, I heard story after story about roommates attempting suicide, getting dangerously drunk, going off their meds because they wanted a "fresh start" (horrible

> "My roommate cut herself all the time. She was a cutter. I once took her to the emergency room and sat with her."
> —junior, UCLA

idea), and doing other self-destructive things. If it happens, approach your roommate (when he or she is sober). Talk to your RA. Talk to people in the counseling center, and talk to your roommate's parents if possible. Understand that a lot of students come to campus with a recognized medical condition or disability that can make them more susceptible to certain behaviors. Also, the onset of mental illness can happen during the college years.

In an emergency, call 911. Remember, passed-out roommates might not get up, meaning they may be dying. In *The Naked Roommate's First Year Survival Workbook*, there's a part of the roommate contract that gives each roommate permission to call the other's parent if either is in imminent danger. Whether or not you've made this agreement, consider reaching out to your roommate's parents if you think your roommate is in terrible danger. Just make sure they are loving and

Emergency Contact

Ask your roommate to exchange emergency contact numbers. Should you need help and can't get it—your roommate can reach out to your lifeline.

caring parents—not abusive addicts who need as much help as your roommate does. Help your roommate and allow your roommate to help you.

Your roommate might not appreciate your help, but people in these situations aren't usually the happiest people to begin with. So, don't let his or her reaction deter you. If you can save your roommate from a dangerous situation, at least try. And if you find that you just need to get away from the situation because your roommate is too messed up too much of the time, then do it. Not everyone can save the world and take care of themselves at the same time.

And if you should find that you're the one who is being spoken to by a concerned roommate, don't just brush it off. Listen. Chances are that you're the one who is wrong and your roommate is right. At least listen.

Bottom Line

If you think your roommate needs help, don't think about it. Call the paramedics, police, or a professional on campus—just get him or her help.

Harlan's Tip Sheet

Naked People, Places, and Resources

- *Check in with your new roommate.* Talk before leaving for school. Figure out what you each of you should bring. Avoid two microwaves, two game systems, and two lava lamps. (That is, unless you have a microwave that's really special to you that you don't want to share.)
- *Avoid judging your roommate via their social networking profiles.* Wait to meet them before deciding not to like them.
- *Make it a rule.* Talk about the things that make you uncomfortable the first time they become problems. Ask your roommate to do the same. Avoiding conversations leads to confrontations.
- *Give your roommate permission to simply be a roommate.* A roommate isn't required to be a friend. Being friends with your roommate is a bonus.
- *Find out how to change rooms.* Typically, you have to wait a certain period of time before moving. Talk to your RA or resident director if you need to move. Every school has its own rules and regulations. If it's an emergency, there are always exceptions to the rule.
- *Give it a few weeks.* Don't be so quick to run away from your roommate because he or she is different. You might be "different" to someone you're living

with. Unless you're in danger, give it at least a few weeks.

- *Call campus police.* Report any illegal happenings to the campus police. If they don't seem to be very effective, call the local police and get them involved.
- *Use your counseling center.* If your roommate needs help, if you need help, or if you want to know how to handle a situation, talk to a counselor or therapist.

Websites Worth Visiting

- Parents, Families, and Friends of Lesbians and Gays
  Website: www.PFLAG.org
  Facebook: www.Facebook.com/PFLAG
  Twitter: www.Twitter.com/PFLAG
- The Trevor Project
  Website: www.TheTrevorProject.org
  Facebook: www.Facebook.com/TheTrevorProject
  Twitter: www.Twitter.com/TrevorProject
- Al-Ateen—Offering hope and help for friends and family of alcoholics
  Website: www.Al-Anon.ALATeen.org
- Anti-Gay Bullying Alliance
  www.Facebook.com/AntiGayBullying
- It Gets Better Project
  Website: www.ItGetsBetter.org
  Facebook: www.Facebook.com/ItGetsBetterProject
  Twitter: www.Twitter.com/ItGetsBetter
- Half of Us—a newer site offering help and support to a college-age audience
  Website: www.HalfofUs.com

Hotlines

- National Hope Network
  1-800-SUICIDE (1-800-784-2433) twenty-four hours
  a day, seven days a week
- National Suicide Prevention Hotline
  1-800-273-TALK (1-800-273-8255)
- Gay and Lesbian National Hotline
  1-888-843-4564
- Need Immediate Help? Call 1-800-273-TALK

(See Tip Sheets in chapters 9, 10, 11, and 13 for more information on sex, alcohol, drugs, sexual assault, and depression.)

A Break to Warn You about Holiday Break

*WARNING #1: YOU MIGHT SEE YOUR PARENTS NAKED.

Since you left for college, your mom and dad have been running around the house, naked, chasing each other. Their love is insatiable.

If you see your parents without clothes on, do not yell, scream, or cry (tempting). Look away, turn, and exit. Your goal is to avoid the visual burn in your brain. Soon, you'll be back at school in the peace and quiet of your own room with your roommate.

> "It gets better the older you get. Coming home as a freshman is a lot different than coming home as a senior."
> —recent grad, University of Missouri

*WARNING #2: YOU MIGHT NOT HAVE A BED (OR BEDROOM).

It was never yours to keep. It was a loaner. If you find a treadmill where your bed used to be, appreciate that your parents are passionate about fitness. If you find a sewing machine in place of your dresser, be grateful Mom or Dad has a new love for fashion. Instead of getting angry and resentful, ask for a new tie and get cozy snuggling on that treadmill under a yard of finely woven silk. Soon, you'll be back at school sleeping in your twin bed with extra long sheets again.

*WARNING #3: YOU MIGHT GET VERY HUNGRY AT HOME.

Your parents have become accustomed to cooking for two (assuming they are empty nesters) or going out to dinner. If you're lucky enough to share a meal with them (assuming they invite you), expect to have one choice of entree. There will be no stir-fry station, no burger bar, and no bottomless salad bar. If you want options, wait until you're back in your SODEXO dream kitchen, meal card in hand.

*WARNING #4: YOU MIGHT NOT BE ABLE TO SLEEP AT HOME.

When you were at school, you had no idea what your parents did or who they did it with. Now, you know when they come and go. Unless they call, or tell you their plans ahead of time, you won't know they're back safely until you hear the door open in the middle of the night. This can cause sleepless nights for loving children when parents still aren't home at 3 a.m. Once you're back at school it will end and you'll no longer worry.

*WARNING #5: YOUR PARENTS MIGHT BE TOO BUSY FOR YOU.

Between going out, working out, sewing, and chasing each other around the house, it might be hard for them to fit you in. Plan ahead. Remind them how they used to love spending time with you. Consider bringing out old family photos and videos to refresh their memories. Ask them when you can plan on dedicated time together. Explain that when you're back at school, they will have all their free time back.

*WARNING #6: IF NONE OF THIS HAPPENS,..

And your parents have one of the aforementioned problems with you (it happens), appreciate that they love you, miss you, and want to spend as much time with you as possible. Be patient and compassionate. This is a big change for everyone. Happy holidays!

Finding Friends

4

Your Social or Antisocial College Life

Dear Harlan,

I started college a month ago, and I haven't made any friends. I have a roommate, but she has friends from her high school and doesn't seem to want to make any new friends. All of the people on my floor seem to have their own groups already, and I don't think I can fit in with them. I think this is a problem for me, because I am very shy, and people see me differently because of it. I just can't seem to get over my shyness, and it is affecting my whole life. I need some advice on how to make some friends, because I don't think I can go through school without them.

—Friendless

Dear Friendless,

Unless you start a club on campus called "Shy People on Campus" and hold meetings in your room, you'll actually need to leave your room to make new friends. (Even if you did start the SPOC club, most people would be too shy to come to the first meeting.)

Considering that most shy people don't like attention and work to avoid situations where they feel like they're being judged, you should work to put yourself in group situations where the activity, not you, is the focus. Activities like sports, academic associations, performing arts, fraternities and sororities, religious organizations, and various clubs and activities will work. Pick a group that doesn't need to select you. Also, a part-time job can be helpful. The idea is to put yourself in rooms with people over a long period of time. As these people become more familiar, you'll become more comfortable and will naturally make friends. It just takes time, work, and patience. And if none of this advice works, head to the counseling office and get help. The problem might be more than just being shy.

Tip #24
The Snow Globe Factor

The Tip
Take advantage of the new beginning. Do not let who you were in high school determine who you will be in college.

The Story
In high school, I was more of a floater, with some redeeming traits. In truth, I was not the most outgoing guy. Yeah, I was sociable, yet only had a small circle of friends. I tried to be involved in school activities, but I did not always belong.

Once I got into college, however, my eyes were opened to a new world of opportunities, friendships, and romance. Because everything was so new and so different, I didn't feel that others judged me as much. Once I figured out that all these people were as out of place and as afraid as I was, it all became so much easier for me to be open, friendly, and receptive to the people around me. I have now become a leader in the classroom, and thankfully in my own life, with all my friends who share the same awkwardness that I once had. The harder the lessons learned, the greater the reward earned.
—junior, Stephen F. Austin State University

> ### A Friendly Fact
> 39.2 percent of surveyed freshmen "frequently" or "occasionally" felt worried about meeting new people.
> —Higher Education Research Institute at UCLA

* * *

Imagine being trapped inside a life-size snow globe—one of those small souvenir globes with water and fake snow inside that resembles an instant blizzard when shaken. If you're unfamiliar with the snow globe, go to Google or Yahoo or Bing and do a search for "souvenir snow globes." I just did the search and found a New York snow globe that would look perfect in any dorm room. A great conversation piece.

> "Roommates and friends of roommates are easy to be friends with at first—it's convenient. But I think they should be one of two groups of friends. I missed out on meeting a lot of cool people who I realized I was more compatible with because I clung onto the first people I met."
>
> —junior, UCLA

Okay, now imagine yourself inside that snow globe. Instead of the "I Love New York" image, substitute your college campus inside the dome. Instead of snow, throw in some fecal matter. Now, imagine shaking the hell out of it. The frenzy that results inside represents the first few weeks of college. At times, it's a sh*tstorm. It's controlled chaos; everyone scrambling to find friends, to find their classes, and to just find their place on campus.

> "Know where I made great friends? The elevator."
>
> —freshman, York University

This is all totally normal. This is what the first few weeks (or even months) of college life are all about. If you know there will be a storm, you can come equipped to weather the conditions.

You're dealing with a lot of new factors—new friends, new classes, new reputations, possibly new roommates, new clothes, and new professors. It's all so new that people don't know you at all—you start off as a stranger. Who you were in high school no longer matters. If you were someone popular, you have to start over. If you weren't all that popular, you also get to start over. There is no such thing as popular or unpopular now, because no one here knows who you are or what you were in high school (assuming everyone from your high school doesn't go to the same school). Everyone gets a new start, and what you make of it is up to you. That said, starting over can be lonely and confusing at times.

> "I never tried to make friends and ended up hanging out by myself a lot. My second semester, I ended up joining a few clubs and meeting new people. After that, I became more sociable and made lots of friends."
> —senior, University of Alabama

When it comes to making friends during the first few weeks of college, it can be overwhelming. So, instead of trying too hard to figure it all out, do what you love doing and you'll naturally meet people with whom you share something in common. It's not about who is interested in you, it's about who YOU find interesting. When you get confused and uncomfortable, lean on what's familiar, like the things you participated in back in high school. Once the snow settles—and once the friendship storm settles—your world will be easier to navigate and you'll find your new friends. Just expect it to be a little stormy at times.

Bottom Line

If you don't like the snow globe analogy, imagine a bobblehead doll with its head bobbing uncontrollably. It takes a while for things to stop bobbling (is that a word?). Once things calm down, you can find balance and lasting friendships.

Tip #25
Shopping for New Friends

The Tip
Do not be afraid to take a risk once you arrive on your college campus. Approaching someone at the food court might be intimidating, but a friendship is the best result!

The Story
Unlike most college students, I did not move away. I went to a university within driving distance from my home in order to save money to go abroad, amongst other reasons. None of my high school friends went with me, and for a long time, I was depressed because I wasn't having the "college experience." Going to a commuter college often means that students go to class, then go home. It wasn't until my second semester (of loneliness) that I realized no one was going to approach me, and I needed to put myself out there! So I started looking for people in the food court eating

> "I'm trapped between going to class and returning to my apartment to study, and I can't make friends this way."
> —sophomore, University of Georgia

alone who I thought would be friendly. It took some guts, but I asked them about the book they were reading, and if they responded nicely, they usually asked me to sit down. I met two of my best friends that way. Try it. Most commuter students (and even noncommuter students) feel lonely and will never turn down an invitation for company.

—junior, San Jose State University

If you want college to be a bigger version of high school, then just surround yourself with people you already know, and skip to the next tip. Go. Now. I mean it!

Still here? Okay, then read on...

Some students leave for college panicked that they won't find new friends. If they're not going to a school with friends, they're not sure how they'll make friends. This is a big worry, but most of the time it's a waste of energy. The reason it's a waste

"Involvement on campus, nonalcohol related, is the way to true friendships."
—junior, Western Illinois University

is because most people come to college without friends, and the friendless need friends. That's why making friends the first few months tends to be relatively easy. Even if you don't find friends the first few months, if you arrive on campus with patience and a plan to find places and people, you'll be too busy to freak out. If you think that everyone already has friends it's typically because they've come to school with friends or they're hanging out with temporary friends (more on that later). There are always people interested in making new friends.

If you're out of your room, living life, and getting involved with college life, doing what you love to do, you'll make friends. It just happens over time. It happens in class, in the residence halls, at parties, with friends of friends, when working campus jobs, when involved with student government, when playing intramural sports, when joining fraternities and sororities, in the laundry room or the library. Like catching a stomach flu or an STD/STI,

"If you want to meet new people, join as many clubs and organizations as possible. I came into college completely alone. None of my friends were attending the same school and I missed my freshman orientation. I didn't think I'd meet anyone. After complaining to my mother about feeling so out of place, she suggested that I see what kinds of organizations there were on campus. I looked into some and ended up joining three clubs my freshman year. It was the best thing I ever did!"

—sophomore,
Eastern Connecticut University

if you expose yourself to the action, it's much more likely to happen.

It doesn't happen if you stay in your room or your car (commuters). You need to get out from behind locked doors. If you're too shy to approach a stranger, find a study group in class. If you aren't living in a place where there are lots of other new students, join clubs, activities, organizations, and religious groups. These are all easy places to make friends. Having a job forces you to be around new people. After you take part in an activity, you'll get to know the people there. Then, with time, POOF, you'll have new friends.

Bottom Line
People are looking for you to be their new friend. Help them find you. Beware: not all friends you make the first year will become lifelong friends (see Tip #27).

Tip #26
Why College Friends Are Different

The Tip
It might seem like you know someone, but it takes time to really know new friends. Be careful.

The Story
I was really good friends with a girl down the hall. My roommate and I had gotten into a fight that weekend. I was talking to one of my new good friends over IM about the situation. Later that night, the roommate of my new friend comes into my room and tells me that my roommate, the one that I had been fighting with, had been allowed to see the IM message that I thought was only being seen by my friend. I couldn't believe that she would do that to me. That's when I learned that it takes a while to trust new friends. From that point on, I've been much more careful with what I tell people. I only tell others the things that I don't mind other people finding out about. New friends are different than high school friends. It takes a while to find people that you know you can trust. In high school, you've known your friends for years. In college, you've only known them for a few months, and you don't really know everything yet.

—freshman, Cazenovia College

* * *

College friends are different than high school friends. They look different, sound different, dress different, talk different, smell different, and have different names (in most cases); they are different people and you haven't had a lot of time to get to know them well.

The friends you have from high school are the friends that you've shared so much with over the years. In a lot of friendships, you've gone

> "You really learn who your friends are and aren't when you get into trouble— the ones who talk behind your back aren't your true friends."
>
> —recent grad, University of Michigan–Ann Arbor

from a boy to a man, girl to woman, bike to car, homecoming to prom, uneducated to educated, single to involved, virgin to nonvirgin (in some cases; see Tip #66), innocent to guilty, and so on. Some friends have even been through elementary school, middle school, and high school together. High school friends are the only friends you've ever known, with whom you've shared a lifetime of memories.

And then you start life in college.

Assuming you don't know people on your new campus, the transition can be anxiety-provoking. New friends take

> "College friends offer a false sense of family."
>
> —sophomore, University of Nevada–Las Vegas

time to grow. Like adjusting to a new pair of shoes, new hairstyle, or new operating system on your cell phone, it takes time to get comfortable with new friends. New friends can't compare to high school friends, so don't compare them.

A lot of people leave for college thinking they will make new friends immediately, and they panic if they don't. But the real problem is thinking that it all should happen so fast. It's not normal. Friendships take a long time to form. Like making fine wine (not that you can legally drink it), it's a process that depends on the essential ingredient of time (not to be confused with the spice thyme, which shouldn't be present in a good wine). Think about high school friends. It took a good two years to form a close friendship. Want lifelong friends? Put yourself in lots of places with lots of people doing things you love to do over a long period of time and friendships will form. Be patient, get involved, meet people, do new things, live life, and you'll naturally build good, stable friendships—or bad, shaky friendships (depending on the kind of friends you're looking to find).

> **"Do not judge people right away. Labels don't hold. Stereotypes don't fit."**
> —freshman, Northwestern University

Bottom Line
It takes time to know who has your back and who is going to stab you in the back.

Tip #27
Friend Today, Gone Tomorrow

The Tip
Don't be disappointed if the people you were best friends with your freshman year are not around by the end of college.

The Story
We met through a mutual friend and become close friends freshman year. We all lived on campus then, not too far

from each other. We were such close friends; we'd even go home together once in a while. We went to parties together. We just pretty much hung out all the time. She was one of my best friends. Junior year we started to grow apart. There wasn't a fight or blowout. We just started to have more work to do. See, when you're a freshman, there's more time to hang out. As we got older, there was much more to do and less time to hang out. When you have two different people and two different majors, you can't always connect. The people that I'm closest with are people that I share a major with. We go to classes together, we study together, and we hang out together. My freshman friend and I don't live near each other at all. It's important to not take it personally if you're not friends with the same people sophomore, junior, or senior year. Don't think there's anything wrong. People grow apart. It's not like high school. Friends come and go.

—senior, Fairleigh Dickinson University

* * *

Take a good look around (assuming you're reading this while at college—otherwise, remember to take a good look around when you get to school). The people around you who you'll soon call friends the first few months of college might not be your friends next semester, next month, or next week. Don't freak out. It's not just you—it's everyone.

Friends made the first few weeks are like seasonal fashion—some lose their appeal after a while. It's not until months into college that you begin to see who your friends are and are not. And that can change, too. A lot of the friends you make the first year of college are what I like to call "friends of convenience." It works like this—the people you tend to be friends with the first couple months of college are the people you tend to be around a lot, like the people in your residence hall, people from classes, people you rush with (if you're pledging a fraternity or sorority—see Tip #35). As you get more involved on campus and put

> "Instead of trying to get involved in everything and be friends with everyone, be intentional about what you do. The deepest friendships develop with the people you spend time with. I spent my first two years juggling my time between many different activities. And as a result, I have many 'Hi' friends. My most meaningful relationships have come as a result of spending time with a smaller number of people."
>
> —junior, Trinity Western University

yourself in more rooms with more people, you'll naturally meet more people. Some will want to be your friend, others won't. That's normal. You don't have to be mean to them; there are enough friends for everyone.

Most new students go through friends like they go through toilet paper the first few months of college (that cafeteria food can be harsh on the system). Know that this friend-today-gone-tomorrow phenomenon is to be expected. At the same time, a lot of the people you meet those first few months will become great friends—even lifelong friends. Not all of them are a temporary convenience.

Important note: should you find yourself without temporary friends those first few months, don't freak out. As you get more comfortable and more involved on campus, you will meet more people who will become your friends. There are people waiting to be your new friend right now. It's just hard to see because a lot of these future friends are hanging out with temporary friends, wishing and waiting to meet someone like you.

Bottom Line
College friends the first year of school are like the weather—hard to predict. They blow in and blow out without notice, and they run hot and cold. But sunny days with bright new friendships are in the forecast.

Tip #28
High School Friends, Cows, and Cats

The Tip
High school friendships will change, but not as much as you might think.

The Story
I went to the University of Michigan and most of my friends stayed close to home. My fear was that everyone would hang out with each other and I'd be left with no one. I was afraid I would be out of sight, out of mind. When I got to school, I got along with my roommate, which helped a lot. I also play some basketball, so I met some guys that way. After a few weeks, I had made some new friends on campus. I stopped worrying so much about being left out when it came to my high school friends. It was easy to stay in touch with friends from home through email and IM. Everyone has cell phones. When we all went

back to our high school for homecoming it was like nothing had changed. Everyone had stories, but it wasn't much different. That's how it's been every time we've seen each other. They come and visit at least once a semester or I see them. I think they like it better here. I'm surprised how little our friendship changed. It's cool—I have my college friends and my high school friends.

—sophomore, University of Michigan–Ann Arbor

✳ ✳ ✳

Worried about your high school friends?

Don't be.

They aren't going anywhere. If you want to stay in touch with them, you can email, text, IM, call, visit, chat, and have them visit you. You'll meet their friends and their friends will meet your new friends. Sure, your friendships will change, but they can change for the better. You can't stay in high school forever (you could try, but I don't know how long you can stay before they'd ask you to leave the premises). Between coming home for breaks (if away at school), seeing each other over the summers, and visiting each other at school, you can still hang out with your friends. If you outgrow a high school friendship, then it wasn't a very good one.

Whatever you do, *do NOT compare your college experience to your friends' college experiences*. If you're having a crappy time and your friends are having an amazing time at another school, don't immediately give up and think that you should transfer. They might be having a terrible time in a few months or in the next year (or they might be covering up the truth because they're having a hard time and don't want to admit it). It might take you a little longer to get comfortable. The dynamics of your college experience are completely unique to you. Your friends might know more people on campus than you do. They might be more involved. They might have an RA who helps them meet people more easily. Who knows, and who cares—all that matters is what's happening with you. Remember, Facebook headlines, tweets, and texts don't tell the whole story. Don't get stuck in the headlines about how everyone's life is better than yours. It's just not true.

My first semester at college was hard. I didn't know anyone. My friends were at a state school having an amazing time (so it appeared). College sucked. I started to feel sorry for myself rather than actually working to find my place in college. I compared my experience to those of my friends at other schools. But they can't be compared. It's like comparing a cow to a cat. Mine was the cow, and theirs were all cats.

See, the title of this tip now makes so much sense...

Bottom Line
Whatever anybody tells you, cow-tipping (pushing cows over while they sleep) is dangerous and mean.

Harlan's Tip Sheet

Naked People, Places, and Resources

- *ATTEND summer and fall orientation programs and events.* If your school says they are optional, make them required. Whether it's a weeklong summer program or week of welcome events, get involved and go to them. If you don't have anyone to go with, then go alone and pretend you're meeting someone. Sure enough, you'll meet someone. You might even meet me if I'm speaking on campus.
- *Get out.* Unless you order carry-out and become friends with the people delivering your food, friends won't come knocking on your door, begging you to hang out. Get out of your room. Study outside your room, get involved, and put yourself out there so people can find you.
- *Take advantage of student organizations.* These are great places to make friends. If you do what you have fun doing, the people you're doing it with naturally become your friends. (See the next chapter.)
- *Do not hang out with just your high school friends.* The biggest mistake is to go to college and remain in your former circle of friends. Branch out. Go with one friend to an event, club, or organization and talk to the other people there. Make sure you meet people during your first year. It's way too easy to use your friends that you came to school with as a crutch.

- *Get in touch with grads.* Before leaving for college, connect with your high school college counselor or the department that deals with alumni relations. Email or call students who are at the school you're going to attend. Find them via Facebook if you don't know them that well. Ask them any questions you have. Who knows, you might even make a friend.
- *Attend welcome week festivities/activities.* Attend as many of the welcome week events as possible. While you might think some of them seem boring, they're actually a good time. Go to the BBQ, see a band, watch a speaker. (It could even be me—I also play the guitar during my shows. Check out my stuff on my YouTube channel: www.YouTube.com/HarlanCohendotcom.)
- *Check out the best places to meet new people on campus*:
  - gym/recreational center
  - student government
  - residence halls
  - fraternities and sororities
  - classes
  - elevators
  - the library
  - religiously affiliated groups and organizations
  - outdoor/adventure clubs
  - club and intramural sports
  - special interest clubs and activities
  - a part-time job
  - through friends
  - through family
  - outside of your room
- *NakedRoommate.com and Facebook.com/NakedRoommate.*

Getting Involved on Campus

5

An All-You-Can-Do Buffet

Dear Harlan,

I'm going to college in a few weeks and I'm more scared than excited about going away to this school. I'll be pretty far from home. I am so scared that I will not find my place and end up quitting. There is no one that I know there. I sometimes get frustrated and depressed because I didn't choose a college closer to home. I feel so stupid.

—No Turning Back

Dear No Turning Back,

If you had chosen a college closer to home because you were afraid of going off to college, you'd probably feel stupid. Either way you'd feel stupid (and you're not), so you made a smart choice.

The most common piece of advice offered by college students for this book has been to get involved. This is how you can find your place, find friends, and find a boyfriend or girlfriend. Leave for college with a plan on how you will get involved. Look to find your place in three different places—one academic place, one social place, and one spiritual place. Put together your plan by visiting your college's website and checking out clubs, activities, and organizations. Use your extracurricular experiences in high school to guide you to similar experiences in college. Talk to older students already on campus doing the things that you might want to do. If you don't know any personally, search for clubs and organizations, find members via Facebook, and send a message. Also, make a list of what looks interesting, then get busy. If you have questions or can't find what you're looking for, contact the student activities office.

If you arrive at school and you don't have anyone to go with to these activities, just go on your own (you can meet other people who are also going alone). Activities like clubs, sports, intramurals, and student government are easy ways to make friends and keep busy. Relax, enjoy, and leave with a plan. And know that help at the counseling office is there for you if you find that it's too much to handle.

Tip #29
Getting Involved: What, Where, When, How, and Why (but not in that order)

The Tip
Get involved sooner rather than later. You'll have more time to explore opportunities and you'll gain a sense of belonging.

The Story
I always felt too afraid, embarrassed, shy—whatever you want to call it—to get involved with organizations on campus. I came to a university with the single focus on performing well academically. After two years of only minor involvement, I threw myself into two positions in my junior year. While

> **"As a freshman at a small school, join as many clubs and activities as soon you get there. I've been a tour guide, president of the campus activities board, and a resident assistant."**
> —sophomore, Endicott College

I love the experience, I find myself attempting to cram everything into my last two years. Getting involved earlier connects you instantly to the campus community and allows you the amazing opportunity to explore practically what your skills and passion are.

—junior, Trinity Western University

* * *

This tip is among the top five most important tips of the book. Don't let the fact that it's Tip #29 diminish its value. This is how you find your places and people who can be in your corner. It's the master key that can unlock the door to the best college experience.

If someone should tell you to NEVER get involved in clubs, activities, organizations, and life on campus, this person dislikes you and is trying to ruin you. He or she is your new enemy. You are being sabotaged. Trust that these kinds of people don't want you to make great friends. They don't want you to find your places in college. They don't want you to discover your passion. They absolutely don't want you to be happy or stay in college for very long. Maybe they want your bed, girlfriend, boyfriend, iPad, laptop, PlayStation, Wii, Xbox, textbooks—it's something you have. Telling someone to NOT get involved is awful, horrible, terrible advice that should be ignored at all costs.

When you think about getting involved on campus, find at least three different activities or organizations to explore. Think social, academic, and spiritual (spiritual is anything that you can do that fills you up with goodness). If you get involved in only one activity, then you risk making only one group of friends. If you can get involved in at least three activities, then you'll most likely find three groups of friends. Having a few different groups of friends is so important. As I mentioned in Tip #3, if one group

> "Freshman year I was a mess. I wasn't involved. I buried myself in schoolwork. I barely had ANY friends. It wasn't until my sophomore year that I finally decided to get a leadership position on campus. I ended up finding my best friends, my favorite bosses, and met incredible people along the way."
> —sophomore, Webster University

of friends does something that makes you uncomfortable (cow-tipping), you can say "No" and always know that you'll still have friends. People with only one group of friends have a harder time saying "No" because saying "No" can leave you with nowhere to go.

Why get involved? Find friends, find your places on campus, get out of your room, find an interest to pursue, find love (it happens), and find a way to impact campus life.

How to get involved? Check out the campus website and talk to people doing the things you want to do. Before you arrive on campus, ask a student leader, peer mentor, or a professional in student life about getting involved. Keep an eye out for clubs and organizations at the fall activities fair. This is

> "A lot of my friends hate going to clubs by themselves, but I've found that it is much easier to meet people and make new friends if you go alone."
> —sophomore, Indiana University

when most of the clubs and organizations set up displays with information on how students can get involved. In addition, find the names of current leaders of the clubs and organizations that sound interesting and send an email with your specific questions.

What to get involved with? Pick at least three clubs,

activities, and organizations that look interesting to you, even before you get to campus.

Where to find your chosen club or organization? Check out the college's website before arriving on campus. Look for the student life pages. You can usually find a long list of registered clubs and organizations. Once you get to campus, talk to upperclassmen, orientation leaders, instructors, and residence life staff, and visit the office on campus that oversees student organizations. Contact the student activities office or the office of the dean of students with questions.

> "Join a student organization the minute you start school. If you are lucky, the upperclassmen in the club will show you tips that would take you months or even years to learn."
>
> —junior, DeVry University

Shy? Take a Leadership Role

Don't just join a club or organization. Plan on being a leader (president, VP, etc.) in the group. Then you will be forced to meet people on a regular basis, plan, and participate in all the activities.

When to get involved? Start looking before you arrive on campus. According to the Higher Education Research Institute, 78.2 percent of first-year students actually get around to doing it. According to NSSE, more than 41 percent of first-year students and 65 percent of seniors report having done community service or volunteer work. Figure out what looks interesting and get the info asap. Try one or two groups or orgs your first semester (or quarter). Work your way up to a few activities and organizations. If you have extra time, try another next semester (or quarter). Plan ahead and get involved sooner rather than later.

A quick note on going to meetings on your own: always assume other people are going to meetings alone. Expect that they are planning on meeting other new members. Do not let all these people down by not going. They want to meet you. And please, *never* judge a club or organization based on attending one meeting. Go to at least three meetings, then judge (use the judge's outfit from Tip #15).

> "Get involved, but don't go overboard. It's about finding a balance."
> —senior, Henderson State University

> "Getting out of my comfort zone was hard, but once I found something that I enjoyed, it was almost like the snowball effect. I met people, and then you meet their friends, and then we all became friends, and then I'd get even more involved. Start early, because I've found that the four (or five, or six, or ten) years go by quickly."
> —junior, Indiana University

Bottom Line

Get involved, make some friends, find your place, and figure out what you love to do—and what you don't love to do.

Tip #30
Clubs and Organizations: A Smorgasbord of Opportunity

The Tip
There is a club or organization on your campus for almost every interest. Get involved with those you are interested in and learn more about yourself.

The Story
Getting involved in campus activities and organizations was how I found my place in college, but it took a few years to get there. Freshman year was all about experimenting and finding my limits. Sophomore year was about finding a student organization that I could give something to and that could give something to me. It was my junior year that I really found my place—on student union board.

> "Join the speech and debate team. It's made me a better thinker, a better writer, and a better student. I also won speech awards! Great for scholarships and grad school."
>
> —junior,
> California State University–Sacramento

It started by getting involved with student government my sophomore year in a program for new students. It was through that program that I met the advisor for union board. He had just started at the university and said to me, "Hey, you need to be on this board." And I said, "Okay." I've met so many incredible people—not just students, but also faculty who can help me in the future. It's helped me find my desire to be a leader and my need for people— I used to think that I wasn't a people person. I now realize that I can talk

to people and work well with people. That's something I never imagined getting from college.

—senior, Iowa State University

* * *

Your college experience is like a buffet of opportunity—instead of all you can eat, it's all you can do. The only limitation is how much time you have to consume the experiences. Start slowly and pick one or two things you can commit to freshman year.

When looking at clubs and organizations on your campus website, dig deep. Not all schools will list activities and organizations in the same places. You might have to click around a little bit. Most will fall under these categories:

- Academic/Professional
- Arts, Media, Music
- Cultural
- Honorary

HAZING WARNING:

If you are forced to do things that make you uncomfortable, DO NOT do them. Get help. Tell the authories on campus and in the community. Florida A&M band member Robert Champion died after allegedly being beaten following a hazing incident in a parked bus. Band members are now facing felony charges. MORE IN HAZING, PAGE 185

- International
- Living-Learning Community
- Political/Environmental/Advocacy
- Religious
- Service
- Social Fraternity/Sorority
- Sports/Recreational/Social
- University Student Government

Some clubs and organizations include politics, women's issues, diversity, public service, alcohol education, religion, athletics, abortion, right to life, singing, gun control, the death penalty, equal rights, gay/lesbian/bisexual rights, volunteerism, leadership, entrepreneurship, student development, campus pride, juggling, video games, break dancing, and role-playing games. (I was recently at a campus and saw a group of students in the midst of some kind of medieval role-playing game in the quad. Either that or they were *really* retro.)

"Join Alpha Phi Omega; it's a national coed service fraternity. We do community service around Fort Worth—blood drives, community rehabilitation, an event call PNO—Professors Night Out. For PNO, we baby-sit professors' kids so that they can go out on the town at night."

—junior, Texas Christian University

You'll find clubs and organizations unique to your campus, and then you'll find national clubs and organizations with individual chapters on campus. If you don't find a club or organization that excites you, start your own. Usually, all you need are a few members and a faculty sponsor. Once you're recognized by the college, they sometimes offer funding. When I was a student at Indiana University, I was a founding member of an improv troupe called Full Frontal Comedy. Whatever your interests, consider starting a club—from a prayer group to a book club to a club that talks about the clubs on campus. Get creative. I met a member of the People Watching Club at Boston University. Like eating? Join the Barbecue Club at the University of Texas–Austin. Their mission:

Naked Trick

Search the member area of www.NakedRoommate.com to contact leaders on your campus. Plug in the name of your school and see who comes up. Chances are, the leaders have indicated that they are nice people willing to answer your questions. Facebook and LinkedIn also can be ways to find clubs and activities on campus.

The Barbecue Club

The purpose of the barbecue club is threefold:

1. to serve the University of Texas and Austin community through barbecue
2. to uphold and promote barbecue consumption and tradition
3. to provide culinary leadership through barbecue while maintaining high standards of barbecue excellence.

And yes, it's worth mentioning one more time—*go to meetings on your own*. Trust me—there will be people there to welcome you to your new club or organization.

Bottom Line

Join a club or start a club. Your campus never knew how badly it needed a Disco Body-Paint Club.

Tip #31
Sports and Athletics: Buckets of College Sweat

The Tip
If you played sports in high school but don't want to play at a highly competitive level in college, look into club sports. They are less intense, involve intercollegiate competition, and take up less time than varsity athletics.

The Story
When I was in high school, I played basketball and soccer. I knew when I arrived

> "I play football, softball, and basketball as part of a league. It's only open to people on campus and it can get extremely competitive."
> —sophomore, University of Pennsylvania

at Boston University that I wouldn't be playing either sport, but I still wanted that intense feeling of competition. The result: women's rugby. Before I got to Boston, I didn't know what rugby was; I had never touched a ball and knew nothing about the positions and rules. The returning players and coach taught me everything I needed to know. Most importantly, my playing time wasn't affected if I missed practice due to intense amounts of homework. Being involved in a sport helped me manage my time and be successful.

—sophomore, Boston University

* * *

Like sports? Scared of gaining the freshman 15 (see Tip #97)? Looking to tackle some people or rip flags from their bodies? If you were (or weren't) an athlete in high school, you can be one in college. And you don't even have to be great to play. You can suck and get good.

Whatever you want to play, you should be able to find it. On

> "Ultimate Frisbee has been my sport. There just needs to be a professional Ultimate Frisbee League."
> —senior, University of Virginia

a decent-sized campus, you've got basketball, football, baseball, soccer, volleyball, swimming, Ultimate Frisbee, golf, lacrosse, rugby, crew, field hockey, softball, fencing, bicycling, bowling, martial arts, archery, cross country, track and field sports, rollerblade hockey, field hockey, ice hockey, luge, and bobsledding (luge and bobsledding are more common at Swedish colleges). Oh yeah, and then there's competitive corn hole.

There are three levels of athletics at most colleges. Varsity athletics are for the elite athletes, club sports are for the serious athletes, and intramurals are for the rest of us. Varsity athletics almost always have tryouts. Club sports are competitive and open to most students who want to play (sometimes there are tryouts). As for intramurals, this is typically the most accessible level of participation. While it can still get intense, it's the easiest of the three to participate in. To find out how it works,

> "One perk of attending a smaller college is that it's easier to get onto the sports teams."
> —sophomore, Ashland University

contact your school's recreational center or the student activities office. And if you want to participate in a team sport and don't have a team, don't let that hold you back. Typically you can be placed on a team. And if you're not into team sports, there's yoga, martial arts, and tons of other options.

Team sports can be found as part of life in the residence halls, Greek fraternities and sororities, and other student organizations (my campus newspaper at IU had a softball team). You may be thinking, *I'd love to get involved, but I'm a horrible athlete.*

> "I'm incredibly shy, so meeting people was tough for me. Second semester I joined the lacrosse club, which was THE best decision I made all year. I'm now playing a sport I love and making new friends while doing it."
> —freshman, Southern Illinois University

Unless you start playing regularly, you'll always be horrible. Start now, and in four years (or more if you're on the seven-year plan), you won't suck so badly. You might even become a team captain—or at least not the worst player. Michael Jordan got cut from his high school basketball team. Remember Michael Jordan? The basketball player?

Bottom Line
Play together, sweat together, and hang out together (after you shower).

Tip #32
Academic Organizations:
Where Smart People Gather

The Tip
There are more than just social fraternities. Talk to your professors to see if there are any professional organizations for your major.

The Story

I had never heard about an engineering fraternity before coming to college. It was midsemester and two professors visited our engineering class with some students in the engineering fraternity. They gave us an overview on how to become a prospective member. Signing up was as easy as picking up a form in the engineering fraternity lounge in the engineering building. Inside there are books, magazines, and refreshments, all maintained by members of the fraternity. For the first two years, I'm a prospective member. It's not until my junior year that I can be admitted. Even then, I have to maintain a minimum GPA, get high marks in all my engineering courses, and get a professor recommendation. Once I'm a member, along with it looking good on my résumé, there are opportunities to contribute to publications and a national database of information that opens doors to internships, job opportunities, and other ways to network with students, professors, and professionals. I'm in a Greek fraternity, but had no idea that there were these types of fraternities, too.

—freshman, Bradley University

* * *

You don't really have to be smart, as in GPA smart, to be in an academic organization, although sometimes you do need to have a minimum GPA to participate.

Academic organizations and/or fraternities (which include men and women) are professional organizations where students with similar interests gather. They offer great opportunities to get involved within your academic department. It's a way to tap into internships and work-study jobs, and help build relationships within your field of study. Many academic fraternities are part of a larger national organization that can open the door to opportunities for internships, jobs, research in your field of study, and networking with students and professionals on other campuses. If you're interested in going to graduate school or have a particular passion, you can use the database to ask members for informational interviews and to build relationships that can help you throughout your academic and professional life.

My girlfriend in college (now my ex) was in the psychology club called Psi Chi. She was on the executive board of the campus chapter. As part of the group, she helped host guest speakers, publicize events, and run the organization. Being in Psi Chi enabled her to get to know a professor who mentored her, helped her get published in a professional journal as part of a research project, and helped get her into graduate school, where she earned a PhD.

> "Be prepared to be offered positions of leadership in clubs and organizations after your freshman and sophomore years. Upperclassmen are always looking to hand over leadership positions to younger students before they graduate."
> —freshman, Lenoir–Rhyne University

How you can join academic organizations varies. Sometimes, you need to be enrolled in a particular field of study to participate. Sometimes, you need to carry a minimum grade point average. You might even need a letter of recommendation. There can be a required number of meetings you must attend. In addition, there can be a small membership fee. To find out about them, talk to your professors, visit the departmental website, and stop by the actual department office to speak with the dean of the department. Do it face to face as opposed to using email. This is a great way to introduce yourself to someone important, and it gives you something to talk about. One more thing to keep in mind—students in these organizations are leaders in the field. These are also students who will make great study partners in the classes you have together.

Bottom Line
Meet smart people with similar interests, find an internship, network to find a job, eat pretzels, and pound soft drinks in the lounge.

Tip #33
Religious Activities: Your Prayers Answered and the Culture Club (not Boy George)

The Tip
Check out the religious organizations your university offers and use them to help ground yourself.

The Story
When I arrived at college I was bombarded with so many different aspects of life and lifestyle choices that it could have been easy to be swayed without the right support system. My closest friends are all the people that I have met as part of the Christian Fellowship on campus. These have been the people who have helped me through turbulent

years, and my faith in God has been strengthened. It is no longer my parents' influence that has connected me with my faith, but it is something that I have chosen for myself and I'm so thankful.

—junior, Northern Michigan University

* * *

There's nothing like a good prayer after a tough week (and more than half of students attending college are doing it, according to the Higher Education Research Institute at UCLA). If you have strong ties to your culture, or religion is running through your blood, then run to the religious organizations and cultural centers on campus. These centers are where students sharing a common interest come together. It's a place to attend prayer services, participate in outdoor activities, take part in public service projects, get free food, and get a chance to travel to locations near and far with meaning—from a trip to Jerusalem, to a trip to Vatican City, to a tour through Latin America. Locally, there are activities such as rafting trips, athletics, hiking, weekend dinners, prayer study, guest speaker events, and other group activities to help bring students together.

Religious Activities

54.8 percent of students are praying/meditating during the first year of college.

—Higher Education Research Institute at UCLA

Whatever your religion, whatever your culture, there

should be a place for you (if not on campus, then near campus). A few examples of religious/cultural clubs— African American Center, African Students Association, Asian American Association, Baha'i Friendship Club, Baptist Student Ministry, Black Student Union, Brazilian Association, Buddhist Club, Campus Prayer Ministry, Catholic Campus Ministries, Chinese Christian Fellowship, Christian Campus Center, Fellowship of Christian Athletes, Hillel Jewish Foundation, Indonesian Student Association, Islamic Center, Japanese Student Association, Latter-Day Saints Student Association, Lutheran Campus Ministry, Lutheran Student Fellowship, Malaysian Students Association, Muslim Student Association, Pakistani Students Association, Taiwanese Student Association, United Methodist Students, Zen Club—and for the ones I missed, I'm sorry (send me a note and I'll include it in the next edition). Whatever your faith, have faith that there will be people and places to celebrate it

"Freshman year I was scared to death of joining any campus activity, but I began to take part in different ministry opportunities on and off campus. I eventually became the leader of senior adult ministry and I am now a freshman family leader."
—senior, East Texas Baptist University

with (and if your faith or culture doesn't have a club or organization on campus, just start one).

As for this whole going-to-meetings-and-events-alone thing (I know, enough with going alone already), if ever there were a place that welcomes new students, religious groups are it. Members will welcome you with open arms. And then, when you find yourself dealing with tough issues, you'll have advisors, spiritual leaders, and new friends to help you along the way.

Bottom Line

You don't have to just pray that you meet people—pray AND meet people, or seek out groups with whom you have cultural ties. Have faith—you will make friends.

Tip #34
The Perks: Travel and See the World for Free

The Tip
Don't be afraid to go on an adventure with a club or activity if you don't know anyone in the van.

The Story
Last spring, I went off campus as part of an alternative spring break program. It was with ten strangers also from campus. We met up and drove twenty-four hours in a van to Miami to build a home for a low-income family. The owner was so happy to have us there. I'll never forget the look on the mom's face when she saw us helping fix her home.

> "We get to go to educational conferences all over the country—Las Vegas is one of the best places. I can't complain."
> —sophomore, Emerson College

She was crying. When we weren't working, we spent time hanging out and walking around South Beach. It was all part of a program at school that only cost about $175. It was a cheap spring break. I even got to wear a bikini. I loved it so much that I'm going on another spring trip as a project leader—despite the strange odor in the van.

—junior, University of New Hampshire

***

This is a perk I never knew about when I went to college. The idea that I could go on an all-expense-paid trip across the country and hang out with thousands of students from hundreds of colleges seems too good to be true. Yes, it's true. Every year, students go to places like California, Chicago, New Orleans, New York, Cincinnati, Boston, Portland, Las Vegas, Seattle, and Boise (yes, even Boise). And the list goes on. I'm talking even international locations (South America, Europe, Asia...). There are conferences, conventions, symposiums, competitions, and educational trips to Europe (sometimes I might even be speaking at them). Usually, travel and a stipend for food are included.

> "Some of our students get to tour the sites in France that are associated with the life and works of the university's patron: Saint Vincent de Paul."
>
> —college life professional, DePaul University

If you're someone who doesn't travel much, this is your chance. I've met students who have never been on an airplane or left their home states. If you're one of those people, this can be your ticket. If you're in a club or organization

> "As part of program board, we've had students travel to Indianapolis, Boston, Cincinnati, then regionals in Portland, and next year they'll go to Reno, Nevada. We travel twice a year. Our students get their air, hotel, and some meals provided. And they stay in nice places, generally in four- or five-star hotels."
> —advisor, Idaho State University

that doesn't travel, talk to the faculty sponsor and see if you can be the first group to attend a convention. Departments have budgets for things like this. All you have to do is ask. Should they say no, then put together a fundraiser and make it happen on your own. Here are some ways to get involved and see the world:

- *Sports.* Travel with your team for away games and compete in national competitions in other cities, states, or countries.
- *Competitive clubs and activities.* Attend regional, national, and international competitions (like those competitions that air on ESPN2 at three o'clock in the morning).
- *Religious organizations.* Travel to other campuses (or countries) for religious retreats and conferences.
- *Clubs and groups with national affiliations.* Investigate your organization's national conference calendar. Executives can often travel for free.
- *Greek life.* Attend regional and/or national conferences (these happen ALL the time).

Birthright

Jewish? Go on a free trip to Israel as part of Taglit-Birthright Israel. Check out www.birthrightisrael.com.

- *Student leadership*. Attend national conferences, regional conferences, and educational meetings. Also investigate summer leadership retreats.

- *Study abroad and alternative spring breaks*. Go to your study abroad office and inquire how you can spend a semester in another country. Often, the price of tuition is the same (or even less).

> "My first alternative spring break trip I went to Phoenix, Arizona, and built houses with Habitat for Humanity. The second year, I built houses with Habitat in Myrtle Beach, South Carolina. Both experiences were life changing."
> —recent grad, Salem State University

- *www.NakedRoommate.com*. Post a question and ask students to share where they've traveled and what organizations or activities made it possible

Bottom Line

Get into a club or organization and get out of town. Packages include free air, free hotel, and free food. Sorry—you'll have to spring for the Pay-Per-View movies.

Harlan's Tip Sheet

Naked People, Places, and Resources

Places on Campus to Find Information

- *Campus info*. It seems obvious, but these people know a lot about the campus, so call them. One college even boasted that the campus operator could give cooking instructions for a Thanksgiving turkey.
- *Facebook*. Follow the campus Facebook page and see updates on clubs, activities, and events.
- *Twitter*. Follow your campus's Twitter feed and get real-time updates on all that's happening on and around campus.
- *Student activities office*. The central hub that oversees campus activities. Typically, student-run clubs and activities need to be registered here.
- *Recreational center*. The gymnasium/field house where students can participate in organized and open sports. Take a walk down the halls and read about events, happenings, and ways to get involved.
- *The office of the dean of students*. The dean's office oversees all of campus. If you have questions, don't hesitate to call.
- *Department/academic offices*. Every area of study has a departmental office. Ask who can lead you to the information you seek.
- *Student leaders*. Talk to your residence life staff, teaching assistants, peer mentors, and any student

who has spent more time than you on campus. They are the experts.

- *Online social networks.* Locate and contact executive members of clubs and organizations via their websites and find the executive board members' information via Facebook. Then send a note with your questions.
- *Spiritual centers.* Walk around a temple, church, or the offices that house spiritual organizations, and you'll see a list of things to do posted on the walls.

Signs and Flyers to Watch for around Campus

- *Activities fair.* Most colleges offer organized events where students can visit booths with members of various clubs and organizations. At the least, watch for signs and posters advertising various activities in the Union, student center, or resident halls.
- *Call-outs.* This is the name for advertisements listed in the campus newspaper or posted around campus inviting students to take part in a club or activity.
- *Philanthropy events.* Participate in charity events organized by students and run by students.
- *Facebook.* For news and events.
- *Department Twitter feeds.* For more news and events.

Greek Life

Behind the Doors, Windows, and Walls of Fraternity and Sorority Life

Dear Harlan,

I'm going away to college next year and would like to join a sorority. I've heard stories of girls going away to college and not getting into a sorority. I wanted to know about the whole process and what happens if I don't get into a sorority. Please help!

—Sorority Searching

Dear Sorority Searching,

It's easy to get into a sorority house. The challenge is not being asked to leave by current members once inside. As a guy, I could never pull that one off.

The process of becoming an actual member and getting into a sorority (or fraternity) house differs from campus to campus. Generally, you arrive on campus and move into the residence halls. RUSH (the caps are for drama) is the process in which potential sorority members meet current members and check out the different houses. Generally, rush takes place in the fall or spring. The rush process consists of organized visits to the sororities on campus, interviews with members, events, and bids (invitations) offered by the sorority and fraternity members.

Rush isn't a perfect process. It can be nerve-racking to have strangers judging you, and it can get a little uncomfortable. Not getting in is *not* the end of the world. It can be hard at first, but once you find your place on campus, you can still be friends with the sorority sisters and then rush again next year. Or you can just do your own thing and have the best of both worlds!

Tip #35
Greek Life: Getting In

The Sorority Tip

The Tip
Don't put on a show for the rush parties.

The Story

There are several girls in my sorority who, while going through rush, put on a huge act about who they were, what they liked, and so on just to get into the sorority they thought was cool. Now that they are in my sorority, they are really unhappy because they have none of the same interests as the girls and they feel like they have to continue to put on a show to fit in.

> "I was told the sorority that wanted me was 'socially awkward' and 'the absolute worst house on campus.' Turned out, it's the best house. Do not listen to rumors. Get to know the people in the house before rejecting it. I almost made a HUGE mistake."
> —senior, Virginia Tech

—freshman, Clemson University

The Fraternity Tip

The Tip

Be yourself and find out what the fraternity is all about.

The Story

Most fraternities will drop a lot of cash and make you feel like you're the most important person during the rush process. There are boat cruises, paintball games, nice dinners, and bagels in the morning. I knew it all couldn't keep happening, but I thought at least there would be bagels in the morning. When rush ended, it all stopped. Don't lose sight of what's most important: the people in the frat. Talk to the brothers and ask questions. Some guys will be straight with you when asking what a typical weekend is like. Don't be afraid to ask. The brothers will respect you more for asking—and if they don't, you shouldn't want to be in that house anyway. Three years later, I'm into Greek life.

—junior, Massachusetts Institute of Technology

* * *

You don't need to be Greek to be in a fraternity or sorority. I'm not Greek and I pledged two fraternities. The term "Greek" comes from the letters of the Greek alphabet fraternities and sororities use for their names. If you're interested in getting an invitation (or bid) to join a Greek fraternity or sorority, it all starts with rush (but please, no pushing to get in).

"I went through recruitment (like Harlan suggested) and after the first night at the informational meeting I became so excited about Greek life! It ended up not being that expensive either. I was so nervous going through recruitment the whole weekend, but by Sunday night when I got a bid from my sorority, I was in tears of joy as I jumped off the stage! I am not one of those typical prissy, materialistic girls and none of my sisters are either. There is a sorority for everyone, and it is worth anybody's time to check it out. Going Greek was the best decision I've ever made and I love it!"
—freshman, Grand Valley State University

REMEMBER: Rush is not about who wants you. It's about what YOU want!

The Sorority Rush Overview

Typically, rush is called "formal rush" because it's a highly organized process lasting several weeks. Each institution has its own way of conducting rush, but this can give you a general idea of how it works. Women are typically required to visit each sorority and meet current members. It's a way for those rushing and sisters in the house to gauge each other's personalities. The current members often sing, dance, and put on shows to welcome visiting potential members. There is usually a short interview with such deep probing questions as: Where are you from? Do you have any siblings? What do you do for fun? Have any pets? Once sorority members meet all the rushees, they invite certain people back for subsequent meetings (sometimes dinner or an activity).

Eventually, bids are offered. Bids are invitations asking those rushing to become members. This is when things can get ugly. Some people who want bids don't get bids—only hurt feelings. Please, do *not* take the process personally. These people have no clue who you really are and what you're all about. It's virtually impossible to really get to know you during this fast-paced process. If you don't get in the first time you rush, trust that you'll have made new friends simply by participating in the rush process. Then you can have the best of both worlds, and should you decide to rush again, you'll have

> "A Greek organization is a group of individuals of similar interests bonded together by common goals and aspirations. These bonds are created through rituals in which all members participate. Rituals are based on common principles such as honor, friendship, truth, and knowledge, to name a few. Each group works to instill these ideals in their members through their everyday activities."
>
> —Case Western Reserve University parent resources website (Student Affairs.Case.edu/greek/parent)

> "My chapter might be considered bottom tier, but I don't agree. These girls challenged me, they helped me grow, and they made me the confident, passionate Greek leader that I am today. There's no way girls like that could ever be considered bottom tier."
>
> —senior, Lehigh University

a ticket in the door. If formal rush is too much for you, informal rush happens all year long, in which you and the members can get to know each other over time.

The Fraternity Rush Overview

Fraternity rush varies from campus to campus, but rush for men is generally less formal than sorority rush. During fraternity rush, it's all about getting to know the brothers and finding out if you mesh with the guys in the house. Organized rush events like attending a sporting event, playing basketball with brothers, cookouts, dinners, and rush parties are typical functions. Once rush ends, the fraternity members hand out bids. If you accept, you become a pledge. Most fraternities have a fall pledge class and a winter pledge class. And again, if you don't get in (and you wanted to), at least you'll have friends who are in who can offer you a bid next semester (it happened to me).

> Have an alternative plan if you're rushing. This means finding other places and other friends outside of the Greek community. Always have options and you'll always make the best decisions.

Questions to Ask Before Signing Up for Greek Life

- *Is the organization officially recognized by the school?* Not all fraternities and sororities are officially recognized by the institution. Check with your campus student life office or the office of the dean of students to see if a group is recognized before signing a bid. If it's not officially recognized, do a lot of research before joining.

- *Is there a Greek advisor?* If the fraternity or sorority is officially recognized, there will be a Greek advisor on campus. This is a professional staff member who oversees the Greek organizations on campus.
- *Has the organization been on probation (or is it currently on probation)?* Contact the advisor or national chapter to find out details about current or past problems.
- *What's the organization's grade point average?* Ask the Greek advisor to help you find this info. If your potential fraternity or sorority has the lowest GPA— not a good sign.
- *Is there a national affiliation?* A lot of fraternities and sororities will have a national leadership in place that will provide guidance and ensure that the chapter is following the rules and regulations and honoring traditions.
- *How much will it cost?* You'll typically have to pay an initiation fee and then an annual membership fee. Make sure you know if you have to live in a fraternity or sorority house as part of your commitment.
- *What's the time commitment?* Talk to members and find out just how much time you will need to commit. Make sure you find out how much it takes up the first year versus the second, third, and fourth year. The first year can be the biggest time commitment.
- *Is this the right fit?* Make sure you know why this is the right fit for you. Make sure it feels right.

A special thank you to Thomas B. (Tom) Jelke, PhD, Chairman of the Association of Fraternity Advisors Foundation; Member of the

National Board of Directors of Sigma Phi Epsilon Fraternity; and CEO of t.jelke solutions, a consulting firm for colleges/universities, fraternal organizations, and nonprofits, for providing assistance with this list.

Bottom Line
If you decide to rush, do not take the process too personally. These people don't know you and have no way of knowing you so quickly. Look at it like this—they should be more concerned about impressing you. They need new members.

Tip #36
Greek Life: The Good

The Sorority Tip

The Tip
Don't pass up on rushing or pledging the Greek system on your campus just because you think you're not "sorority material."

The Story
I thought the exact same thing when I started college. I told myself, "I don't need to pay to have friends." [Monthly dues are sometimes associated with Greek organizations.] I pledged a sorority on a whim during my second semester freshman year. I loved the girls I pledged with, and even wound up being elected vice president of the sorority my junior year. That brief tenure as vice president taught me

quite a bit about running an organization of that size, and it also looks nice on a résumé.

—graduate student, Montclair State University

The Fraternity Tip

The Tip
Frats can offer you much more than beer.

The Story
I never in a million years pictured myself in a fraternity. I soon discovered that some guys I met weren't the typical frat guys I thought they were. They were a colony, which is one of the first stages in the creation of a chapter. I wanted to join after one meeting. That was five years ago, and I have now held two different executive positions in the chapter and joined five other campus organizations that I never would have even known about if it weren't for my brothers. I am now a senior approaching graduation, and I have held five executive offices in four different organizations, and all because of a colony I helped build. I not only have a great group of friends, but I also have one impressive résumé.

—senior, Pittsburg State University

* * *

According to the North American Interfraternity Council

44 percent of all U.S. presidents have been Greek.

37 percent of U.S. senators are Greek.

23 percent of U.S. congressmen/women are Greek.

31 percent of all U.S. Supreme Court Justices have been Greek.

30 percent of Fortune 500 executives are Greek.

Having pledged two fraternities, dated women in sororities, and unsuccessfully interviewed five times to be a live-in houseboy at sororities when I was in college (not true), I've seen the good, the bad, and the ugly parts of Greek life. This is the tip about the good.

Personally, I think Greek life can be a great life. It gives you an instant group of people your age to hang out with, a social life, opportunities to get involved, and a comfortable place on campus. Members often live together (not all fraternities and sororities have houses on campus or require living in the house), eat together, sleep together (in separate beds), party together, play together, study together, and go through pledging together—it helps to quickly form a tight bond. You have a common identity—the history and the reputation of your campus chapter. And once you graduate, you have a network of support that can help you professionally. And no, it's not about buying friends—it's paying dues to help run an organization and build relationships (inside and outside the Greek community).

And an added bonus: Greeks tend to fill many of the top student leadership positions on campus. It's not uncommon for a campus to have a relatively small Greek population and a disproportionately large number of Greek members filling the most influential posts of campus clubs and organizations. Greek life can be a springboard to getting involved in (or even running) a variety of activities and organizations on campus.

The Best Parts of Greek Life

Leadership opportunities. Each organization usually elects an executive board consisting of a president, vice president, secretary, social chair, rush chair, philanthropy chair (for fund-raising and community involvement), and several other chairs or positions. Outside the inner workings of the house, representatives of fraternities and sororities work with other leaders on campus to organize campus events. Seasonal rituals like homecoming, alcohol awareness events, dance marathons, acting/singing competitions, and community service events are often opportunities for Greeks to get involved and to meet other Greeks and non-Greeks.

> "Join a Greek organization! At the very least rush them and see what the deal is. I came to college with a very anti-Greek view of things. I was under the impression that all fraternities were just like *Animal House*, doing nothing but partying and hazing their pledges. I went through my entire freshman year uninvolved and not feeling particularly like a student. At the beginning of my sophomore year, I was finally convinced to rush. The moment I set foot into the house I felt a connection that I hadn't felt with anyone in years. The entire experience was remarkably life-changing."
> —junior, Drexel University

Social opportunities. As a member of a fraternity or sorority, your social life is kind of just there for you. You just need to show up. There are date parties, formals, and other social events (where a fraternity and sorority may pair up). It's an easy way to make friends inside and outside your house. Besides these events, there are often team sports and campus-wide activities and philanthropic opportunities.

Diversity. Between national affiliations, volunteer work, service on campus, and other activities, you can meet as many people as you choose to. Most national fraternities and sororities have national conferences annually where you can meet people from chapters around the country with similar interests and a common bond.

Philanthropy. One of the least talked about parts of Greek life is the opportunity to participate in life-changing events that raise millions of dollars for hospitals, shelters, and other organizations. There are dance marathons, food drives, bake sales, service projects, performances, and other events that provide leadership opportunities for Greek members. Service is one of the areas of Greek life that gets little attention. But it's invaluable.

Academics. Some houses have better GPA averages than others. On many campuses, Greeks are the most academically successful. It helps to be in a fraternity or sorority that values academic achievement. Whatever it is that your house is known for, chances are, when you become a member, you'll follow the same path.

Networking. Greek life can last a lifetime. Beyond graduation, there is a strong network of active fraternity and sorority members who stay connected. Greek life doesn't stop once college ends. This strong network can be valuable when looking for internships, looking for a job, going to grad school, relocating to a different city, or just looking to hang out with new people.

Bottom Line

Greek life can be a great life. Most people outside the Greek system don't always understand, appreciate, or see the value of going Greek.

The Tip
Don't be afraid to de-pledge if it's not the right fit.

The Story
I became close friends with a girl through a team sport my freshman year. She was a year older and someone I liked hanging out with. She invited me to come to dinner at her sorority house a couple times. Then she invited me to rush her house. Once I got into the sorority, I was just friends with two or three people. The rest I didn't have much in common with. It's funny. They were supposed to be the "cool" sorority, but it was just a bunch of girls who weren't cool in high school, but then thought they were cool in college. I couldn't stand it. I found out that I'm just not someone who likes to be in a house with fifty other girls. I didn't like any part of it. And it cost money. They told me that I would have to move into the house, so I de-pledged. This all happened a few days ago. I just stopped going to chapter meetings and left a message on the president's phone. I'm not the sorority type and now I know it. Some people are, but it's just not my thing. They might not understand, but that's not my problem.

—sophomore, college withheld

* * *

Everyone and everything has a good side and a bad side (my left side is my most attractive side). Greek life is no exception.

In all fairness, this tip is the bad side of it all. If you can't handle reading the bad side, please feel free to look away. As good as Greek life

can be, it can have some serious drawbacks. But simply being aware of the bad and ugly parts can help you avoid some of the potential problems in this and the following tip.

The Potential Problems

Isolation and lack of diversity. When you're in a fraternity or sorority, it's easy to isolate yourself from the rest of campus. It takes effort to use the opportunities provided to you by being involved with Greek life to get involved outside of your fraternity or sorority. Some people go Greek and close off their social circles. It's much better to keep yourself open to the best of both worlds. It's great to belong to a group, but the group should never keep you away from meeting people—Greek and non-Greek.

Social pressures. When you're part of such a tight group, it's normal to feel intense pressure to do things you don't always want to do—like drinking, drugs, sex, and partying. Statistically, those involved in Greek life tend to drink more. It's a fact. That said, some fraternities and sororities like to party more than others. Find out which house fits your personality and set of values. Whatever the people in the fraternity or sorority do will most likely be the things that you'll end up doing. Most members buckle to the pressure (but still, a select few do not). And if you create a world of options on campus, where you have a couple of other groups of friends outside of your fraternity or sorority, you will never feel the need to buckle to the pressure because you'll always have more friends. Let me be clear, you can be sober, stay sober, and be a Greek member.

Loss of identity. Define your Greek life. Do not let your Greek affiliation define you. Use Greek life as a gateway to get involved in non-Greek life too. It's easy to let the group define you. It's like this: you're in a new place, surrounded by new people, and all you want is to feel like you belong. Pledgeship can take unique people and roll them into a big blob of dough from which cookie-cutter members are formed. Some people lose their identities and become lost in the group.

Complacency. It's easy to not get involved outside of the Greek circles when your social life is pretty much taken care of for you. It's easy to just go with the flow. Make a real effort to meet people and to participate in activities outside of the Greek circles.

False sense of superiority. Some people think they're better than others on campus because of the letters on their chests. Never forget that these letters will end up in a box in your closet once you graduate. People don't tend to wear their Greek letters to work. If you think you're better, you will turn people off to you and your organization.

Bottom Line

Greek life makes it extremely easy to be a leader, but just as easy to be a follower. Choose to be a leader.

The Tip
Pledging activities are always a choice. Don't demean yourself—especially to the point of physical harm—just to fit in.

The Story
Our college's pledging program is undergoing a crackdown from the administration. Many alleged pledging activities have been the focus of concern in recent years—such as pledges not being allowed to sleep, being kept outside all night, and so on. But when one fraternity's pledges were reportedly observed at a party covered in what appeared to be vomit and urine, and being kicked down stairs, another Greek group's members decided to alert authorities. I'm a member of a nonhazing sorority myself and we're suffering the consequences. As a result, the school is implementing an indefinite suspension of pledging pending appointment of a faculty-student-staff "task force." We think it's time— no student should be allowed to abuse another just for the sake of "belonging."

—senior, Cornell College

＊＊＊

And now, this is where the chapter gets ugly. If you haze someone, you can go to jail. If you allow people to haze you, the results can be devastating. Forget "tradition." The police, lawyers, parents, friends, family, and judges don't care. Don't believe me? Google "fraternity, charges, hazing" and search NEWS. It's very easy to get caught up in the groupthink. Students almost die—and do die—from hazing. Please, *never* put up with hazing. Not familiar with hazing? Let me help you out:

Hazing

The term "hazing" means any conduct or method of initiation into any student organization, whether on public or private property, which willfully or recklessly endangers the physical or mental health of any student or other person. Such conduct shall include whipping; beating; branding; forced calisthenics; exposure to the weather; forced consumption of any food, liquor, beverage, drug, or other substance; or any other brutal treatment or forced physical activity which is likely to adversely affect the physical health or safety of any such student or other person, or which subjects such student or other person to extreme mental stress, including extended deprivation of sleep or rest or extended isolation.

> "Don't do it if you think it's wrong in your gut. Brothers who give you a hard time aren't people you'll want as friends."
> —recent grad, University of Illinois

Source: Chapter 269, Section 17, Crimes Against Public Peace, The Commonwealth of Massachusetts, www.MALegislature.gov/Laws /GeneralLaws/PartIV/TitleI/Chapter269 /Section17

Every college and state has strict rules and laws against hazing. If you're the one doing the hazing, you could be arrested. If you're the one who is being hazed, you can have people arrested (record it on a cell phone and use it as evidence—assuming it's admissible and legal to record). Do not just accept it as a normal ritual. If you change the culture, tradition will change.

> "If someone is hazing you, report it to nationals, the proper authorities on campus, or me."
> —Harlan

If you ever feel that you're being put in an uncomfortable or dangerous situation or that you're being forced to do something that you know isn't right, don't do it. Leave an anonymous message with the dean of students. Leave an anonymous message with the national chapter. You can have your parents leave a confidential message (and then you can say that you never knew about it). Hazing is stupid. It's not necessary. Make sure that you protect yourself and your friends. The biggest problem is that sometimes, new members get lost in the group mentality and can't see the real dangers. They forget they have options and feel powerless when someone tells them to do something absurd or dangerous. Alert people who can step in and stop whatever it is that's happening. And yes, this happens all over campus (team sports and the performing arts are two other places where hazing commonly happens), not just in the Greek community—but

Hazed? Know Someone Being Hazed? Call the Hazing Hotline:

Report incidents of hazing anonymously. Call toll-free: 1-888-NOT-HAZE, or 1-888-668-4293.

hazing in Greek life is a tradition that doesn't need to continue.

I'll end this tip with a link to a video you should watch about a student who was hazed and didn't survive. The fraternity members in this video agreed to participate in it as part of a legal settlement. Honor the life of Phanta "Jack" Phoummarath and watch the video (and share it with others). Here's the website: www.InMemoryofJack.com.

Bottom Line

If pledges stopped tolerating hazing, the hazing would stop. Report hazing. You can email me anonymously and I'll do my best to pass along the word to the right people on campus and in the national organization. Send your note to: harlan@helpmeharlan.com, subject: Hazing.

Harlan's Tip Sheet

Naked People, Places, and Resources

Definitions
- *Greek advisor:* The person on campus who works with the fraternity and sorority leaders to make sure procedures and rules are being followed.

- *Dean of students*: The dean of students oversees the entire campus. If there is a serious problem or concern in a fraternity or sorority, the dean of students will get involved.
- *Interfraternity Council (IFC)*: This is the governing body of the recognized fraternity chapters on campus, made up of representatives from each fraternity. The IFC works to provide programming and leadership opportunities within the Greek community, and also makes sure policies and procedures are being followed.
- *Panhellenic Association*: Every woman who joins a sorority becomes a member of the Panhellenic Association (often referred to as Panhel). The association brings sorority members together to work toward common goals for the benefit of the community. A council made up of a representative from each sorority governs the Panhellenic Association.
- *National office*: Most Greek organizations have a national office that oversees each chapter. Contact the national office if you can't find resolutions to your problems within your chapter.
- *Dues and initiation fees*: Fraternities and sororities usually charge a one-time initiation fee and membership fees. Inquire about specific costs before accepting a bid.
- *Philanthropy*: Most chapters organize charitable events to help raise money for an important cause.
- *Executive board*: Each Greek organization has an internal governing board made up of members who run different aspects of the house. Usually there is a

president, vice president, secretary, rush chair, social chair, philanthropy chair, and many more chairs.
- *Hazing:* See definition in Tip #38.

Hazing Hotline
- Anti-hazing Hotline—to report incidents of hazing anonymously, call the toll-free number: 1-888-NOT-HAZE, or 1-888-668-4293.

Websites (with links to national fraternity and sorority sites)
- Association of Fraternal Leadership & Values Website: www.AFLV.org
  Facebook: www.Facebook.com/TheAFLV
  Twitter: www.Twitter.com/AFLV
- National Panhellenic Conference
  Website: www.NPCWomen.org
  Facebook: www.Facebook.com/NPCWomen
  Twitter: www.Twitter.com/NPCWomen
- National Multicultural Greek Council
  Website: www.NationalMGC.org
  Facebook: www.Facebook.com/NationalMGC
  Twitter: www.Twitter.com/NationalMGC
- North American Interfraternity Conference
  Website: www.NICIndy.org
  Facebook: www.Facebook.com/NICFraternity
  Twitter: www.Twitter.com/NICFraternity
- Northeast Greek Leadership Association (NGLA)
  Website: www.NGLA.org
  Facebook: www.Facebook.com/MyNGLA
  Twitter: www.Twitter.com/NGLAGreeks

- Southeast Interfraternity Conference (SEIFC)
  Website: www.SEIFC.org
- Southeast Panhellenic Conference (SEPC)
  Website: www.SEPCOnline.net
- Stop Hazing Information (by state)
  Website: www.stophazing.org/laws/states-with-anti
  -hazing-laws

Life Inside the Classroom

Assuming You Wake Up and Go to Class

*If you're REALLY concerned about succeeding inside the classroom, check out *The Naked Roommate's First Year Survival Workbook*. You'll find more tips, strategies, and Naked exercises to help you make the most of life inside the classroom. If you're just looking to get a C, D, or F—don't bother.

Dear Harlan,

I'm a sophomore in college and stressed over a class. I have to take two years of a foreign language to graduate, and I've taken almost a year and a half of Russian. The end seems so close, but I just don't think I can take it anymore. The class is very difficult and it requires a much larger time commitment than I have been able to offer. Compound that with the fact that I have found myself completely unmotivated to work on Russian, and I have a class in which I do poorly and I feel miserable. There are two weeks of class left in the semester, and I don't know whether or not I should bother to keep going. Even after studying for hours, I failed yet another test, and it doesn't look like it's going to get any better.

It's 4 a.m., and I still can't sleep, because I know I have to wake up and go to this class. I feel terrible, and it's really been hurting my other work, not to mention my general quality of life. Is college really supposed to be like this?

—Rattled by Russian

Dear Rattled,

My original reply was in Russian, but I figured the semester would be over by the time you translated it, so I translated it back to English for you. Listen, man (or woman)—talk to your professor and explain the situation, preferably in English. Tell him or her that you really want to pass and will do whatever it takes. Professors can be surprisingly flexible in these situations. Offer to meet with him or her several times before the end of the semester. Suggest getting an incomplete and doing extra work over the break, when you can focus solely on Russian. In the meantime, meet with your academic advisor as soon as possible. I don't know if your professor knows you or not, but the better a professor knows you the less likely you are to fail.

To sum this up for you—go to class, talk to your professor, talk to your advisor, and figure out a way to make this work. Yes, this is what college is about. But no, you don't have to handle this on your own. Turn to the people in your corner. Unless you're going to be a translator for the United Nations, this class won't break you. Get some sleep and relax.

Tip #39
To Go or Not to Go

The Tip
You can miss classes once in a while, but you have to be very strategic about it. If you miss a lot of classes, your grades suffer.

The Story
I've learned that college is about figuring out how to make the best possible use of my time. It's not as if I'm sleeping through classes, but sometimes I've found that it's better to miss a lecture if I have to work on a paper or study for something else. The rule is that I'll never miss a lecture around midterms or finals, and I'll never miss a section. The teachers know if I'm there or not because there are usually only about ten

"No matter what time you schedule your first class, you'll find a way to sleep through it."
—junior, DeSales University

or fifteen people in a section. In lectures, they don't know if I'm there. It also helps that most of my professors post their notes on their websites. One professor refuses to put his PowerPoint presentation online because he feels that it's not fair for students who go to class. There have been a few rare occasions where I've been tired or run-down and missed class, but that generally doesn't hold me back from class.

—freshman, Harvard University

* * *

Are you sitting in bed, blowing off class, and reading this tip? If you are, at least you're doing some reading—be proud. Deciding whether to go to class or not is one of the hardest choices you'll face in your college career—that and whether or not to secretly borrow clean underwear from your roommate when you run out. The attendance question regularly stares you in the eye—every morning when the alarm goes off (assuming you've even set it). Deciding whether or not to go to class is a new freedom that you have in college; in most cases, you're free of parental supervision, attendance offices, and questioning principals (but some professors do take attendance). If you *choose* to, you can sleep late, watch TV all day, play video games, enjoy a four-hour breakfast at the buffet, go to the gym, go to a party, hang

"It took me until my last semester to realize that if I went to class nearly every time, the exams were a zillion times easier because I already had a grasp on the material. Now that I'm in grad school and going to every class as expected, I'm finding it a breeze."
—graduate student, University of Texas

out with your boyfriend or girlfriend, hang out on Facebook, Skype, or just lie in bed imagining all those things that you could be doing—which can be exhausting, leading you to fall asleep again and miss your afternoon classes too.

The choice to go or not to go is yours, but with every choice come consequences. In this case, the consequence could be missing essential material, missing a pop quiz with no makeup offered, missing material that will likely be the key to the next exam, losing out on extra credit awarded for simply attending class, getting poor grades, and failing out of school. From time to time you will find yourself unable to make it to class. It happens. Just make sure that you can at least do the following to cover yourself:

> "Don't get in the habit of skipping classes. As your classes become more difficult, it's more important to go."
> —junior, Manhattan College

○ Some instructors will award credit just for attending class. Make sure to find out your instructor's attendance policy. Ask your instructor or teaching assistant if the information is not in your syllabus. Either way, you should still go to class.

> "When picking your classes, pick something you are interested in learning about. If you are not interested in the subject, then you will not want to get up to go to class."
> —sophomore, Angelo State University

○ Instructors have been known to give quizzes to start class. Not being there or coming late means failing the quiz (bummer). Know what you've missed and do damage control. Even if you don't get to retake the quiz, making the effort can help you in the future.

○ Get notes from a friend in your class. The only catch is that you need to actually go to class so that you can make a friend who can share notes with you. And then, when your new friend is out of class, you'll be the one sharing your notes. WARNING: it's tempting to just use all the online resources your instructor makes available, but many instructors will test what's actually discussed in class.

○ If you should get sick or miss classes because of reasons beyond your control, you have options. You can drop a class before it counts against you. Talk to your professors and your academic advisor—but be sure to do something. A dropped class doesn't typically count against your grade point average. An F can and will hurt you.

> "I came to school with a 4.0 GPA and thought that college would be a breeze, just like high school. The first few weeks I went to class religiously and then the party invites started coming. It seemed like the weekend started on a Wednesday and ended on Tuesday. I was usually too tired to go to my early morning classes and didn't feel like putting much effort into the other ones. It wasn't until the report cards came out [and] I realized my GPA had plummeted to a 2.5 and I lost my scholarship that I realized I had to do something about it."
> —senior, Northern Michigan University

○ If you find that you're consistently missing class because you're nursing a hangover, downloading porn, or that you're still partying in the morning while your class is in session, there's a pretty good chance that you need some professional treatment. That's not normal (see Tip #82).

○ If you find that you're missing so many classes that you forget where your classes are located and which days you even have them, ask yourself this question: why in the hell am I here if I'm never going to classes? I might be better off buying a Ferrari with my tuition money.

○ Sitting in class and playing games on your phone, texting people on the other side of the room, and watching seven seasons of *The Office* on your computer counts as sitting in—NOT actually being in—class.

Bottom Line
Missing a class is equivalent to paying hundreds of dollars for a ticket to a show and then not going. Unfortunately, you can't scalp tickets to English 101. Even more unfortunately, your instructor isn't Katy Perry.

Tip #40
Nice Professor, Nice Professor

The Tip
Professors are your friends. Don't be afraid to get to know them.

The Story
I started college completely intimidated by my professors. I was afraid to talk to them and even approach them. In

high school, the teachers were pushing me, but in college, I had to push myself. I had to be the one to seek out help. In Philosophy 160, I understood most of it, but a few paragraphs confused me. There were about two hundred people in the class. I went to the professor's office hours, and he was in the room with a dog at his feet. I thought that was kind of interesting. He read the paragraph and broke it down to me. He cleared it up in a matter of minutes. I went back to him whenever something was confusing and he was happy to help. All of my professors wanted to help. One professor even invited some students to his house for dinner. His wife made us dinner. I was surprised that my professor and I became friends.

—freshman, University of Washington–Seattle

"Make a commitment to visit each professor's office hours at least once a term. My biggest regret from college has been not getting to know my professors—and not just because of letters of recommendation from them. Professors are some of the best people to talk to about the fields you are interested in. They can provide helpful advice on grad school, papers, and college life. I missed out on meeting so many professors."

—senior, UCLA

* * *

Scary Facts about Professors

55.5 percent of surveyed freshmen "frequently" or "occasionally" felt intimidated by professors.

—Higher Education Research Institute at UCLA

Professors are often some of the most intimidating and interesting members of the college community. Amazingly, half of students report being frequently or occasionally intimidated by them. There's no need to tiptoe around your instructors as if walking barefoot around the mold spores in the community bathrooms. (A quick note about community bathroom floors: for God's sake, always wear flip flops!) In reality, professors are some of the kindest, funniest, smartest, warmest, most interesting, and most misunderstood people you'll meet in college. Your professors should be people in your corner. It's a no-brainer.

One of the biggest mistakes students make is not getting to know their professors. Your professors want you to talk to them. They want to help you. They want to share their passion with you. They choose to teach. They want to be

challenged by you. They want to be approached by you. Do them a favor and ask questions. Allow them to get to know you. Unlike high school, most of them are not going to track you down. They might not even know your name—but it's not their fault. In college, you need to be the one to get to know your professors. Approach them.

"By going to one of my professor's office hours I was able to have the opportunity to work with a professor on a research project that helped me get into the graduate school of my choice. Take advantage of office hours."

—graduate student, Bowling Green State University

Engage them. Sure, a few will act like they've got a pole stuck up their professor rear ends or they will appear to have left their personalities in the faculty lounge, but most aren't like that. Most won't push you around just because they can. On some campuses, you can go an entire semester (or quarter) without ever actually talking to your instructor. And if you enter the classroom through the door in the back of the room and your instructor enters through the door in the front of the room, you might not even cross paths. It can be that severe. While researching this book and my book for parents of college students, professor after professor urged me to encourage students to make it a point to introduce themselves. The better a professor knows you, the better your chance of passing a course or getting additional help along the way. Professors can offer you extra help in the way of tutoring, rescheduling exams if you miss one, and giving you an extra point or two for all your effort. They can offer mentoring and support during college and after college. They can offer letters of recommendation for graduate school or for campus jobs or activities. And they can offer a friendship that can last far beyond your college years. The problem is that a lot of students don't want to approach their professors because they are too intimidated

"Test dates can be flexible with some professors if you check with them. My professor was totally cool about changing a test date because I was away at a conference. All I had to do was ask."
—junior, Texas Christian University

"Every year just before the first big exam, I have waves of nameless strangers at my door, suddenly trying to figure out what has been going on the first two months of class. At this point, there is little I can do for them, except ask awkward questions ('Did you read the book? Do you have the book? How often have you been to class?'). When someone I have already met comes in, the help comes easier to both of us."
—college professor in Texas

or don't want to look stupid when asking a question. But really, these professors are there for YOU. Besides, they need for you to ask questions—even easy ones. If you knew everything, they would have no reason to exist. Give them a purpose. Make an effort to get to know your professors. Don't be shy. Just say, "Hi, I'm blah blah (if that's not your name, then say your name),

> **"If your professors don't know you, don't expect any favors."**
> —freshman, Eastern Illinois University

and I just wanted to introduce myself to you." Oh, and if you should ever struggle in a class, don't worry about feeling embarrassed or looking stupid. Your instructor wants to help you. Getting help is the smart thing to do. Not getting help is the opposite of smart.

Also, see if your teacher is on Twitter. You might gain some added insight into your instructor's life outside the classroom. As for Facebook, you might not want to make a friend request. Then your professor will know that you weren't really out sick, but had one too many cups of manhito juice at the taco and toga party.

Quick warning: if you're checking out a professor using www.RateMyProfessors.com, confirm what you read with real-life students on campus, face to face. Not all students grade their professors fairly.

Bottom Line

Professors want you to do well, but unless they actually know your name (not just your user email name) and your face (not just your Facebook profile pic), they can't help you do well.

Tip #41
How to Get an A (or almost an A)

The Tip
To get an A, follow these seven steps to academic success, created by me, an average student:

Step 1: Go to class regularly and on time.
Step 2: Do all assigned homework.
Step 3: Take notes.
Step 4: Be in tune with your professor.
Step 5: Take advantage of tutoring.
Step 6: Organize.
Step 7: Have a positive attitude.

Attention Students with Documented Learning Disabilities:

Register with the office for students with disabilities and let your instructor know. If your instructor understands your challenges, he or she can be more sensitive to you and your needs. Take advantage of special accommodations available to you.

The Story
In high school, I was never really able to get good grades. I never understood why. I studied a lot, I did my homework, but somehow I always struggled.

When I got into college, my mentality changed. I decided to completely redo my habits and take on a new form of scholastic work. I decided to come to every single class, write down what the professors would say, and I would study only what I was told to study. And, to this point, after six consecutive trimesters, I am maintaining a 4.0 GPA. I am the vice president of the prestigious Alpha Chi National Honors Society, Iota Illinois Chapter, and I hold lectures and speeches teaching other students just how easy it is to get good grades. I know that if students follow these seven steps, I can ethically guarantee them good grades (As and Bs).

—junior, DeVry University

* * *

Before I tell you how to get an A, appreciate that more students than ever are arriving on campus with A averages. According to the Higher Education Research Institute, in the last ten years, increases have continued to occur in the proportion of students reporting an A-average, reaching a high point in 2006 of 24.1 percent. This means that getting an A won't be as easy as it was in high school. If you ever struggle academically, find your people and places. Instead of keeping your grades a big secret, find support.

Here are my tips within the tip for getting an A:

- *Go to classes*. Obviously, you need to be there to listen, learn, and absorb.
- *Sit near the front of the room.* The closer you are, the harder it is to Snapchat.

Naked Celebration

Celebrate your Cs, Ds, and Fs BUT ONLY in September and October. Rejoice because it's not December or January and the grades aren't final. Get help. Talk to your instructor, go to the academic resource center, get tutors. Celebrate and get help before the grades are final.

- *Make sure your professor knows who you are.* Introduce yourself to your professor. Do it in class, during office hours, and around campus.
- *Do readings ahead of time.* If you're familiar with the readings, you will naturally absorb so much more of the lecture content in class—and retain it.
- *Study your notes the night after you take them.* Conscientiously review your notes the night after the lecture. Again, the material will stick with you this way.
- *Look over your syllabus before going to class.* The syllabus is the schedule of what's to come. It helps to know when the exams are approaching.
- *Get help before you need it.* If you're having trouble, don't go for help the day before the final. Go as soon as the trouble starts.
- *Go to office hours.* Every professor has office hours set aside for students to come in and get extra help. It's like a free tutoring session.
- *Take advantage of teaching assistants.* Think of them as personal academic assistants. Sometimes they can slip up and give up sensitive information by mistake.
- *Form study groups.* Find people in class who can challenge you, share notes, and pool resources to help everyone master the material.
- *Ask about extra credit.* If you're not making the grade, ask to do extra work.

Tweet a Meet-Up

Want to form a study group? Ask your professor to create a hashtag for your class (example #IU-Chem101-Cohen). Then tweet a meet-up time and place to study. The tweet will look something like this, "2night 8:00 study group at 3rd flr main library. All are welcome #IU-Chem101-Cohen."

- *Question exams when you get them back*. Many professors will change your score if you care enough to bring up a confusing question on a graded exam. It's worth trying.
- *Find out from upperclassmen how a professor grades*. Some professors only give out a few As while others give out many more. It will help you to know how hard you need to work in the class to earn an A.
- *Find old exams*. If it's legal, study off of old exams. You might find a few questions on the new exam that are the same or similar. At the very least, old exams can help you focus on important information.
- *Talk to former students*. Talk to people who have taken the class and ask about the best ways to study and how the professor tests. Many colleges have websites where students list information about professors' procedures and grading styles.
- *Avoid cramming if possible*. You'll retain information longer if you study way ahead of the exam. Cramming

A math professor's guide to making the grade

(1) Take all prerequisites before your first collegiate mathematics class. (2) Attend all classes and arrive at least ten minutes early. (3) Buy your textbook early and skim the first chapter. (4) If possible, sit close to the front of the class to reduce any distractions. (5) Find a study partner and try to meet several times a week. (6) Constantly monitor your attitude and study habits. (7) Do not be afraid to ask questions—often high school students think asking questions is a sign of weakness. This is not true in college. (8) Seek help from the Math Lab and/or your professor. (9) Consider taking your math class in a short term where you can focus only on this one course. (10) Keep up on a daily basis and remember, for every hour in class, you should study at least two hours outside the classroom.

might help you pass, but you need to retain information for final exams. (That said, I crammed too much.)

- *Go to exam reviews.* Before exams, many professors or teaching assistants will offer reviews. These are priceless rundowns of the material typically on the exam.
- *Grades can be negotiable.* Fight for a higher grade by all means possible (without breaking any laws or codes of conduct). When the professor says, "If I do this for you, I'll have to do it for everyone," counter with, "If everyone cared as much as me, I could understand, but I'm the only one here—the only one who cares enough…"

Bottom Line

The bad news: not everyone can get an A. The good news: most people don't want to do the work to get an A. You can.

Tip #42
How to Just Pass

The Tip
Unlike high school, you actually need to study in college.

The Story
I came to college as a straight-A student, and never really had to study too much in high school. It came as a surprise to me when I got two Cs and just two Bs my first semester. When I met my boyfriend, I soon came to copy

his study habits. Instead of trying to cram it all in the night before, give yourself three solid days to study for your test, and then on the night before, review everything that you've already studied. This will take major pressure off in the hours nearing the exam. This tip has made me face the upcoming exam well ahead of time and not try to avoid it until the last minute. Your grades will reflect the time you put into them—unlike grades in high school!

—senior, Juniata College

* * *

If you find that you just can't put in the time you need to get the grade you desire, you can at least ensure a passing grade by using the following advice from Tip #41:

WARNING: Shocked, embarrassed, or upset with your grade? NEVER keep it a secret. I struggled. We all struggle. Don't struggle alone. Get help. If you can't get academic help, find a mental health professional. Grades are NOT a reflection of self-worth. If they were, your author wouldn't be worth very much.

- Go to class.
- Go to the review before the exam.
- Study old exams (if it's legal).

- Find a study group with people more motivated and/ or smarter than you are.

If you can go to class and manage to actually stay awake, you should achieve a low C or a solid D (although those grades aren't really worthy of the word "achieve"). Basically, if you go to class and do minimal work, there's a decent chance you'll be able to slide by.

Additional note: for classes that involve essay exams on specific readings, you'll need to read the book or at least have someone explain the book to you. This is why it helps to surround yourself with smart people who are more motivated than you. If you ask them to explain it to you and they respond, "Why the hell should I tell you?" reply, "If you tell me, then you'll be able to go through the material while explaining it and you'll have a better grasp of it all." If they say, "But I already know it," tell them, "Yeah, but it helps to talk it through. Besides, it's not like I'm going to affect your grade. Just tell me enough to pass." If it's still a problem, try, "I'll get you into a party." It's a win-win situation.

Additional additional note: when it comes to the math and accounting classes with number-oriented themes, just going to class and doing nothing else could land you a D or an F. If you're not great with numbers, be aware that you need to do more than go to class.

> "Share your exam schedule with your roommate so that, if need be, you can wake each other up."
> —freshman, College of the Holy Cross

> "It took a while to get used to the fact that I didn't have to raise my hand to go the bathroom. I could just get up and leave when I wanted to leave."
> —senior, Northwestern University

> "I never studied or did much work in high school. I completely bombed my first college test and had horrible grades on my homework. I quickly learned that I actually had to study."
> —freshman, Purdue University

If you're good with numbers, you can still just go to class, review, and pass.

Bottom Line
Minimal work + minimal attendance + minimal effort = minimal grades.

Tip #43
How to Fail

The Tip
Too much partying and no studying can be your downfall. Drinking at college can be a lot of fun, but it can also be your worst enemy.

The Story
I say that I am a college sophomore, which is true, considering that I dropped out of college a year ago, and after three years of attending I was a first-semester sophomore, with a 1.5 GPA. That is a far cry from the 3.65 GPA I graduated high school with. I was all set to go to college, but once I got there, I realized that the easiest places to meet people on campus were parties and bars, and it's much easier to talk to girls after you've had a couple…Eventually this progressed to going out most nights of the week, sleeping too late to get to half my classes, and being too hungover to

> "I lost control, lost my scholarship, and now I'm working my butt off to stay in school."
>
> —sophomore,
> South Dakota State University

go to the other half. Just because no parents are around to stop you from doing things that you probably shouldn't be doing—like drinking—is no reason to dive in headfirst.

—sophomore, College of William & Mary

* * *

If your major in college is failing, and you succeed, you fail. And that's not good. Ironically, failing takes work. If you want to fail—follow each of the following rules. To pass, just do the opposite:

○ Sleep through your classes (in class or in your bed).

○ Skip class and then don't do the readings. (FYI: According to the NSSE, one out of five first-year students and seniors reported that they frequently came to class without completing readings or assignments.)

○ Pretend to buy textbooks (tricky you).

○ Avoid your professor when material starts to get confusing for fear of looking stupid (causing you to fail and look stupid).

○ Never go to review sessions before tests.

○ Avoid getting help and blame the prof when you fail.

○ Refuse to borrow notes when you miss a class.

○ Go to a class drunk, high, or hungover (or all of the above).

○ Attend class and play video games online with people from your study group.

○ Use your video camera on your phone or laptop to tape yourself not paying attention.

○ Download porn and write online reviews during class (exception: if attending a human sexuality course, this might help you pass).

○ Play hide-and-go-seek during class, but spend your time hiding in another classroom.

○ Miss an exam and don't bother to ask for a makeup (although it's rare to get one, you need to at least ask).

○ Look at someone else's exam for the answers.

○ Show up for an exam and look for the answers on someone else's exam who is also failing.

○ Show up for an exam and get caught cheating.

○ Stream music on your phone or computer while wearing sound-canceling headphones in class. You need to listen to pass.

○ Refer to your teacher as Professor Stupid and the teaching assistant as Professor Stupid's Assistant.

○ Date the professor and cheat on him or her.

○ Date a professor and then cheat with another professor and have them both find out (a sure way to fail two classes).

If you care to pass and want to pass, you can find a way to pass. Professors want you to pass. Teaching assistants want you to pass. The people who tutor for free want you to pass (yes, there is often free tutoring; ask your academic advisor, instructor, or res life staff). I want you to pass. The guy who just passed by you wants you to pass. The children playing in the park want you to pass. The barking dog wants you to pass (that's what he's barking). You have to want to fail in order to fail. It takes effort. That said, should you find that you're doing your best and still can't pass, make an appointment with a therapist at the counseling center. The problem might be more than just a "tough course."

Bottom Line
Report Card of a Failing Student
Grades: F F F F F D
GPA: 0.2
Status: Moving Back Home

Tip #44
The Cheat Sheet

WARNING: Don't be a dumba** and cheat.

The Tip
When it comes to cheating, technology is your friend—and make sure cheat sheets are small enough to eat.

The Story
I've gotten answers via instant messenger, programmed off of my laptop, and entered into my calculator. One time, I heard about a guy on another campus who was failing one course. So he went to the final exam to help the rest of the class. He went into the exam and left about five minutes later. The answers for the test were posted outside the classroom for people to check once they finished. He then text messaged the answers to everyone in the class. And with technology, there isn't hard evidence to convict any of the cheaters. And although I have actually made cheat sheets small enough to be eaten, I've never had to eat them.

—junior, technology school in Michigan

* * *

You'll have the opportunity to cheat, but it's stupid, wrong, and lazy. It's all about integrity. And cheating makes you lose it. Sadly, cheating has come a long way over the years (but it can still get you expelled). The rise of technology has taken dishonesty to a new low. Between phones that snap photos, text messaging, cheating while tweeting, hackers, smart phones, and video surveillance, cheating has been taken to a whole new high-tech level. And of course, the old-fashioned method of looking at someone's paper still happens.

"If you're buying a term paper online, chances are someone else has bought it too. If you both hand it in, it'll be hard to explain it to your professor as one big funny coincidence."
—senior, Boston University

If you decide to cheat, you can get thrown out of school, but that's not a huge deterrent for most students. Besides possible expulsion, you're paying thousands upon thousands of dollars to get an education. You pay for it—why not use it? You can get by and pass your classes without cheating. Instead of an A, you can get a B or a C. Not going to classes, cheating to get by, and then graduating is a waste. And if you're someone who is cheating so that you can get a good enough grade to get into a graduate school, that's even dumber, because then all the cheating will only leave you behind, having to cheat to catch up. It's such a cliché (forgive me for this piece-of-crap cliché), but you're really cheating yourself out of an education, out of personal integrity, and out of so much that college is supposed to be.

If you should cheat and get busted, don't use the excuse, "I didn't want to disappoint my parents by getting a poor grade." Getting expelled for cheating is far more disappointing than getting a bad grade. If you find that you're having a hard time passing class, get help before you feel the need to cheat. Some people have a rule that they'll only cheat on courses that don't matter to them, but those courses soon will matter when they get expelled after getting busted. And if you're someone who is taking a class pass/fail and you cheat, you deserve to fail.

All that said, if you do cheat, I hope you get caught (sorry, but I do). If you do get caught, accept the consequences. Oh, if you should decide to buy a paper or copy someone else's work, know that many papers are automatically screened for plagiarism using sophisticated software that's standard on many college campuses. There's no way to convince a professor that it's just a weird coincidence. Professors can also use other technology to detect if your writing is original. They can set up devices to survey the class via live video. While your professor looks busy working on her laptop, she's actually watching you via streaming video on her monitor (not that I've heard of a professor doing this, but it's not a bad idea). People who cheat deserve to get caught. (For more information, cheaters, you can flip to Tip #62 in the relationship section of the book.)

Bottom Line

If a professor sees you looking at someone else's test, just tell your professor that you were checking to see who else got the answer right. When you have to see the dean of students, tell him or her the same thing. When the dean throws you out, you can later tell it to your kids when explaining why mommy or daddy was expelled from college.

Tip #45
The Art of Reading (or not reading) the College Textbook

WARNING: Do not skim this part.

The Tip
If you go to class every day, you can do less reading and more skimming.

The Story
I'll be honest, I don't read the textbook before class. Sometimes I'll just skim it, but not word for word. Mostly, I'll read it after the class and then I'll highlight the points the professor has made. I'll use sticky notes to highlight. It keeps it cleaner so I don't have to worry about cleaning the pages. Unless I know a professor will ask questions about the reading or is giving a quiz, I'll do the reading after class. It helps to manage my time better. There just isn't enough time to do all the reading. Besides, each professor uses the text differently. Some will test from the book and some will test from class materials. I've even had professors eliminate entire chapters. Now, when it comes to buying books, I like to wait until the first week of class. I want to be sure about what we need and what we don't need. Some books end up not even being opened. It's all about the professor.

—sophomore, Lasell College

* * *

College textbooks are to professors like body soaps are to your new roommates—not all use them the same way. Some never use them.

I'll never forget it—I cried three times when buying my college textbooks for the first time. Once when I saw the price, once when I saw all the pages I had to read, and once when I tried to carry them (the weight of the plastic bag cutting into my hand brought tears to my eyes). To think that you're going to have to read thousands of pages of text over the course of sixteen weeks is insane. There aren't enough hours in the day to read all the pages in the books. Even if you did want to do all the reading, assuming you aren't a speed reader, you couldn't do it all.

> "I don't really have to read the textbooks. The teacher tells us the most important things. If I get confused, that's when I use the textbook. When highlighting, I pick the type that's in bold."
> —freshman, University of Georgia

Don't worry, don't panic, don't freak out—a lot of it is just for show. See, your professors need to assign reading—it's part of their job. They know that not everyone will read every page. Unless they test you on it before discussing it, don't worry about reading every word on each page. The text is more of a guide. It's a way to reinforce what was discussed in class and clear up any confusion. Once you get to class, you'll get a feel for the style of your professor and how you'll use the textbooks (this is assuming you actually make it to class).

Naked Plug

Check out *The Naked Roommate's First Year Survival Workbook* to help you with your reading, time management, note taking, and other essential skills for classroom success. There's a huge study skill section. Or don't check it out...

If you're feeling overwhelmed, ask your instructor the best way to work through the mountain of text. You might get inside information.

How to Navigate through All the Text

Read it, skim it, or find a smart friend who has read it or skimmed it.

When it comes to reading for English lit, if the book has been made into a movie, see the movie with a friend who has actually read the book. Ask him or her to explain the differences. Smart professors test those questions. If possible, see if there is an audio version of the book available to download or rent—this way you can "read" while you drive or work out. CliffsNotes (www.CliffsNotes.com) or SparkNotes (www.SparkNotes.com) are helpful for offering you plot points and character background info, but they won't always give you the whole picture. Either read the whole thing yourself, or ask the smart friend who has read the book to look over the CliffsNotes or SparkNotes and give you an oral narration. It helps to hear the story. Of course, do the reading if you can do the reading, but if you just can't because you don't have the time, be resourceful. If there are several books to read, have each person in your study group read one and rotate being the "smart" one.

When highlighting textbooks, many used textbooks come with their own highlights. Be careful; some previous users are morons. Even if he or she is not a moron, he or she might have had a different instructor who used the text differently. Or he or she might just be a bad highlighter who uses the highlighter to create designs on the page—not to take notes. Assuming you don't get the book from someone who just finished the same class with the same professor, use a different highlighter color. Once you're in class, you can decide if the highlighting you've inherited will be a good guide.

Bottom Line
Should this book be required text, and should you get tested, this is the part of the book you'd be tested on. The answer to the question is "Sacagawea." If you're reading the answer after getting the quiz question wrong, I'm so sorry. But I warned you at the beginning of this tip not to skim this one.

Tip #46
Take Notes Here

The Tip
Sit near the front of the room.

The Story
It seemed obvious, but I was in the last row most of the time. I found myself putting my head down and taking a nap. Other times I would write random notes. Sometimes I would make jokes with my friends. I would stare at a girl a few rows ahead of me. I would watch the clock. In classes where I had my laptop, I would send instant messages or check out the sports scores. I was in class in body, but I

was really in other places. I thought I would just absorb material, but I wasn't even listening enough. After mid-terms, and seeing my shockingly poor grades, I moved up to the front of the room. It's like you become so much more a part of the class. It's harder to get distracted because the professor is right there looking at the people in the front row. Being close to the action kept me more interested and helped me listen, which helped me to become much better at taking notes.

—junior, University of Southern Indiana

* * *

Seriously, take notes here. Please write in the space below.

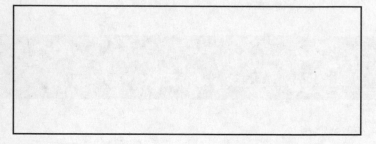

This doesn't seem like the most exciting tip, but you're wrong. I'm actually eating fire and walking on shards of glass while writing this one to add some excitement.

Every instructor has his or her own teaching style. Come to class with an idea of the topic(s) that will be discussed. Use your syllabus as a guide for taking notes. Go online and use classroom resources. Come to class with a few pens and loose-leaf paper (this way you can rearrange your notes and add other people's notes). Find a seat close to the action. It helps to see the board to keep you involved. As a rule—anything written on the board or presented in PowerPoint is important. Even if you have online access to lecture notes following class, writing them down will help you retain the information. Professors emphasize the most important points by writing them, speaking them, and repeating them. Listen for key phrases that are intended to emphasize key points. If they say it more than once, there's a good chance it will show up on the test.

As you attend more classes, you'll get a better sense of the style of your professor. You'll begin to hear words that emphasize more important parts of the lecture. For example, hearing the words "This is important" is a good sign that it's important. Listen for summaries at the end of class. If you're unsure what's important, ask your instructor, "If you were taking notes in your own class, how would you know what's most important?"

When class is finished, review your notes that night or the next morning. Talk through them out loud and put material in your own words (this actually helps). Highlight key points. Write a summary sentence or two. If you have time, rewrite your notes. Rewriting in your own words gives you an opportunity to process the information and concepts.

Post-exam tip: after the exam, look over the notes and see what was tested and whether the information came from lecture or readings. You can have a better sense of how your professor designs his or her exams.

One more note on notes. You might come across professional note-taking services that sell notes taken in your actual classes. Sometimes these services violate the school's policies. Regardless, never rely solely on these notes. If you miss class, use both the professional notes and other students' notes from class.

Bottom Line

If your instructor writes it, repeats it, or reflects upon it, write it, remember it, and take note of it—chances are, you will be tested on it.

Tip #47
Do It in a Group

The Tip
No one is smart enough to always study alone. The group will save you.

The Story
Before coming to college, I never studied with anyone, except maybe once when there was a group project. There wasn't so much pressure or material to cover on high school exams. I would just show up and pass. In college, I had class with a few people from my hall. We would go to class together and then study together. If one of us missed class, we would share notes. What was nice is that one of the people had a friend who knew the professor from the previous year (he was

> "It was during a group project in the business school that I met my boyfriend and fell in love. The professor told us that it will happen in some of the groups. He was right."
> —senior, Indiana University

a sophomore). A week before the test, I had to leave town for a week due to a family emergency. Earlier in the month, I had missed classes because I was sick. The group completely saved me. They went to the review and shared the review notes. They even had an old test from a test file. I ended up getting a B and that was better than I could have hoped for. There's no reason to study alone.

—junior, University of Maryland

* * *

If you're looking to pass your classes, pass around notes, and make a pass on someone in your class, find a study group. The study group is one of the most powerful tools for classroom success. It's a way to pool all of your resources— you can share notes when someone misses class, discuss topics that will be covered on the exam, and work through confusing material by listening to friends who have

Bet You Didn't Know (or didn't want to know)

95.9 percent of surveyed freshmen "frequently" or "occasionally" discussed course content with students outside of class.

88.2 percent of surveyed freshmen "frequently" or "occasionally" asked questions in class.

91.9 percent of surveyed freshmen "frequently" or "occasionally" studied with other students.

60.7 percent of surveyed freshmen "frequently" or "occasionally" skipped class.

46.4 percent of surveyed freshmen "frequently" or "occasionally" received tutoring.

33.8 percent of surveyed freshmen were "frequently" bored in class.

41.7 percent of surveyed freshmen felt that their courses "frequently" inspired them to think in new ways.

—Higher Education Research Institute at UCLA

spoken with the professor or teaching assistant. It's also a way to hang out and make studying a good time (or just not a terrible time). Besides getting a better grasp on material, making friends, and getting on the dean's list, you might even find a little bit of lovin'.

Imagine this. It's a long night of studying before your first exam. Everyone is tired and wants to call it a night. You and the object of your affection want to cram a little more in before calling it quits. You decide to grab a late-night snack. Suddenly, that hard calculus problem turns into a titillating conversation that's punctuated by a first kiss. As the textbook digs into your side, and the scientific calculator into your thigh, you ignore the pain and focus on that kiss. Not only do you get an A on the exam, you have found a new study buddy that gives you one more reason to make it to class.

> "Ask for help before you need it. Tutoring and study groups make C students B students and B students A students."
> —advisor, Central Michigan University

Please be aware: there is no guarantee that your study group will lead to crazy mad love, but it *will* help you do well in class and get crazy mad good grades.

How to start a study group: after the first few weeks, people will start to look familiar. A couple weeks before the exam, ask a few people who interest you if they want to get together to study. Find a place to meet (like the library). Don't be afraid to be the one to put it together. Once you get together the first time, it will be easier to do it again. A cool way to make it happen can be via technology. Create a class hashtag (#) so you can

> "What's great about college is that when you get homework, it's not like you're going home alone. There are a lot of people around who can work together in a group. It sounds bad, but it helps to have everybody do some work and then come together."
> —freshman, Harvard University

connect via Twitter (talk to your instructor and see if he or she can come up with one to communicate to the class). You can also start a Facebook group for the class. Use the invite function to put together study groups. Use technology to stay connected and connect outside of the classroom.

Bottom Line
Study groups can get you more than just a passing grade; they can create a perfect opportunity to make a friendly pass at someone in class.

Tip #48
Old Exams, Sharing Notes, and Mostly
Legal Ways to Pass

The Tip
Old exams, old exams, old exams. Find out who has the best test files.

The Story
I was surprised to find out that my sorority kept a test file. They had old exams from just about every class. What happens is, you take a test, and then you bring it home. (Most professors allow you to keep exams.) The other part that shocked me was that the professors would then use similar test questions, sometimes the exact questions. It's common knowledge that after a test is completed, students will keep the test. I guess some are just lazy. Once in a while a test that shouldn't have gotten out there got

out there, but I never did anything that was unethical or illegal. Some professors will number each test and collect them after the exam to make sure that no one takes them home and keeps them on file. It's amazing how a test from ten years ago can show up years later. The test file is a huge resource that helped me, although not on the longer blue book exams.

—sophomore, University of Kansas

✳ ✳ ✳

Time is limited, and how to maximize your time while studying is crucial. Because you have a full schedule, you'll need to be smart about studying. At the same time, you don't want to do anything that will get you thrown off campus for cheating.

Old exams and older students are two of the greatest keys to mastering current exams. Many fraternities and sororities, or even local stores, have test files with past exams (make friends with the Greek members in class).

> **"I love my sorority. I also love their test file."**
> —freshman, University of Georgia

Assuming it's legal—and on most campuses it is—these are great guides to how a professor will test you. (I mention that it might not be legal because some professors don't want their old exams to get out.) There's no better predictor of what will be on a professor's exam than the key points and ideas tested on a previous exam. Oftentimes, test questions are taken right from old exams and put on new ones.

Another huge resource is someone who has recently taken your class. Get experienced students in your corner. Become friends with them (find them on Facebook). Ask what they wish they had known before taking the course. Even ask if you can check out their old notes. Ask how the professor grades. Get the inside information and use it to your advantage. Some classes have smaller discussion groups where the teaching assistants give the grades. Some TAs grade more easily than others. Ask, ask, ask the people who were in your seat before you.

When it comes to sharing notes to prepare for exams, some students have a gift for writing (or typing) at high speed and maintaining remarkable comprehension. Sit in different seats throughout the semester, get to know the smart people, and check out other people's notes. Also, don't be so quick to shun the kiss-up kid in the front who seems to be best friends with the professor. It's not always *what* you know, but *who* you know and what *they* know. Be smart, be resourceful, and do it legally.

Bottom Line
Old exams are the best study guides available. But as a rule, if an exam is older than you, it might be too old.

Tip #49
The Major Issue: Picking One

The Tip
Don't sweat finding a major right away. And don't worry about changing it should you find out that your heart's not into it.

The Story

I graduated high school and went to a technical college with hopes of becoming a computer programmer.

My parents and friends had always told me how well I worked with computers, so I figured it would work well for me as a major. Only after I got there and took classes was I able to realize that my heart wasn't into it. I pushed myself into the major too soon rather than giving myself time to figure out

that my heart was into writing. I switched my major and transferred colleges so I could follow my heart.

—junior, Washington State University–Vancouver

*** * ***

Most students change their majors at least once. You might change it monthly. You might change it in a year. You might have just changed it since reading the previous sentence. What you're thinking you'll end up doing today will most likely not be what you'll end up doing tomorrow. The point? Majors will change.

The best tip is to relax when picking a major. Don't let the world (or your parents) tell you what to be. Try a general direction, take a step, and see how it feels.

Get an internship or part-time job and talk to people doing what looks interesting (use LinkedIn, career counselors, and alums). Get a taste of what interests you. If you find that it's not what you wanted, great— just change majors. If

> "It's never too late to realize you have made the wrong decision. I changed majors from engineering to English my junior year. I'm happier, healthier, and thankful. It's hard to make a big decision like that because you have to admit that you made a mistake."
>
> —senior, Binghamton University

it is what you like, great—stay with your major. Things to think about when contemplating a *major* change:

- DO NOT let future income be your ONLY motivating factor in choosing a major. But do make sure you can pay back loans and understand the range of income your degree will help you secure.
- DO NOT worry that the field you're choosing is too competitive. Someone has to do it—why not you? If anything, the path you head down will lead to answers that you could have only discovered by going down that road.
- DO NOT buckle to parental pressure. If your parents are forcing you to do something that doesn't feel right, don't do it. You're the one who will have to wake up every day and go to work. Not them. Find people doing what you want to do and report back to your parents. Listen to them. Then do what feels right.
- DO NOT be afraid to change your major. Make sure you seek support on campus when contemplating major change.

When you figure out what you want your major to be, talk to your academic advisor and put together a plan. Try to graduate in four years, if possible. You might need to take summer classes to help you graduate in four years (see if you can take summer courses at home and transfer the credits). Switching majors can sometimes hold you up. Don't be afraid to change what it is that you want to do. It's only the rest of your life.

> "Choose a major not based on money, but what you love to do. What you do will be a major part of your life. If you love what you're doing, the money you've always wanted will eventually come."
> —senior, University of Arkansas–Pine Bluff

Bottom Line

Most students will change their major at least once. Many more than once. But most do not change it ten to twenty times. That's too many.

Tip #50
Advice on Your Advisor

The Tip
Always make a serious effort to get to know your advisor.

The Story
It was about four weeks into my freshman year of college. I was meeting new friends, staying up all night, and having a blast. But when class time came, I'd drag myself in half asleep and sit around waiting for my next chance to nap. I

was interested in my classes, but expected that if I needed to be doing something, my professor would tell me. When fourth-week grades came out, I realized I was doing awful and didn't know what to do. Luckily, one of my professors was also my advisor, and somehow saw in me the potential to be a better student. He took me aside and set up a meeting. We talked about my personal and professional goals and what I should be doing now to achieve them. It was a day that changed my entire college career. I became a more involved student and realized that my teachers weren't going to come to me—I needed to make the effort. I continued to hang out and have a good time, but also made the classroom a high priority. My advisor turned out to be not only a tremendous asset but a good friend. He's written countless letters of recommendation for me and given me tons of educational and emotional support.

> "I didn't find out that it was 'acceptable' to drop classes midsemester until I talked to upperclassmen. My advisor didn't go over dropping courses with me, either. There was a calculus course that I was taking that I was pretty much failing since day one. I didn't know that it was okay to drop a course and pick it up at a later time. Maybe you'll do better when you are less busy or if you have a different professor. If I would have known that, I would not have a bad grade on my transcript."
> —junior, Western Illinois University

—senior, Gannon University

* * *

Let me introduce you to your academic or college advisor.

Having a good advisor in your corner can help guide you, support you, and help you graduate on time (or close to on time). Your academic advisor is the person in the advising office (not a coincidence) who guides and supports you along your college journey. Your advisor is your point man or woman with whom you discuss selecting and registering for classes, selecting a major, switching a major, dropping classes, and dealing with uncomfortable situations inside the classroom and within your department. Your advisor can be an amazing source of information—he or she will inform you of requirements, procedures, deadlines, ways to get in classes, and places on campus to find answers when he or she doesn't have them. You can usually speak to your advisor face to face, via email, or with a call. Meet with your advisor on a regular basis—not just when a crisis hits. Make an extra appointment to check in and ask general questions and get general advice. Think of your advisor like Google, but with a pulse and heartbeat. An advisor who knows you before a crisis hits will be better equipped to be an advocate when you really need help. Navigating the steaming piles of bureaucracy found on many college campuses can be a tough task. It's extremely helpful to have someone in your corner fighting for what's important to you.

* *

⚠ **Beware:** Not All Advisors Are Created Equal

* *

The Good Ones: these advisors listen, ask questions, and allow you to answer them. They point you in the right direction based on what you say, what you need, and how you feel. Good advisors champion for you when you need someone to fight for you. Good advisors get back to you with answers to questions. Good advisors refer you to the people who have answers to your questions if he or she can't answer them. Good advisors do all they can do to guide you during your college journey and make sure that you graduate on time with a degree that fits you. Good advisors will encourage you to reach out to them without hesitation. They can even help once you leave campus.

The Not So Good Ones: these advisors don't listen, rush you, and appear to be overwhelmed, overworked, and underenthused. They do not champion on your behalf and don't help you navigate the system. If you find yourself with an advisor who doesn't work for you, find an advisor who meshes with your personality and encourages you to be your best. Make sure to check to see that the path your advisor is advising is the best path. You want to graduate with the degree you desire as quickly as possible. Just to be safe, talk to upperclassmen who are doing the things that you want to do. If you find that every advisor on campus is no good, the problem most likely is not the advisors, but you.

Bottom Line

Get to know your advisor. It can be the difference between graduating in four years and graduating in five, six, seven, or eight years.

Tip #51
Pick a Number, Any Number

The Tip
Not getting into a class is not the end of it. Don't let the system beat you down. If people with power know you, they can make exceptions.

The Story
Coming from a smaller high school and going to a larger college was a lot to take in at first. After going through registration, it just seemed like I was one of the masses. Everything had a system that the students plugged into. I remember not getting into a freshman English lit class second semester and dealing with the process of trying to get in. It was like dealing with a utility company at times. It wasn't until I physically went to the class and actually talked with the professor—by the way, something my older brother told me to do—that I received the attention that I hoped for. The professor allowed me to sit in on the class. After about two weeks, she let me in. While there is a system and it's easy to get lost in the system, if you talk to the people—the real people who are making decisions—you don't have to be just another number. That seemed to be what helped most of all.
> —sophomore, North Dakota State University

✳ ✳ ✳

If your name is actually a number (for example, if your name is 50 Cent—what up, Fiddy), you won't mind being just a number in college (or currency). If your name is not a number or currency, you might not want to be just a social security number, student ID, or other random number when you get to college. And this can happen in big and small colleges.

The difference between high school and college is that in high school, your teachers knew you. They might even have known your family members. Your high school kept track of you during the day. It was hard to slip through the cracks. And if you did, your parents would be notified.

In college, it's easy to float through the system. Education isn't mandatory anymore. Being an individual is much more of an individual choice. You are the one who is now responsible for making sure that you are not just another number, and that takes work on your part. As someone who went to one school with thirty thousand students and another with forty thousand, I know. My first freshman year, I felt like I didn't matter. It wasn't until my second freshman experience, when I put myself out there and made my voice heard, that I felt like an individual.

It all starts in class. Whether it's a lecture with two hundred students or a classroom with twenty, you need to be the one to introduce yourself to the professor (and do it before midterms, so if you need help, your professor will know you). Then it continues with finding friends. You need to introduce yourself to new people. You need to get yourself involved. You need to sign up for clubs and activities. You need to show up to play on a sports team. You need to be the one to allow people to get to know you. You can establish who you are, what you do, and where you're going. Unless you let people know who you are, you may be just 54665 (or 54668 or 54675) to everyone. And that can happen at any college.

Sometimes, within the college bureaucracy, you can get lost in the system. Some people just take it and get pushed around. Others take action. Before rolling over and letting the college push you around, make your voice heard. Be an individual by meeting the people who can make exceptions to the rules and regulations. You won't know unless you try.

Bottom Line
At times, you might feel like just another number. When it happens, speak up and don't stop talking until you are number one!

Tip #52
Time for Time Management
(this will be fast!)

The Tip
Plan for your success and use a planner.

The Story
Using a day planner probably was the single best aid to time management I've found. Whether you use an electronic planner or the old-fashioned paper-and-pencil version, this tool is indispensable for keeping your priorities, deadlines, and other important dates in order. I prefer a nonelectronic planner because it does not crash, it is not likely to be stolen,

I don't have to learn a new handwriting style, it doesn't have a battery that will run out (and erase all my data), and it will still work if I drop it or leave it in the sun (or freezing cold) all day. The bottom line is that you have to find a system that will work for you. Talk to a friend who uses a planner and try to develop a system of using it that works for you.

"Time management is all about corner cutting. If I had to do all the readings, I'd never survive. My brother taught me to work in groups, to know what's important to read, and to go to section."
—freshman, Harvard University

—freshman, UC–Berkeley

* * *

If you don't have the time to read this, you need to make the time. Imagine this is a Facebook update with a video of your favorite celeb, or imagine these words are being spoken by a very attractive man or woman that you want to get to know better. This will only take about one minute and fifty-six seconds (I timed this chapter).

We all manage time differently. College is about finding your individual balance. The more balance you can achieve, the easier it will be to juggle all that you need to do in a day, or a week, or a month. That's why it's so important to take the time to know yourself, so you can better manage yourself, your relationships, and your emotions. Then you can have time to do the things that are important to you. A good part of this book

"I got to campus and instantly wanted to get involved with everything. I forgot that I was there primarily for an academic life. Over my college career, I've learned to prioritize what's important."
—senior, Allegheny College

has been about managing life inside the classroom. The second part of this book is about helping you solve all the other problems outside the classroom—dating, relationships, sex, etc.—the issues that take up the most time and energy. If you can manage life inside and outside classes, you will find the time you need to manage your life. Then time management will be less about survival and more about the freedom to make choices.

> "Study before you go out at night. Don't say you will get up in the morning to study because you won't!"
>
> —freshman,
> Southern Illinois University–Edwardsville

The most important tip for time management: when you need help or have questions, ask the people in your corner who can give you the answers or point you to the answers. Be efficient. Don't wait. Save yourself time by asking for help before you need it. There are professionals who are trained to help you manage your time. In addition to getting help, keep the following tips in mind:

1. Use the first semester (or quarter if you're not on the semester system) to figure out how much you need to study to achieve the grades that you're looking for. Because you're in college to learn, you're better off overstudying than understudying. Getting a low grade your freshman year can haunt you. It's like a weight that pulls your GPA down throughout your college career.

2. Create a routine. Treat college like your job. Sometimes you can have an hour or two-hour break between classes. If you have a break, stay on

campus. Do your readings, review your notes, or work on an assignment that's due in the future. The problem is that if you go home, you can get tired or distracted. Find a place on campus where you can do your work. If it's done, you'll have the night free.

3. If you find that you're falling behind, don't panic. Get help immediately. Talk to your professors, a teaching assistant, and veterans of the class. You don't always have to read every page of every single book.

4. If you have to have a job, start with fewer hours and then build from there. You can always add more once you figure out how much time you need to dedicate to your classes. Sometimes when you have a job and a full schedule, it's easier to study because you know when you have to get it done. Being busy can actually help.

5. Get some kind of planner or organizer. Get it out of your head. Figure out your week before starting every week. College doesn't offer as much structure as high school—you need to be the one to structure your time. Write it down and stick to it.

> ## What Time Is It? Time for Time Management Facts!
>
> 52 percent of surveyed freshmen felt that it was "very easy" or "somewhat easy" to manage their time effectively (15.3 very easy/36.7 somewhat easy).
>
> 44.4 percent of surveyed freshmen "frequently" felt overwhelmed by all they had to do.
>
> 23.9 percent of surveyed freshmen used "online social networking" six or more hours per week.
>
> —Higher Education Research Institute at UCLA

6. If you're having a hard time managing your schedule, find out if there is help on campus. Contact the orientation office and ask. Many colleges offer time-management resources for new students.

7. Get help before you *need* it. This means that you should get help when you get that first bad quiz grade or mess up an exam. It's too late to wait until the final exam to get help.

8. Be patient and give it a semester (or two quarters). It's hard to know how much time you will need until you go through one cycle. And appreciate that not everyone works at the same pace—you might need more or less time than your friends or siblings.

9. Sometimes doing more can be easier than doing less. When you have places to be and people to see, you can be more focused and directed.

Bonus Tip

Consider attending college near a state that is in a different time zone. Then when you need an extra hour, you can always get it. Just remember, you have to give it back when you cross back over the state line again.

Bottom Line

Save time and have the best time by asking for help before you really need it. If you can take the time to get help, you'll save time and find time.

Tip #53
Wine Tasting, Bowling, and Other Important Electives

The Tip
Take an elective that has nothing to do with your major. Choose something that you've always been vaguely interested in but never had the time or resources to explore. And don't be afraid to take classes at a community college.

The Story
The best elective that I took was actually at a community college. It was costuming for theater class, I took it because it seemed interesting and it was something I'd always been curious about. Taking that class is what led me to major in costume design at Cornish. This same thing happened to my brother. He took astronomy on a whim as an elective at a community college and now he's an astronomy major at the University of Hawaii. If you're not sure what you're interested in doing, go to a community college or just take some classes there. It saves money, and most credits from community colleges transfer.

—junior, Cornish College of the Arts

* * *

I started playing guitar as part of a group lesson. It was a one-credit class. Every week, we met in one of the residence hall lounges and jammed. It was so cool that I took a classical one-on-one guitar class the next year. There was no extra charge for it. Graduate students taught the course. That's how I learned to play guitar. I didn't know that I'd start writing and playing music as part of my job later in life. It all started with taking a class that looked cool and had absolutely nothing to do with my major (you can listen to my music at NakedRoommate.com). I had a couple extra credit hours that would have just been thrown away, so I figured, why not?

My brother took a wine tasting class in college. My good friends took a bowling class. A girlfriend took a self-defense class (no messing with her). There were other electives like aerobics, judo, tae kwon do, archery, ballroom dancing, racquetball, art, acting, pottery, crafts, film appreciation, sex and sexuality, the history of rock and roll, and so many others. Instead of just taking the classes you need to get through your major, take some electives you would never think of taking. Learn how to code or fix a computer (life skills). If you don't like the class, then drop it before it counts against you. See if you can audit the class (no credit given). Don't just take a class because you think it will be easy. Take a cool elective because it's interesting. These classes can stick with you for a lifetime.

> "The best classes are those that do not have your best friends from your dorm in them. It was my business and accounting electives that helped change the course of my future."
> —freshman, University of Mount Union

I scoured colleges and came up with some classes worth taking; the most popular ones tend to be ballroom dancing and basic swing dancing. Here's one from a college in Wisconsin: class students read selections from *Chew* magazine and debate "The Art of Eating" and "The

Primal Cheeseburger." The final project involves tracking a food product to where it all began before it was manufactured. For example, when dealing with ketchup, they track the tomatoes all the way back to the farm. Factors like distance, pesticide use, and whether it was farmed on a corporate or family-owned farm are part of the debate. They even eat food in class. And yes, there really is a wine tasting class and a history of rock and roll class. Oh, and if you're attending the University of Virginia, you can try to get a seat in ENWR 1510 (accelerated academic writing). The title of one particular section is, "GaGa for Gaga: Sex, Gender, and Identity." The class analyzes how the musician pushes social boundaries through her work.

Bottom Line

If you have extra credit hours, don't throw them away. One elective can become the course that changes the entire course of your life. Or, you can try to sell your extra credit hours on eBay (is that legal?).

Harlan's Tip Sheet

Naked People, Places, and Resources

Classroom Vocab

- *Syllabus*: The guide to the class: required readings, rules, regulations, and procedures, as well as a course outline with important dates for exams and projects.
- *Teaching assistants (TAs)*: Sometimes called "teaching fellows" or other names. Typically, graduate students or undergraduates that teach sections or lectures under the supervision of a professor. Go to them for help. These people know things that can help you.
- *Sections/Labs:* In addition to lectures, classes may have sections or labs. These offer a more intimate setting and one-on-one teaching. At larger colleges, these are often taught by TAs.
- *Semesters/quarters/trimesters*: Some schools have semesters (two semesters = one school year), some trimesters (three trimesters = one school year), some quarters (four quarters = one school year)...pretty basic.
- *Incomplete*: The mark you get when you don't satisfy the requirements for a class.
- *Pass/fail*: Some classes are offered as pass/fail. You don't get a letter grade, just a pass or fail.
- *Auditing*: Sitting in on a course, but not for credit or a grade.

- *Drop/add*: The process of dropping courses and adding new ones. Be careful—most schools have a deadline after which you can't withdraw from a course without it showing up on your transcript and affecting your GPA. There may also be different names for this process. Ask upperclassmen.
- *Waitlist*: If a class is full, you can be put on a waitlist. Always approach the professors; sometimes they will make exceptions if you beg to take the class.
- *Sitting in on a class*: If you're waitlisted, ask to sit in on a course. More often than not, a professor will just allow you to officially join the class.
- *Office hours*: Time allocated for students to meet with professors and teaching assistants to get extra help.

Additional Resources

- *Departmental websites*. Visit the website of your department on campus. Often you can find out about new classes being offered, updated procedures, and protocols. Visit regularly.
- *Department Twitter feeds and Facebook pages*. More departments are using Facebook and Twitter to post updates and communicate with students about deadlines, events, and opportunities.
- *Free tutoring*. Ask your professor, advisors, or resident assistant where and when it's available. If you need help with writing papers, usually there is free help for students in a writing center.
- *Office hours*. If you can't always make the regular hours, most professors will try to be flexible.

- *www.RateMyProfessors.com*. Students rate their professors on this site according to easiness, helpfulness, clarity, and rater interest. However, always confirm what you read with a student in person—not all the ratings are fair. Also, see if your school has its own system available to review professors. Many schools offer a way to see reviews posted by other students.
- *www.NakedRoommate.com*. Search the member area to find students on your campus who can answer questions about life inside the classroom.
- For more study tips and time management skills, get your hands on *The Naked Roommate's First Year Survival Workbook*.

8

Dating and Relationships

Your Higher Education in Lust, Love, and Loss

* * *

Sixth Edition Naked Message

If you can't handle NO, you're not ready for YES. Tattoo it on a body part you see on a regular basis (maybe, a little severe). But this is true of dating, relationships, and sexual consent in college. The problem with dating is that we suck at NO. We hate it. Students get drunk, hook up, and do whatever they can to avoid having to face the possibility of NO. We hate rejection. I hope the following chapters (and my book on dating) can help you rethink dating, relationships, sex, love, and intimacy. Really, if you can't talk to that guy or girl in English class while sober, how can you talk about consent? This chapter, my advice column, videos, and books can help.

* * *

Dear Harlan,

I am a freshman in college and living in a coed dorm. I met this girl in September who lives down the hall. I have had a slight crush on her since then. Just recently we had a four-hour conversation together, which is the longest I have ever had with anyone. That night I found out she liked a fellow coworker, but she recently gave up that crush because he is under eighteen. I am confused as to what I should do. Should I continue to talk to her or should I tell her my interest?

—Dazed and Most Definitely Confused

Dear Dazed,
My longest conversation with a woman was for just over five hours. It was in high school. It cost $1.99 a minute. She really liked me.

Here's a quick way to clear this up in under a minute of talking time. Walk up to her and say, "I had so much fun the other night. Let's do it again, but next time, let's get something to eat." That's all it takes. Then it would be a date.

The door of opportunity is open. Your chance is here. The time is now. You should continue talking to her and express your interest. If she's interested, great. If not, assume that it's because it's too uncomfortable for her to date someone on the same floor. To not say something would be the greatest risk of all. At least give her a chance to be more than just a friend. She deserves a chance. Just don't wait too long. The more time that passes, the closer to eighteen that underage coworker of hers gets.

Tip #54
The Rules of College Love (or just lust)

The Tip
Relax, chill, and talk to the people you want to date without getting stuck in your head.

The Story
I was way too worried about what girls thought about me and how I could get as many as possible to hook up with me. I'd either say nothing or say the wrong things. It took over my life. Until I relaxed, found a life in college, and stopped trying so hard, relationships eluded me. I was too intense and uptight. Once I relaxed, it became so much more manageable. It took me a few years to figure it out, but now I'm there and much happier.

—junior, University of Illinois–Chicago

* * *

Please note: this tip can get you a date. If you put cologne or perfume on this page and rub it on you, it can be even more effective.

Dating and love are 90 percent amazing and 10 percent BS. The secret is never allowing the 10 percent to take up 100 percent of your time. Some of you might plan on hooking up in college (note: a hookup can be anything from a hug to procreation). Some of you might plan on dating in college. Some of you might plan on finding your future husband, wife, or partner. Dating in college works like this: if you're in a room long enough, you will hook up. If you're in a room with alcohol it can often happen faster (NOT recommended, bad idea, put down the bottle NOW). Anyone can find someone warm if they are in rooms long enough—but not everyone can find a healthy, long-lasting relationship built on trust and mutual respect. Whatever you desire, I can help you find it or keep it.

It all starts with appreciating and believing that you live in a world of options. The truth is there are thousands of people who want to hold you, love you, and spread love oils on you (if you're into that). NEVER NEVER NEVER forget that you live in a world of options. Thousands of people will want you. Millions will not. Focus on the ones who

> "Don't date just because you think you're supposed to date. There is a lot of pressure when you go to school to get involved with someone. It might seem like finding a relationship or finding someone to be with will help make things better, but it doesn't make it better. Wait until you find someone who can appreciate you for everything that makes up all the parts of you."
> —sophomore, Angelo State University

want you and move beyond the ones who don't. If you don't believe thousands will want you, make it 100, or 50, or 10 people. But there are options. If you don't believe me, consider spending a semester studying abroad in China or India so you can meet some of the billions of people who will want you. If you still don't believe me, make an appointment with the campus therapist.

Five Steps to Finding a Date While Fully Clothed and Totally Sober (from my book *Getting Naked*)

1. *Embrace the Secret Truth.* The Universal Rejection Truth of dating and relationships says that thousands of people will want you, but millions will not. Focus on who you want. NOT who wants you. Rejection is as normal and natural as breathing oxygen. To fight the URT is to fight nature. Once you accept the truth, you can come out of rejection denial. Rejection denial is a dark and dangerous place where you think everyone you like should like you. When someone doesn't want what you want, you hate, fight, and hide. BUT once you accept the truth, you can give people permission to not always want you. Like deodorant, once you apply the URT to your everyday life, you will no longer stink at taking risks. The answer: give the world permission to want you and NOT want you. Then, focus on what YOU want.

2. *Train (preferably in a thong).* In order to take risk after risk and tolerate rejection, you need to do work. I call this training in your thong. Training means acknowledging what makes you uncomfortable and working to be your personal best in your physical, emotional, and spiritual thong. It involves looking in the mirror (in

> ### Want to Date? Tell Him or Her
>
> Before getting physical, make it clear that you like to date before hooking up. Then make it clear you would love to go on a date (then hook up).

a thong) and acknowledging your favorite and least favorite qualities. It's working to change what you don't love (in a healthy way) and learning to love the things you can't change. It's turning to people in your corner who can tell you what you need to hear and what you want to hear. Once you begin your training, you can start to put yourself in more rooms with more people. You can say what you think and do what you feel without fear and regret. It's the difference between living a life driven by passion and living one paralyzed by fear.

3. *No excuses.* Excuses are things we create to cover up the insecurities hanging out of our thongs. Instead, let excuses lead you to answers. When you can't say what you think or do what you feel, ask yourself why. When you find yourself making an excuse, ask yourself if you're using excuses to avoid taking a risk because you're afraid of rejection or if it's a valid reason.

4. *DO IT.* Say what you think. Do what you feel. Remember, no matter what happens, it will be a success. Success is not about YES or NO. Success is taking action. Taking the risk = guaranteed success.

5. *Celebrate, reflect, and repeat.* If the risk goes as planned—awesome. If not, that's awesome too. Celebrate the fact that you have the testicles or ovaries to say what you think and do what you feel. If the risk doesn't go as planned, figure out why. If you've trained for the sport of taking risks and are

comfortable in your thongs, you can discover why you're not getting what you want. Once you find answers, repeat steps 1–4 until you get what you want.

WARNING: If any of this is too uncomfortable for you, make an appointment with a therapist on campus. Finding a date, finding love, and getting married doesn't mean you are comfortable taking risks—it just means you were probably in a room long enough or in a room with alcohol and met someone when you least expected it.

Bottom Line
Thousands of people will want you...millions will not. NEVER let the ones who don't want you keep you from meeting the ones who do.

Tip #55
The College Hookup

The Tip
If you're looking for something noncommitted, ambiguous, and uncomfortable, then the hookup is the perfect love—I mean lust—connection.

The Story
I came to college never having had a serious boyfriend. I met this guy on my floor a week after getting here. We hung out a few times and made out—nothing more. I thought we were together, but he didn't think so. To me, hanging out

meant something. Once I joined a sorority, it all became that much more blurred. Just because you take a guy to a dance doesn't mean that you're a couple. It doesn't even matter what happens when you're together. More than once, I thought things were more than they were. As time went on, it became clear that the lack of clarity was the only clear part of it all. The best advice I'd give to myself or to freshmen is to talk about what you want before you get involved with someone. It makes it so much easier. Don't be afraid to be honest. If someone won't hang out with you, then you're better off without him. Unless you are the one to talk about it, no one will talk about it. That's when things kind of get weird. Talk about it and make up your rules as you go along.

> "Don't develop feelings over a text message. I didn't follow my own advice and pretty much ended up heartbroken, because I got so excited that something might happen."
> —junior, California Lutheran University

—senior, Northeastern University

* * *

The college hookup is the most common of the college relationships (although "hookup" is an insult to the word "relationship"). The hookup is an intimate encounter involving anything from kissing to full sex, void of any commitment. It's easier than dating because you don't have to state your intention. You can just let nature take its course. Due to the lack of communication involved with the college hookup, it's set up to be a confusing and ambiguous relationship. The college hookup can fall into one of the following seventeen categories:

1. The Drunk Hookup:
   an alcohol-induced connection
2. The Friendly Hookup:
   friends who go way beyond friendly
3. The Rebound Hookup:
   broken up and looking for some Band-Aid lovin'
4. The Cheating Hookup:
   no dignity here—see Tip #62 for more on this one
5. The Desperation Hookup:
   looking for anyone—and I mean *anyone*
6. The Online Hookup:
   a high-speed connection
7. The Who's Next Hookup:
   the love junkie who can't get enough
8. The Ex Hookup:
   reliable, dependable, and oh-so-easy
9. The Visitor Hookup:
   here today, gone tomorrow (a.k.a.: hit-and-run)
10. The I-Love-You Hookup:
    love at first sight (until the morning light)
11. The Convenience Hookup:
    the closest person with a pulse gets some
12. The First-Week Hookup:
    action exclusive to welcome week
13. The I-Just-Want-to-Have-Fun Hookup:
    it's all good fun until someone falls in love
14. The Weekend Hookup:
    I love you Friday, I love you Saturday, but don't
    call me Sunday
15. The Sympathy Hookup:
    a charitable donation (it's always generous to give)

16. The Help-Me Hookup:
    hooking up with a teaching assistant, resident assistant, or inappropriate helper
17. The Repeat Backup Hookup:
    a go-to guy or girl who is the backup love buddy (a.k.a.: the 3 a.m. text message booty call)

The problem with hookups—once the hookup is hung up, confusion ensues. Because there isn't a lot of clear communication before the hookup, there is even less afterwards. Yes, a few hours ago you were locked in each other's loins; post-hookup, you're too afraid to text or say hi. And this is why the hookup becomes the drama of your morning, afternoon, and night. It eats up all of your energy. Seeing the person, thinking about the person, contemplating texting the person—it's an emotional whirlwind. *But it doesn't have to be that way.* All you have to do is talk to your partner before you get naked (or partially naked). Ask what happens after the hookup. If your hookup partner is too busy getting naked to listen, then he or she is not the right partner— that is, unless you're looking for confusion, questions, and drama. Going slow or saying NO teaches you what

> "It's fun to look out of my window in the early morning on the weekends. That's when you see all the people taking the 'walk of shame' in their clothes from the night before. These are the people who hooked up and have to walk home in the morning. It's something worth seeing."
> —junior, Western Illinois University

> "I have a lot of girlfriends who have a lot of regrets about past hookups from freshman and sophomore year. If you have regrets, don't dwell on it—just don't do it anymore."
> —junior, University of Vermont

someone wants. Impatient people who don't listen to you do not care about you or your feelings. They care about getting laid and hooking up. If you say what you want before you get naked, you will know what you're getting into (or who is getting into you). As a rule, if you demand respect, you will command respect. That is, unless you prefer to be disrespected.

Bottom Line

The College Hookup = confusing, unstable, and often resulting in itching, burning, and a visit to the health center.

Tip 55.5
The Most Important Relationship

The Tip
It's okay to be single.

The Story
Don't get so wrapped up in dating, in finding your significant other, that you lose yourself in the process. I spent most of my freshman year in relationships with different guys. By the time sophomore year began, I realized that I was having trouble picturing myself alone, without someone by my side. And then, one of my other guy friends confessed that he had feelings for me. But I knew I wasn't ready. Don't make the same mistake that I did. Spend some time getting to know yourself for

who YOU are BEFORE you lose yourself in someone else's arms.

—senior, Eastern New Mexico University

* * *

If you don't love yourself, you're always going to be depending on someone to love you. You'll always be looking for someone to save you. The most dangerous part of falling in love for the first time is that if you don't love yourself, there's way too much at stake. I know. It happened to me.

When I found love, I didn't even like myself. I was a teenager with a terrible self-image. A little background—I was really overweight until my junior year in high school. I weighed about 192 pounds on a 5-feet-2-inch frame my freshman year in high school. A girl once told me I was too fat to date. This set me up to feel totally defective, uncomfortable, and never good enough. Then, something happened. I fell in love.

A popular, intelligent, and beautiful woman loved me. She was a swimmer, student council treasurer, and in the homecoming court. I loved her more than I loved myself (not too hard). When I went to college we did the long-distance thing. She was a senior in high school and I was a freshman in college. As I struggled, she thrived. The relationship began to deteriorate. At one point, her dad compared our relationship to a dying puppy—urging her to shoot the puppy. She dumped me. I was devastated.

It took me years to realize what I did wrong. I NEVER loved myself. I never worked to love myself. I still work on it. It's a lifetime project. The greatest gift you can give yourself and your future partners is to work to love yourself. I call this process training in your thong (metaphor). I could call it getting comfortable in your skin, but a thong shows all our biggest fears and insecurities. There are three things you need to do in order to train to love yourself:

1. *Train in your physical thong.* Look in the mirror and examine yourself physically. If you don't love what you see, ask yourself what you can do to change what you don't love and tolerate what you can't change. Turn to five people, put yourself in three places, and be patient while you create change. Work on it. Appreciate that your least favorite qualities will be the things others love about you (example: my protruding ears have become an asset).

2. *Train in your emotional thong.* Look in the mirror and reflect on your secrets, fears, and insecurities in the mirror. Change what you don't love and work to tolerate what you can't change. Reach out to your five people, put yourself in places to work on you, and be patient. Turn your fears and insecurities into a source of strength.

Like *Chicken Soup for the Teenage Soul*?

Read my story "Loving Yourself First" at www.HarlanCohen.com. It's included in *Chicken Soup for the Teenage Soul III*.

3. *Train in your spiritual thong.* The best way to describe this—what do you have in your life that gives you pleasure that no one can take away? What makes you interesting? What fills you up with happiness? Put yourself

in places where you can sweat, play, and pray. Do things you love to do. Turn to people doing things you would love to do and people who can direct you. And be patient. It takes time to get GREAT at doing new things.

Loving yourself is about getting comfortable in your skin and knowing that you're attractive, good enough, and interesting with or without a partner. When you love yourself, you can say what you think, do what you feel, set boundaries, demand respect, command respect, and live a life driven by passion.

Bottom Line
Love yourself first and you will always have love in your life.

Tip #56
Close-Distance Relationships

The Tip
Don't date anyone who lives on your floor in your hall.

The Story
We started dating in November of my freshman year. He lived down the hall on the same floor, which is how we met. In the beginning, it was fun because I had someone to date who lived down the hall. It would be easy to spend the night together. I didn't have to get up early to

go home because I was already home. Right before finals week is when it got very frustrating. If I wasn't in class or I wasn't with him, he asked where I was and why I wasn't with him. And then people were asking about us—and it wasn't fun anymore. We just kind of decided it was too much and we wanted to be friends. Once I broke up with him, I found more friends on the floor and became so much closer with them. I got to see my roommate more and now we're best friends.

> "If I could start all over, I would tell someone not to rush into a relationship. If you rush into something, it may feel too perfect and then, when it ends, it crushes you. I wish someone had told me not to get too involved too fast. I'm someone who got crushed."
> —freshman, Lynn University

—junior, Northern Illinois University

***

Messing around with a neighbor (a.k.a. "dormcest" or "hallcest") might seem great when it's all good, but when it goes bad, you want to be as far away as possible. The person who was once your convenient love becomes your inconvenient nightmare neighbor. Don't be so quick to date next door. It can go bad as fast as it begins.

Remember that part about being able to walk down the hall to your room in the morning after shacking up? It's no longer a good thing. And the part about sharing a dining hall and seeing that person at every meal? Meals together will now make you sick. And also,

> "I met my girlfriend in the laundry room. I was sitting on top of the machine waiting for my clothes to dry and she was sitting next to me on her washing machine."
> —freshman, Virginia Tech

that part about having so many of the same friends you both hung out with? Now that's just too uncomfortable. Then there's seeing who he or she is now dating. Things close by are good until they go good-bye, and most relationships will go bye-bye at some time or another. Think twice before grabbing that person close by just because it's convenient. Besides, it's just lazy. There is a lot of love in a lot of places if you're willing to take the risk to find the loving.

> "Dating your teaching assistant might seem like fun, but the fun ends when you break up and have to see your TA in class. Besides, it's completely against the rules."
>
> —grad, Indiana University

That brings me to relationships of convenience. What seems good and easy turns out to be the complete opposite. Things like hooking up with a neighbor down the hall, someone at work, or with your good friend's ex are just bad ideas—especially when it comes to hooking up with an ex. It's convenient, it's easy, and really, it's also lower than low. Sure, it's hard to meet attractive people, but it's also weak to prey on a good friend's ex. Assuming that most relationships don't last forever, when the love fades, you'll be left without your girlfriend or boyfriend and without a close friend.

> "He promised nothing would happen and that we'd just talk. I fell for the act and next thing I know I'm in his room, in his bed, and he is trying to shove his tongue down my throat. I left. The night ended up being embarrassing for me, frustrating for him, and a nightmare for the rest of the semester."
>
> —freshman, Michigan State University

If you want to find some lovin' that won't leave you jobless, friendless, or afraid to leave your room at night, follow Tip #29 and all of chapter 5. There are plenty of partners. We each have thousands of options (many don't live in the same country or speak the same language—yet another reason to take a language of the Orient). Don't choose the easy or lazy route when it comes to finding love. Chances are you'll only be left lonely and full of regret and in hiding from your neighbors.

Bottom Line
Shortcuts to love tend to be the fast route to long-term troubles.

Tip #57
Long-Distance Relationships (LDRs)

*PLEASE READ THIS TIP CAREFULLY:
I want to be clear: again, I think long-distance relationships can work. The following tip and story is NOT my advice. It's one student's opinion. More after you read this tip.

The Tip
Don't hang on to a long-distance love just because it's safe and secure.

The Story
When I came to college, I had been seeing a guy for about a year. He was my first serious boyfriend. It was a great relationship in high school. He went to a community college at home while I went away to a new place and experienced a lot of new things. We decided to stay together, even though we are a few hours apart. It worked. We both had the same cell phone plan so we would call each other

for free at least once a day. We saw each other every other week. Trust was never an issue. The relationship was safe—it allowed me to meet more people at college, but still know I had a boyfriend.

> "While long-distance relationships sound like a challenge, they tend to be a disaster. I ended up being cheated on, despite my girlfriend's constant critiquing of my decision. I always wanted to believe it would work and did a great job convincing myself it was worthwhile. Don't delude yourself—no matter what you had, it won't translate hundreds or even thousands of miles—no amount of IM, cell phone conversations, or planned trips can reverse the fact."
> —junior, UCLA

Fast-forward to my sophomore year. I ended up meeting a guy in March. At the time, I was having doubts about my high school sweetheart, but stayed together because, again, it was easy and familiar. Meeting this other guy made me realize there are other options that I could be secure with. I'm not the type to cheat, so I decided to end things with my boyfriend before anything happened. My boyfriend was surprised—I told him that if it was meant to be, we would find each other again. Because he was my first boyfriend I needed to see what was out there to better define what I needed in a relationship. We're still good friends.

—junior, Towson University

∗ ∗ ∗

Want a great long-distance relationship? Plan to be even happier while apart. YES, it's possible. And it's not a bad thing. Being sad isn't a testament to a good relationship. It just means you're sad. Before I continue, I want to be clear—if you have a relationship that you think is worth hanging on to, DO NOT be so quick to get rid of it just because you're going to college. If you're 100 percent committed to the relationship, there's a chance it could work. But if you're not 100 percent committed, don't even try. And whatever you do, never lie, never cheat, and never pretend—you'll only taint it forever.

Long-distance relationships (LDRs) in college have never been so cheap and easy—that is, with free long distance, live streaming video, email, text, Twitter, Facebook, Snapchat, Pinterest, cheap flights, and weekend visits. But still, the emotional toll of not being hand in hand, face to face, lips to lips makes it too hard for most couples to survive.

The hardest part of being in an LDR is all the emotions. LDRs can often isolate you from the world. Instead of thinking about college life and how to make a life in a new place, people tend to lean on their old relationships, which keeps them from meeting other people who could become close friends. They can take up too much time and too much energy, and leave you feeling more alone and lost than ever once the relationship ends (and

"College is the only time in life that you can be selfish, self-absorbed, and experimental. I spent too much time arguing on the phone with my long-distance boyfriend instead of socializing, joining organizations, and making friends."

—grad student, Salem State University

most do). And considering most people in love don't love themselves too much—being away from the only love in your life can be terrifying. I know. I was one of you.

LDRs often act as a crutch that keeps people from meeting new people and having new experiences. The flights, the road trips, the emotions, the good-byes—it's hard, and for most people, it wears them down. And now, with so many ways to stay in touch via technology, it's that much easier to be in one place physically, and somewhere else emotionally (see Tip #8).

If you decide to do the long-distance thing, keep the following in mind: trust is the glue that keeps you together, express yourself if something is bothering you (never let it build up), be completely honest, and make sure you have a life outside of your relationship. This is why you need to work to have people and places on campus. If you want to take a break, be honest. Never, never, never cheat on your partner. Cheating will ruin everything that you've worked so hard to build. Cheating makes getting back together nearly impossible. If you can survive the distance, learn to be

"I think that probably the one thing that's making my long-distance relationship work is the fact that my boyfriend and I had been good friends even before we started seeing each other. Otherwise, I doubt that it would work. For all of those people out there who are involved in a healthy relationship that is long-distance, hang in there. It will only get better."
—junior, Salisbury State University

happy while apart, and make it through it all, you'll have the rest of your life to spend in a close distance relationship.

Bottom Line
Learn to be happy while apart and have a long happy life together. ☺

Tip #58
High School Bitter Sweethearts

***

REMINDER #3
This Tip and Story is not my advice...it's from a student. My advice is
coming soon.

***

The Tip
Don't take your high school girlfriend or boyfriend to
school. Break up when you leave for college.

The Story
I know it sounds harsh, but take it from someone who
goes to an all-girls school. All the girls I knew my freshman year who had boyfriends
had lots of problems socially.
They would spend a lot of time
on the phone with their boys
and not getting to know their
hallmates or classmates, nor
doing their work. Also, you
don't want to go out, party, or
get to know other guys because
you'll feel like you're cheating.
Whether your boy is still in high school or going to school
nearby, dump him at least for your first semester—you'll
understand later!

> ### Quick Note from Harlan
> In earlier editions of this book, some people confused this student tip for my advice. For my take on high school sweethearts, keep reading the rest of this tip.

—sophomore, Hollins University

* * *

Here's the BIG question: Should you keep or lose your high school sweetheart?

My answer?

Do NOT be so quick to ditch it. Enjoy it while you've got it. Until you get to college, until you go to classes, until you figure out what it's like to be in college, don't be so quick to cut all ties. Besides, it's nice to have a close friend to keep you balanced during an unstable time. Figure it out once you get there. Big deal if you miss out on a few weeks of random hooking up. It will still be there if you want to experience it.

"My ex-girlfriend and high school sweetheart transferred to my school following our first year at college. We gave it the 'college try' but it didn't work out. 'Relapses' were common, but the committed relationship never worked. Much earlier, we should have resolved to go our separate ways instead of maintaining a friendship. The friendship led to closeness, which developed into romance, which never worked. Cyclical and bad."

—junior, UC–Davis

Plan on staying together until it doesn't feel right. That said, if you have serious doubts before you go into college, and you know it doesn't feel right, then just end it. If you have doubts when you get to college, then it's not right; take some time and space to figure out what feels right for you. If you have doubts while reading this book, then it's not the right thing, so end it.

"Don't dump your girlfriend from high school just because you think you're going to college and will find other girls."

—freshman, University of Southern Indiana

Here's the best tip: follow your heart. Be honest with your significant other. Respect what he or she has to say (whether you're on the giving or receiving end).

And do not cheat. It's tempting to have your high school sweetie in the wings while you date your entire campus, knowing that you always have something or someone to go home to, but cheating is bad. It's not loving, it's not necessary, and it only taints what you once had. Make sure that if you are staying together it's because your high school sweetheart is your first and best choice—not because you are too afraid of being single. You have endless options—never, ever forget it.

Hate Your Ex?

Hating is easier than moving forward. It's safe. It's predictable. It keeps you from getting hurt again. When you're tired of hating, give your ex permission to date people who aren't nearly as interesting or as attractive as you. Then you can move forward.

Bottom Line

High school relationships don't always pack well when taken to college. They can be extremely fragile and need to be handled lovingly and carefully or they can easily break.

Tip #59
Imaginary Relationships and Online Dating

The Tip

Don't be afraid to say something to someone you're interested in. The longer you wait the bigger deal it becomes, until it becomes too big of a deal to act on.

The Story

If you're interested in meeting someone in your class, don't just sit around imagining what the relationship could be. Find out if it's going to happen. While you're sitting there waiting and daydreaming, some other guy will come along and ask her out. Then all you'll be left with is a fantasy. It happened to me my first semester. There was my dream girl in history class. I just sat there drooling during lecture. When I finally found the courage to talk to her, it was too late. I found out before talking to her that she was dating someone else. I had put so much into our relationship. We had practically been dating (in my head) for the entire semester. I later found out that she had liked me, but it never happened. As I've progressed through my college life, I've become a lot less shy. That's helped me learn to live in reality and make some friends and more.

—senior, Illinois State University

***

No, you're not imagining it. This is two tips in one (no, there's no additional cost).

Imaginary Relationships

When looking for love in college, it's easier and safer to sit and fantasize about what someone might be like to date. Now, with Facebook, you have more material to fantasize with than ever before in the history of fantasies. You can imagine the first kiss. Then the first date. Then it's the first night together. Then the first time you say "I love you." Then you're a couple. Then you're visiting each other's home for the weekend. Then you get engaged. Then you get married. Then you have kids. Then you have a family. And yet, you haven't even met the person who is now your husband or wife. Avoid falling into the imaginary relationship world. When you have feelings for someone, just say something. If you can't say what you think or do what you feel, turn back to Tip #54 and check out www.GettingNakedExperiment.com. There is always a chance that someone might not return your feelings. Should that happen, the good news is that it's easy to find another imaginary relationship.

Online Dating

It can be hard to meet people on campus. It can be hard for people to find you. Online dating allows people to find you. It helps you find them. The challenge is filtering through the people who are looking to be rescued from the land of the single and searching and the people who are looking for the same things you want. Number 1 rule of online dating—if you can't date offline, you're not ready to date online. The online world is filled with people who are too afraid or too insecure to experience love in person, but can only experience it through chatting, photos, and phone conversations without ever meeting. Until you can see your partner, touch your partner, and kiss your partner (should you be so lucky), it's not real.

"We met online and talked for about six months. When it came time to meet her, she was nothing like she described to me. I couldn't get past the fact that she had lied. I'm relieved that she was only a liar and not dangerous. I didn't even tell anyone where I was going or what I was doing when we met."
—senior, University of Florida

If you do go the online route, make sure the first date is in a public place, make sure your friends know where you are and who you're meeting (you can even take a friend with), and make sure it's not in a remote location. Also,

> **"Online dating is convenient. It's easier to turn a relationship on when you want it and off when you don't."**
> —senior, Salve Regina University

make sure the person you're seeing knows that your friends and family are aware of what's happening. And really, if you need to keep it a secret, you're not ready to be so involved. It shouldn't be happening. When it comes to online dating, there are thousands of amazing potential partners, but there are also too many bad people out there to give anyone the benefit of the doubt. Make it about what you want, not about who wants you. To avoid online dating fatigue, switch services every few months.

Tinder Alert

Don't get too hot too fast. Yes, you can find love on Tinder, but you can also get pregnant or get an STI. Go slow. Text. Talk. Meet during daylight hours while sober.

Bottom Line

Making love with your mouse might seem safe, but it's not real. And if you're sharing your computer with a roommate, it's not sanitary.

Tip #60
The Friendly Relationship

The Tip
If you're interested in being more than friends, tell that friend, and don't let "no" keep you from still being friends. You never know what might happen later.

The Story
I told her my freshman year that I was interested in being more than friends. She said she didn't see me that way. She just thought of me as a friend. I was upset, but I liked hanging out with her and didn't let it bother me. We stayed friends. I was there when guys came and went. I never tried to make a move. We just hung out. I had a couple relationships along the way. It wasn't until our senior year that we finally got together. It just felt right. She said that if I had never mentioned that I wanted to be more than friends, she might not have looked at me that way. The more I dated around, the more she began to realize that I was the one she should be with. I never let her not wanting me ruin the friendship. If a friend isn't interested, don't run from the friendship. It's friends who turn out to be the best relationships. You only risk ruining the friendship if you're someone who isn't all that secure to begin with. Tell if you're interested.

—senior, University of Missouri

* * *

You find yourself hanging out all the time with a friend of the opposite (or same) sex. You're both from the same city. You both hate your roommates. You spend time talking about all your sad past relationships. You eat dinner in the cafeteria together. She lets you nibble on her chicken strip. You let her dip her French fries in your ketchup. You go out to parties together. You drive home together during holiday break. You poke each other on Facebook. You're in each other's cell phone plans so you can endlessly talk without worrying about losing minutes. You are the best of friends, and then one night, at about two in the morning, you look at him or her and think, *What the hell? I think I'm in love*.

The problem with being the friend who wants more is that most friends who want more never let their feelings be known. They secretly want more, but do nothing. No, wait—they complain to all of their friends that they are always the friend and never the boyfriend/girlfriend. They hide in the "friend zone." It's safe, it's easy, and it's secure. It's also painful, uncomfortable, and empty. Keeping your feelings a secret is not nice.

The key to avoiding the friend zone is to let a friend know that you have feelings for him or her when you have these feelings. Afraid it will be weird? Give your friend

Want to Date a Friend? Ask Yourself Three Questions:

1. Do you have more than one friend?

2. Do you give your friend permission to NOT want you?

3. Are there other people you can see yourself dating (other than your friend)?

Answer YES to all three questions and you are ready to tell a friend you'd like to be more.

permission to not share your feelings. Make it clear that you're okay being friends but wanted to share your feelings. The trick—you have to be okay with rejection—or it will get weird. Once you share your feelings, you've accomplished your goal. Your friend will always know that you want to be more than a friend. When your friend is ready to be more, it will happen. Or it will never happen. It doesn't have to be weird.

> "He told me he liked me as more than friends our sophomore year. I was shocked and rejected him. We stayed friends. Two years later, I fell in love with him. We're now married."
> —grad, Northwestern University

It's only weird if you make it that way. It's only weird if you refuse to give your good friend permission to NOT want you. So don't make it weird. You'd be surprised how much more attractive you appear once you express your interest and move on. The more comfortable you can become with taking risks the easier it will be to say what you think and do what you feel.

Bottom Line

A true friend would tell a friend, "I'm attracted to you." And that friend would honestly respond with how he or she feels. And then life would go on...o bla di o bla da, life goes on...(it's a Beatles song reference).

Tip #61
Gay/Lesbian/Bisexual Relationships

The Tip
It's very hard to date someone who's not out. If you're gay and want to date, then come out and be who you are.

The Story
I've been out since high school. When I got to college, I started dating someone who was not out at all. It was freshman year. We met at summer camp the year before. I was the first person he came out to, and to this day I'm still one of the few. He went to a local college and none of his friends knew he was bi.

When it came to our relationship, things would be fine when were alone, but when we went out in public he would become wicked homophobic. Even when we were in places that I felt comfortable and where he knew no one, he would still give me a dirty look or say "not here." I'm not a big PDA person, but I at least like to be close to someone. I like to be myself around my friends, and especially with a boyfriend. After about four months, it was too much. I told him I couldn't do this anymore. I said, "You're not ready for this. I don't want to force you to be someone you're not." He was upset, but understanding.

—sophomore, Wentworth Institute of Technology

* * *

A lot of you reading this are gay, lesbian, bisexual, transgender, queer, or questioning. For a lot of you, college might be your first time dating someone of the same sex in the open or behind closed doors. Whether you're out or not, some campuses have openly gay communities and others have more of an underground scene.

A great way to gauge the climate is to check out the groups and organizations on campus that address sexuality. Typically, these groups have names like LESBIGAY Alliance, the Gay Student Union, or something with "gay, lesbian, bisexual, and transgender" in its name. Send an email (or Facebook message) to the board members who are involved with these groups and organizations (you should be able to find information for such groups and organizations on your campus website). Ask members about gay-friendly residence halls, hangouts, and hot spots (and cool spots) on campus. There might even be a LGBTQ center on campus. It's also a good idea to contact the office of the dean of students and to inquire into local resources for the LGBTQ community.

If you're not sure if you're gay, lesbian, or bisexual, take your time to figure it out. Just know that if you do experiment, from what students have told me, the gay community can be a place where everyone knows everything. Meaning, if you're not out, other people will find out that you're gay once you start dating on campus. Make sure your partner knows if you're out or not. Otherwise, he or she might talk (still, he or she might talk).

Remember to find people in your corner who have been there and done it. Having LGTBQ friends and allies on and off campus will always give you someone to lean on. Should you get uncomfortable, you need to have people who can support you. A strong foundation of people and professionals will always help you be balanced and find perspective.

If you find that it's too difficult or too uncomfortable on your campus to be yourself, consider relocating to a campus that's friendlier to gays, lesbians, and bisexuals. If you can't transfer, look to see if there is a gay, lesbian, bisexual, or transgender community on a nearby campus. Just find yourself a community.

One more note—if at any time you ever feel threatened, bullied, confused, hurt, or hopeless, please know that things WILL get better. If you don't believe me, check out the It Gets Better Project at www.ItGetsBetter.org. If at any time you EVER feel like you're going to hurt yourself or need help, please reach out for help. Regardless of what anyone says or makes you feel, you deserve to be loved and deserve to share your love. NEVER forget it. Check out the resources at the end of this chapter to find help and support.

Bottom Line
Just be true to yourself. If you don't know yourself, then take the time to figure yourself out.

Tip #62
Cheaters, Users, and Abusers

The Tip
If you think someone might be cheating, there's a good chance that something is happening. Listen to yourself and your friends.

The Story

I didn't suspect anything until a good friend told me that my boyfriend had hit on her. I thought she was just jealous. Then another friend told me something similar. I kind of distanced myself from them. I didn't want to hear anything. A few months later, I noticed that he was getting strange calls on his cell phone. I'd ask him and he'd tell me it was just about studying. When it came to email, he had a separate account and a password that he guarded. When I asked him, he made me feel like the worst person in the world. One time, he went out of town and I decided just to double check. I was able to check his voice messages and found out that he was seeing his ex. When I went to the computer, I was able to look at old mail and saw that other girls had been writing sexual messages about their past and future. I was devastated. When I accused him, he accused me of being controlling and jealous. Yeah, right. Luckily, my friends who were trying to protect me took me back. If everyone tells you something is wrong and you think something is off, trust that something is wrong.

—junior, University of Massachusetts–Dartmouth

"I was in a relationship that lasted a couple years. We broke up at least four times and got back together every time but the last time. I didn't like the way we argued and screamed and yelled at each other. He would apologize and tell me that he'd change and that he wouldn't be possessive or be jealous...and I would believe him. That's how it was for two years. Finally, I told him I was out and finished. My friends told me that I was in an abusive relationship. It was abusive mentally and they were right."

—freshman, Loraine Community College

＊＊＊

Defining the Cheater

Cheaters are selfish, lazy, and confused people who don't have the testicles, or the ovaries, to say how they feel to someone they supposedly like or love. Instead of being honest, they lie, deceive, cover up, rip out hearts, and scar innocent victims forever. Cheating is NOT about love—it's about lying to yourself and the people who like or love you. If the world would stop putting up with cheaters and their selfish, destructive, and hurtful ways, cheating might stop. Sadly, too many people who are cheated on don't think they have other options because they don't know how to find a date (see Tip #54 for instructions on how to find a date while sober). Subsequently, these people put up with cheaters and their cheating ways.

> ### Cut This Out and Put It on Your Mirror
>
> I know AT ALL TIMES there are people who will love me, support me, and respect me. I NEVER need to put up with anyone who hurts me, disrespects me, and degrades me.

To the Cheated On

Don't ignore it. Do not make excuses for inexcusable behavior. Think twice before accepting someone's apology. You have options. Don't just put up with it, get used to it, or justify it. No matter what that cheater says, he or she doesn't respect you. Unless that person gets serious help (I mean therapy resulting in major life changes or offering you complete confidence he or she has changed and deserves ONE and only one chance), do not take him or her back. It's easy to promise change, but few are willing to commit to change.

If You're Being Abused

Never justify being physically or emotionally abused. It is NEVER your fault and it's NEVER acceptable. You might think, *But I love him or her.* And yes, you love being loved, but there is other love—better love. If love means being battered, physically or emotionally, then you don't need a romantic relationship, you need help. Turn to the people who are paid to help you. Without your parents so involved in your daily life, you need to be responsible for you. If you're in an abusive relationship, use your resources on your college campus to get out. Talk to counselors on campus. Get support. Do not get used to it. NEVER FORGET THAT YOU LIVE IN A WORLD OF OPTIONS. YOU DESERVE TO BE LOVED AND RESPECTED. Despite what your abuser says, you have endless options. Again, NEVER FORGET IT! If you do get used to it, when will it stop?

National Domestic Abuse Hotline (www.thehotline.org)

Abuse victims can call 1-800-799-SAFE (1-800-799-7233).

The Big Question

If you knew that you had thousands of men or women who wanted to love you, respect you, and treat you the way you deserve to be treated, would you ever put up with anyone who hurt you, ignored you, alienated you, disrespected you, disrespected your family, or made you feel like anything less than how you deserve to feel?

THE ANSWER: NEVER.

REMEMBER: You live in a world of endless options.

To the Cheaters and Abusers

Rather than making someone feel like less so you can feel like more, manipulating, cheating, and hurting someone, and ruining that person's life, have some integrity and get out of the relationship. Get help. Stop wasting everyone's time. If you're hitting your partner or controlling him or her by saying degrading, demeaning, or negative comments, stop it and look in the mirror. YOU NEED HELP. It doesn't say much about you if demeaning, controlling, manipulating, alienating, and abusing someone is the only way to get that someone to love you. That's not love. It's abuse. Help and support are available. Please get it.

Bottom Line
People who love each other do not hit each other. NEVER.

Tip #63
I Have No Life Other Than My Relationship

The Tip
Do not make someone your world. You'll feel confused and empty, and you'll end up searching for yourself.

The Story
I entered my freshman year of college with an optimistic and even naïve mind-set. I thought that everyone out there did not have the capability to hurt anyone, let alone me. I met this amazing, talented, caring, and loving individual who took my heart the minute I saw him. I knew that by the end of the semester I was going to have to talk to him.

After weeks of contemplating how I was going to approach him, I finally did it. We instantly clicked.

Weeks after our encounter, we were official. He and I were together all the time. We were one. Every weekend and every chance we had to spend with each other, we did.

Things moved incredibly fast and soon we were so involved with each other that it seemed as though he was my present, my future, and my world. I was so in love with him that I forgot who I was and what I stood for. Sometimes, things came up that I did not particularly agree with or was uncomfortable with, but I was so scared to lose him that I shut them out and forgot about them. I got lost in his presence and warmth. I never thought that this person would be the one to give me my first heartbreak. I cared for him so much that I was willing to take any aches and pain to spare him.

> "Don't let relationships hold you back from the things you want to do on campus."
> —senior, Misericordia College

He broke up with me. He did not feel the same way about me anymore. It took me months to discover myself again. It took me months to realize that you should *never* make someone your world; they should be a part of *your* world. If someone cares for you enough, they will respect you and want you for every inch of soul that you are. Be true to yourself, take care of yourself, and *do not* put somebody's well-being over yours, because the world is not as caring as you may think.

—sophomore, Eastern Illinois University

* * *

One day, you park your Winnebago of Love and realize that you're in the middle of nowhere, friends are gone, college is gone, and life isn't about you, but instead who you're with. Welcome to the land of "I have no life other than my relationship!" Population: 2.

It can happen without you ever even realizing it. It starts when you fall in love. No better place to be than with the love of your life, right? The things that used to occupy your time aren't as interesting or as important as the person you're with. It's better than spending time with friends. It's better than spending time with yourself. It's better than spending time with strangers you could be meeting in clubs, activities, or organizations. There really doesn't seem to be anything or anyone else in the world that makes you as happy. And then...

- Friends and family get hurt and pissed off. And it's true, most relationships don't last as long as most friendships. Even if you think it's going to last, it's not likely to last. And it's friends and family who will help you when it ends.

- You become so dependent on this one person for your happiness that you end up putting up with things that you should never put up with. You don't think you have options and start feeling trapped. Having isolated yourself from the world, you are left with little or no life outside of your relationship. With no outside life, and few options when it comes to other people to hang out with, you tend to hang onto crappy relationships that should be trashed.

- It's hard to grow, make friends, and find new experiences when your only experience is that relationship. So many people I've talked to wish they hadn't made their relationship their whole life. It just takes up so much time. And there are so many other things that you can be doing. You can still have a relationship, but find balance.
- You become so isolated and so alone that your relationship becomes a crutch that you need to lean on in order to find balance. Eventually, the crutch gives way and you fall hard.

Bottom Line
Don't abandon yourself, your family, or your friends. Should you get dumped, you'll be left with no one. Should you not get dumped, you'll be too afraid to dump a toxic partner. That's when things go from bad, to the rest of your life...

Tip #64
I Got Dumped and No Longer Have a Relationship

The Tip
Always believe that the worst is over and things can only get better with the friends you have around you.

The Story

I broke up with my boyfriend of three years and it was a messy ending. I came into college just beginning this relationship and I regret the last three years of college because I had limited myself to just one person. I had friends from all over calling me, coming over, and taking care of me. Never underestimate that your friends will always be there and the old ones will never stop caring. It's not easy breaking up with someone in college, especially someone you were serious with. However, you will get through it and make new friends.

—junior, Texas A&M University

* * *

There's breaking up with a first love, then there is sitting naked in a bathtub filled with angry bees while covered with honey. No, this isn't a kinky fantasy; it's an analogy that illustrates how much each of these situations can sting.

It's so unbelievably painful to lose love, especially your first love. It's the first person you've loved and who has loved you so completely. It's deep, it's excruciating, it's intense, but it does pass over time. One thing to never forget—first love is like a drug. It's intense, powerful, and will make you do crazy things. But it's not sustainable. Appreciate that first love happens once, but there will be more love, better love in your future. Here's a guide to help you survive a breakup:

Phase I: Get Upset

Cry and get emotional. Avoid hiding your feelings. Don't hook up with the first person who shows you attention for validation (yes, you're still desirable). Allow yourself to get upset—do it alone or do it in a place where there are mirrors. I like to cry in a mirror (helps me see the raw emotion, plus it's a little more dramatic). Allow yourself time to grieve the loss of the relationship. It's a bonding experience with yourself.

Phase II: Know That You're Still Desirable

Never forget that you're hot. Too many times people panic and think, *No one else will love me.* This is why so many people run into rebound relationships. That thinking is wrong, wrong, wrong. (Not a typo; yes, I wrote it three times. It's really that wrong.)

You always have options—thousands. Breaking up is all part of the dating process. Most couples break up. Sure, some will get married, but then

> "When my girlfriend of two years broke up with me, I went through at least two months of depression and then a period of about three or four months where I was doing stupid things because I really didn't know who I was. Finally, I found what I thought to be my true self."
> —junior, Rutgers University

about half of those people will end up breaking up (it's called divorce). Breaking up can be brutal, but it's part of the process. It's better to be free and available to be with someone who appreciates all you have to offer than to be with someone who isn't sure what he or she wants!

Phase III: Surround Yourself with Friends and Stay Busy

Lean on friends. Let them tell you things like: you're better than him or her, it's her/his loss, he/she never treated you well, I never liked him/her anyway, you're hot. It's all true. Listen and stay busy doing things (not your ex). Put yourself in rooms doing things you love to do. Get your heart rate up. Sweat. Lose yourself in something other than alcohol, drugs, or random strangers. And find a therapist, counselor, or psychologist to guide you.

Phase IV: Take a Break from Dating

This can be for as long as you need. But give yourself time to rest and recoup. Wait until you heal before getting back out there. Have a good time hanging out with your friends again. This time is gold.

> "The beginning of my sophomore year my girlfriend of two years left me. So many emotions went through me all at once, and my body couldn't handle it. After several days of not eating, I was finally rushed to the hospital, because I was so weak I couldn't get out of bed. If that wasn't bad enough, rumors started circulating that I went crazy, and tried to kill myself, which only made matters worse for myself, my family, and my now ex-girlfriend. My grades took a major turn, I was rapidly losing weight and not only looking but feeling unhealthy. It took almost six months to get my feet planted back on the ground and realize that there is more than one person that can make you happy."
>
> —senior, Clark University

Phase V: Avoid Running Right Back to an Ex

If you're running back to an ex out of loneliness and insecurity, you're running toward trouble. If you're running back because the relationship is the healthiest thing in the world for you and the space apart provided clarity, then proceed with caution.

Phase VI: Get Back Out There

When you do get back out into the world, you will be so much smarter. Learn from your past relationship. Celebrate what you experienced. Trust that it will only get better.

Bottom Line

Sitting naked with bees in honey can sting, similar to a bad breakup. But it gets better over time (assuming you're not allergic to bees).

Harlan's Tip Sheet

Naked People, Places, and Resources

Definitions

- *Creepin':* Regularly viewing someone's personal online profile without that person knowing you're watching him or her. Following someone's status updates, looking through his or her pictures, seeing his or her friends, reading notes, reading blogs, and repeating these actions on a regular basis are all part of creepin'.
- *Realantasy:* A combination of fantasy and reality most commonly found in online relationships and imaginary classroom relationships.
- *The Universal Rejection Truth of Dating and Relationships:* Thousands will want you, but millions will not.
- *Rejection denial:* A deep, dark, dangerous place where you think that everyone you like should like you. When someone you like doesn't like you, there's

a big problem. But the problem is that you never give people permission to not like you.

- *Self-rejection:* Rejecting yourself before ever allowing anyone the opportunity to reject you.
- *Rejection by circumstance:* The reason or circumstance that someone isn't giving you what you desire.
- *Raw rejection:* No matter what you say or what you do, some people will never like you for reasons you can't, or choose not to, change.
- *Training in your thong:* Working to be your personal best so that you never allow people who do not want you to keep you from taking risks and finding all the people who will want you.
- *The Getting Naked Experiment:* A call to action to help people say what they think and do what they feel. Check out *Getting Naked: Five Steps to Finding the Love of Your Life (While Fully Clothed and Totally Sober).*

Websites

- National Sexual Assault Hotline
  1-800-656-HOPE (1-800-656-4673)
  Website: www.RAINN.org
  Facebook: www.Facebook.com/RAINN01
  Twitter: www.Twitter.com/RAINN01
- National Domestic Violence Hotline
  1-800-799-SAFE (1-800-799-7233)
  Website: www.thehotline.org
  Facebook: www.Facebook.com/NationalDomestic
  ViolenceHotline
  Twitter: www.Twitter.com/NDVH

- National Teen Dating Abuse Hotline
  Website: www.LoveIsRepect.org
  Facebook: www.Facebook.com/LoveIsRespectPage
  Twitter: www.Twitter.com/LoveIsRespect
- It Gets Better Project
  Website: www.ItGetsBetter.org
  Facebook: www.Facebook.com/ItGetsBetterProject
  Twitter: www.Twitter.com/ItGetsBetter
- The Getting Naked Experiment
  Website: www.GettingNakedExperiment.com
  Facebook: www.Facebook.com/WhatsYourRisk
  Twitter: www.Twitter.com/TweetYourRisk
- Dating Websites
  There are too many dating websites to list. Pick a big one (www.OkCupid.com, www.Match.com, www.PlentyOfFish.com, or www.eHarmony.com) and pick a more niche site (based on religion, sexual orientation, or other interests). Make sure to give it at least a year!

Best Relationship Advice (Yes, I'm Biased)

- Help Me, Harlan!
  Check out my nationally syndicated advice column. You can see an archive of thousands of letters and answers on my website at www.HarlanCohen.com.
- www.NakedRoommate.com
  Ask questions and get answers from real college students.

9

Sex

Having It, Not Having It, Hearing Other People Having It

WELCOME TO THE SEX CHAPTER!!!
Yes, it's getting hot in here. Sorry, but before turning the page, you need to consent. Do you promise to ask yourself and your partner the following questions before getting naked:

1. Did your partner say or clearly indicate YES?
2. Did you say or clearly indicate YES?
3. Is everyone who said or indicated YES sober?
4. If you say NO during sex, is your partner prepared to stop?
5. If your partner says NO during sex, are you prepared to stop?

If consent is unclear, don't have sex. YES means YES. Clear consent is about protecting you and your partner.

Sign here: _____

Dear Harlan,
I always told myself that I would wait to have sex, but last week, in the heat of the moment, I kind of lost my virginity and now I regret it. My problem is that he

still wants to see me, but I'm stuck on this guy who lives a floor below me and who I hooked up with once last month. We didn't talk much after that, but now I see him everywhere. He's always smiling at me. I really like him and want to start something more. What should I do to make him notice me again? Should I just forget about the guy I lost my virginity to? I need help.

—Extremely Confused

Dear Extremely Confused,

You can always have sex with the guy you now like—that will get him to notice you (for at least a minute). And NO—I'm not serious...

You "kind of" made a mistake losing your virginity, and now you kind of have to fix it. But before doing anything, figure out why it happened. Think about what you're using sex for. If it's to get a guy's attention, find a better technique. Slow down and be careful.

Now, regarding your situation—talk to the guy you slept with, just in case you and the sex actually meant something to him, and assure him that he didn't do anything wrong. Let him know that it just doesn't feel right to be a couple. As for the guy a floor below you, it seems that you already have his attention. Start with a conversation and keep your clothes on, so as to not get his attention using sex. You might not be a virgin anymore, but you can still "kind of" wait to have sex with another guy.

Another thing to keep in mind—be careful when using sex as a way to get attention. Things like bad reputations, sexually transmitted infections, and children (that you'll give birth to) can end up following you around for years. And then, when you do find someone whom you want to date for more than a night, the past might become an issue.

Tip #65
Deciding to Do It

The Tip
Make sure the first time is with someone comfortable.

The Story
When I got to college, I was a virgin. I had dated, but never felt ready. I had kept my virginity. When I came to college, it was easier to have sex. People talked about it as if it wasn't a big deal. Hearing all the conversations made it matter less and less. I ended up losing it my freshman year to a guy that I was kind of dating. It wasn't great, but he made it comfortable. He was also a virgin. We talked a lot. He was surprisingly sensitive. The most important thing is to make sure that it's with someone comfortable. It wasn't physically all that great and it was much more comforting to be able to talk about everything. I could not have imagined doing it with some hookup from a party. I know a lot of friends who lost it to someone who they barely knew. That, I would have regretted.

—junior, University of Montana

* * *

If you've already done it, DO NOT skip this tip. In fact, I'm going to give back your virginity just for visiting this tip. Here. It's back. I can do that. It's part of being an advice columnist and author. So, for all you virgins and nonvirgins, it's safe to assume that some of you are planning on having sex in college. And a lot of you are planning on NOT having sex. Considering that roughly 80 percent of students graduating from college have done it, many of you who are planning not to do it might decide to do it in the future. Just in case you choose to, keep reading...

When deciding to have sex, keep the following virgin questionnaire in mind. If possible, copy this checklist and keep it close to you when making your decision. You have my permission to reproduce it and keep it in your pocket. If you don't have pockets, keep it in your sock. If you're not wearing socks, then stash it in your underwear. If you're not wearing underwear, then it's probably too late...

> "My friend was a virgin for eighteen years and he said to her, 'You look like you listen to rock music,' and then she lost it."
>
> —freshman, University of Nevada–Las Vegas

○ Why do you want to have sex with this person?

○ Can you discuss sex with this person?

○ Are you able to offer and get clear consent while sober?

○ What will happen after the sex?

○ If you say NO or WAIT, will your partner listen and wait? (Practice this.)

○ Are you single? Is your partner single?

○ Do you have contraception (including condoms)?

○ Have you asked your partner about herpes, genital warts, and other sexual souvenirs?

○ Do you want to give this person something so special? (And no, you can't get it back once it's given. If anyone says that, that person is trying to get you in bed again.)

○ Have you talked about what would happen if someone got pregnant?

○ Are you doing it because you want to or because you're feeling pressure? (If you're afraid the sex won't be around tomorrow, it's not a good idea to have it today.)

○ Are you sober? Is your partner sober?

○ Are you afraid sex will ruin the relationship?

○ Is this decision in alignment with your values and religion?

○ Will it be awkward to see the person the next day?

○ Is it happening in a comfortable place (not while your roommate sleeps)?

○ Does it feel 100 percent right?

○ Do you know the person's first and last name? Can you spell it? Can you pronounce it?

Besides the whole sexually transmitted infection thing and pregnancy scare factors, there is the emotional factor. Sex is intense and it can bring on a flood of emotions. Unless you're sure it's right, and unless you're with someone who makes you comfortable, it's not right.

Bottom Line

When in doubt, don't do it.

FYI: Some STDs/STIs can be transmitted even when a condom is used.

Tip #66
Deciding Not to Do It

The Tip
If you can't talk about sex with the person you're going to sleep with, then you obviously aren't mature enough to have it.

The Story
I met my boyfriend at college. We started going out about one week into school and seemed to be really compatible. We talked about everything, including sex. I told him that I didn't want to ruin my chance at life by getting some disease or becoming pregnant, because honestly, I'm just too selfish right now to have a whole other human being depending on me. We talked it out, and still do, and he completely respects my decision. Talking about it even made him respect me more, and made him feel like I really trusted him and felt comfortable enough to share that sort of thing with him. If anything, talking about waiting has brought us closer together.

"I'm not gonna lie, I really wanted to have sex. He had his pants down and asked me. We were more than friends, but not yet official. I got to thinking a little harder and decided it was a bad idea, since we weren't official. I told him no. It turns out that we never dated. I am so thankful that I did not lose my virginity to him."
—sophomore,
San Diego State University

—freshman, Redlands College

* * *

Sex is always available. Waiting is always a choice.

According the National Institute of Virginity (this isn't real), a virgin walks by you every 3.5 minutes. Actually, I made up that statistic and the Institute, but the point is that virgins are all around you. They're everywhere. It's just that not everyone flaunts it. A truthful stat reports that more and more teens are waiting longer to have sex.

Some wait for religious reasons. Some don't want to risk getting pregnant. Some aren't emotionally ready. Some just haven't found the right partner worthy of the honor. And then there are the reluctant virgins—those who want it, but can't get it. But really, if you want sex badly enough, you can find someone who is desperate enough, lonely enough, intoxicated enough, or affordable enough (not recommended). Choosing to have sex is easy. Waiting until it's right—that's the challenge. Virgins make a choice. It's not a curse—it's a gift.

If you're a virgin, hang on to it for a while. Whatever you do, avoid losing it by accident, while drinking, due to pressure, or out of fear of losing someone. Never feel pressured to get rid of it. Make sure that when you confide in a partner that you're a virgin, you also make it clear that virgins can be extremely sexual and sensual people. Being a virgin doesn't mean being a prude. It just means that you don't sleep around. Many virgin men and women have confided in me—some people don't always want to date a virgin (clearly they don't understand that virgins can still be sexual). Still, there are a lot of people who find virginity extremely attractive. There are so many people who will be so excited to *not* make love to you, *not* have to worry about pregnancy scares, *not* have to worry about STDs/STIs, *not* have to deal with contraception, and *not* have to deal with all the emotions that go along with having sex!

And to you virgins who judge people who want to have sex with you—just stop. Some people want to be in a sexual relationship built on love, mutual respect, and trust before marriage. It's a personal choice, just like not having sex is a choice. Respect their choices and be sure to remind them that you're worth the wait. Also, make it clear that being a virgin doesn't mean that you're not sexual—in fact, you can explain what you'll do and won't do—that might pique their interest and clear up the confusion.

Bottom Line
Being a virgin doesn't mean you can't have sex. It means you choose NOT to have sex. And that's hot.

Tip #67
Doing It Way Too Much

The Tip
It's easy to have sex once you start. Pace yourself.

The Story
I started off as a virgin in college. It wasn't for religious reasons; I just didn't find the right person to be with. I lost my virginity the first month in college. Once it was gone, it became so much easier to have sex. There wasn't the pressure of, "Wait, hold on, oh my god, I'm a virgin. Ahhhh."

What happened to me next is the bad part. I kind of started being too promiscuous. I'd go out, party, and come home with some different partner. No, I never got an STI that I know of or anything like that, but I was with some people

"It's just expected now; you go to a party, you hang out, and then something sexual will happen."
—senior, Alfred University

who I would have never been with normally. I lost control. It seemed like fun at the time, but I wish that I had, let's say, been more selective. It's hard when you see the people you slept with freshman year on campus like at the library or at a game. I'm not proud of the past.

—senior, University of Oklahoma

* * *

If you've been trying to read this tip but keep getting distracted because you keep having sex (with someone or alone), then you're probably doing it too much.

For some students, sex is used as a way to escape reality; for others it's a way to feel connected. With no curfews, no parents, and no one other than yourself to watch over you, the decision is yours to make.

Be aware—the most common problem with new students is that sex is sometimes used as a crutch to make it

"Losing your virginity doesn't have to mean losing high standards. Despite losing my virginity, I have yet to have sex with another person."
—freshman, Gonzaga University

through the whole transition (this includes the use of online porn). Look at it like this—a new student on a new campus is

naturally uncomfortable. One way to feel connected for ten minutes, or five minutes, or thirty seconds (depending who you're with) is to have sex. It's a quick fix, a fast connection, and a way to feel like you're not alone.

Fast sex (or random sex) is often just a temporary distraction from a bigger problem. It's an ego boost, it's a drug, it's an escape, it's a way to feel comfortable in an uncomfortable place. Beware: it can even be an addiction. The problem is that when the sex ends, you can end up hurt, pregnant, with an STD/STI, with a bad reputation, in a dangerous relationship, or confused—wondering if someone likes you for you or only for the sex and leaving you feeling even more uncomfortable and alone.

> ### Doing It Way Too Much... Alone?
> Porn addiction is real. If you're missing classes, avoiding real life interactions, or are unable to have real sexual encounters—get help.

Besides using sex as a crutch, there's also the "he/she's too easy" phenomenon. This is when a guy or a girl has sex, enjoys the sex, but is then disappointed because the sex was so easily offered by his or her partner. It's a post-coital loss of respect. In retrospect, the partner wishes the sex had been denied for longer. The longer the wait, the better the couple can get to know each other. The better they know each other, the more meaning behind the sex.

"Just because a girl has sex doesn't mean that she's a slut."
—junior, Angelo State University

There's really nothing to be gained from having sex too soon (other than STDs/STIs and possibly children—see tips to follow). Want to get to know someone? Keep your pants on.

Having sex too soon is best described by using the analogy of building a new house—until the walls are up, the roof is shingled, the plumbing is in place, the electricity is flowing, and the carpets are installed, entering the house can be dangerous. Should you go into someone's "house" too soon or invite someone inside yours, always use a hard hat. You never know what you're getting into or who was there last.

Be Prepared for a Sex Emergency

Consider carrying two condoms with you just in case one breaks or tears while it's being put on. Both men and women are equally responsible for preventing STIs and using contraceptives, and both should carry condoms.

—The BACCHUS Network, www.SmarterSex.org

Bottom Line

If you're having sex again while reading this tip, it's definitely way too much. Visit SAA-Recovery.org/ for info on sex addiction.

Tip #68
The One-Night Stand

The Tip
Make sure sex is consensual. "No" means no. That goes for the person saying it and the person being told it.

The Story
When a guy is getting into a random hookup, he needs to make sure it's consensual. I have a good female friend on another campus who was intoxicated and was with a guy who wasn't intoxicated. They had sex. She says that she never consented to it. She pressed charges because she

thought that he took advantage. Guys are in a vulnerable position when engaging in a one-night stand. I'm extremely careful. I won't do anything with any woman unless she says it's all right. It's just not worth it.

—freshman, Earlham College

***

The scene: It's a hot night. You're at a party. The music is playing. You've had a long week. Midterms were hell. You just broke up with your boyfriend/girlfriend. You've had a couple drinks. You're looking to relax and blow off some steam. You then find yourself kissing someone you never imagined kissing. You think, *I've never done this before, it's college, I'm looking for some love, and someone to hook up with*...Things get intense. The heat is blazing. You can either end the night by getting his/her number, or you can just go home together and do it. What you do is up to you. It's one night—one night that can cause weeks, months, or years of aggravation and problems.

> "As a rule, we'll only stop our friends from taking someone back to their place if they're in a relationship or if the person is totally unattractive. Beer goggles can do that."
>
> —senior,
> University of Nevada–Las Vegas

Reasons to avoid the one-night stands:

- Condoms are not always effective in protecting you from the elements. It's hard to know where or with whom your partner has been. It's even harder to trust him or her to tell you the truth.
- Sex makes some people crazy—they have a one-night stand and then want to spend the rest of their life with you. Can you say stalker?

- Someone might be in a relationship, or living with someone who might not take kindly to you having sex with his or her partner.
- It's hard to know if you've gotten someone pregnant or gotten pregnant.
- It's uncomfortable to see your one-night stand around campus days, weeks, months, and even years after the sex happens. People who have seen each other naked can never look at each other the same way again.
- If drugs or alcohol are involved, you don't know for sure if the sex is consensual.
- You might change your mind and your partner might not be willing to listen—this is when things get dangerous.
- It's confusing and fleeting, and can consume your time and energy the next morning, when you work through the drama following the walk of shame.

Yes Means Yes

California passed a new law that requires sexual partners to get clear consent while sober. This means anything other than clear consent can be interpreted as sexual assault.

$$* * *$$

If a one-night stand happens (and it does happen for some people), be smart about it. Make sure it's what you want. Make sure both of you understand that it's a one-night thing. Make sure that you use protection and that you ask your partner about his or her sexual history. Make sure you are alert, awake, and aware.

Bottom Line

You might be asking, "If the hookup sex happens during the day, is it still considered a one-night stand?" The answer is, technically, it's a one-day stand. But you can still call it a one-night stand to help others understand.

Tip #69
Pimps, Hos, and Reputations

The Tip
News travels fast, especially on a smaller campus.

The Story
When someone does something with someone, other people on campus will know about it. The smaller the campus, the faster the news travels. It can be as bad as high school. A guy will know if you're a girl who sleeps around or doesn't sleep around. What you do becomes public knowledge. I'm a pretty good girl when it comes

"Never sleep with more than one person in a fraternity or sorority. Everyone will know what you did."
—senior, Ohio State University

to what I do, but the one time I did hook up and went a little too far, I heard about it from people who barely knew either of us. Everyone loves to talk about who did what with who. What you do will totally follow you around. On a bigger campus, that's not so true. It's easier to get lost in the crowd, but it's not true on a smaller college campus—not at all.

—junior, DePauw University

Reputations are like bad gas—they can follow you for a very long time.

The smaller the campus, the more the reputation sticks to you. When it comes to what happens in the bedroom (or at the library, or in the laundry room, or wherever you find yourself in an intimate moment), news travels fast. People talk. They talk a lot. And now, with Facebook, texting, Twitter, Tumblr, Snapchat, and sexting, news travels even faster. You might as well put the story of your affair in the campus newspaper (no explicit photos, please).

You might not realize it, but when you sleep with someone, there's a good chance other people will find out (especially if you are in someone's room while that person's roommate is sleeping). When you sleep with someone and then sleep with their friend, there's an even better chance that someone will find out (especially if you're sleeping with them both at the same time and in the same bed). If you sleep with someone and then sleep with their friend and then sleep with two more of their friends, everyone will know. Then you will either be known as easy, a manwhore, a manbo, a slut, or some other expression that isn't all that endearing. And then, when you do find yourself wanting to have a serious relationship, the person whom

Sex Fact

College students reported having the following number of sexual partners (for oral sex, vaginal, or anal intercourse) within the last 12 months: 12.5 percent of men and 8.7 percent of females report having 4 or more sexual partners.

—ACHA-NCHA-II Executive Summary Fall 2014

you want to take you seriously won't. And even if he or she does want to be with you, the fact that you've slept with his or her friends makes it close to impossible. It takes years to change reputations. Be careful making them.

Should you make a habit of sleeping around, bring a change of clothes with you so that you don't have to take your walk of shame in your evening wear. There's nothing more obvious than a woman in a miniskirt and sequined top or guy in an all-black outfit walking the streets at nine in the morning on an eighty-degree day.

Bottom Line
Quick note: it's hard to deny sleeping around if you've slept with most of the people on campus.

Tip #70
Sexual Souvenirs

*Note: STDs and STIs are the same thing.
*Second Note: Listen to "The Chlamydia Jive" and "The Syphilis Song" at www.NakedRoommate.com and www.HarlanCohen.com.

The Tip
Herpes isn't an end-all. We all have baggage.

The Story

My friend and I decided to hook up when I was visiting him. We discussed our status and our last time being checked for STIs. Two weeks later, I got symptoms I immediately recognized as herpes. A trip to the doctor and a culture told me what I already knew. I called my mother and told her the news, holding back tears. Funny enough, it turned out both she AND my aunt have it. I contacted my friend from before, and at first he thought I put HIM at risk. Turns out he did not know that the cold sores on his mouth were herpes and transmissible genitally. He gave it to me when he gave me oral sex. The first few months I was very afraid to date or hook up. The word herpes was frightening, but I decided to say it until it wasn't anymore. I tell anyone and everyone that I have herpes if the conversation goes that way. It's baggage, but it's only a small addition to my closet of issues and flaws I've accumulated. And that closet is just part of the house that is me—which I believe is full of so many wonderful things that make me worth dating! Funny enough, when I did have to relay the news to a crush, I was more worried that he DIDN'T care. We've been dating over six months, and it's been a year since I contracted herpes. I've remained outspoken about it and it's brought only good to my life. Every time I tell my story, I meet another person who contracted either herpes or another STI, and they

> "Girls should definitely get a Pap smear every single year, whether you are 'sexually active' or not. I had very little and non-risky sexual contact and ended up getting HPV on spring break, which I would not want anyone to have to go through."
>
> —sophomore, Miami University (Ohio)

always are grateful to meet someone else who has it. When we don't talk about it, it remains this stigma that it only happens to dirty, gross people. But it can happen to anyone having sex—of any kind!

—senior, University of Kentucky

* * *

Some people come home with a souvenir shot glass from college. Some people come home with a T-shirt bearing a school mascot. Some people come home with herpes, genital warts, and chlamydia. If your hobby is collecting STIs, college is THE PLACE to do your collecting. The challenge—you don't always know who has them and who doesn't have them. People don't wear signs or T-shirts saying, "Hi, I've Got Herpes." (Visit my website to get your sex souvenir T-shirt.) The STI truth is that—brace yourself—one in five college-age people have at least one (and some say the percentages are even higher).

> "My roommate freshman year caught pubic lice from the bathroom toilet. She wasn't sexually active and realized what had happened after a red and raw rash broke out."
>
> —senior, Manhattan College

> "One of the girls I know just got genital warts. She was sleeping with this kid who was pretty active. She was scared to confront him. She didn't want to accuse him, but she wanted to inform him in case he didn't know so he wouldn't give it to someone else."
>
> —junior, Western New England University

According to the U.S. Centers for Disease Control and Prevention, in the United States, one of every six teenagers and adults is infected with genital herpes. Women are more commonly infected than men, and it is estimated that one of every four women has herpes. Health experts estimate that there are more cases of genital HPV infection than of any other STI in the United States. Chlamydia is the most common bacterial STI. It's known as a "silent" disease because the majority of infected people have no symptoms (this is why it's so important for sexually active women to get annual or semi-annual checkups).

> "It's been two years since I found out I contracted genital herpes. At first, it made me feel worthless, like what did I do to deserve this? After turning to alcohol to try and cope and waking up in a hospital room from drinking too much, I decided to talk to the counselor at school. It was very difficult to speak about it…Through counseling I realized I wasn't a bad person. And that it was much more common than I thought. Just because I have herpes doesn't mean I won't be loved. Since being diagnosed and reaching out for help, I've had a sexually active relationship. The herpes made me more cautious about who I share myself with…I don't see that as a bad thing."
>
> —senior, Southern Vermont College

Beyond the whole physical side of STIs, there's the emotional part of it. With many of these STIs, once you get them, they stay with you for the rest of your life, and they change your life. You have to tell your future partners. As for how you get these things, while condoms are effective, they don't always protect you. So, if you plan on rubbing yourself against someone else, cover up and be sure to get their sexual history.

Should you suspect that you have a sexual souvenir, get tested

> "We had a chlamydia outbreak on our campus. My best friend had a genital warts outbreak on her campus."
>
> —junior, small campus in Indiana

quickly. Many STIs can be detected with relatively little discomfort. A little urine or blood, or a few cells can do the trick. Should you test positive, there is treatment available to eliminate or help control outbreaks. If you are positive for an STI, consider getting professional support if you experience feelings of shame and humiliation. I can promise you that you will still be desirable and loved. Millions of people live healthy and loving lives with sexual souvenirs. While STIs like HPV and herpes can't be cured, they can be managed.

Another huge problem is that some STIs do not show symptoms or do not show up in tests. Unless a man shows symptoms of HPV, it's not possible to know if he has it. Chlamydia can have no symptoms in 50 to 75 percent of cases, although it can show up in tests. If gone untreated, it can lead to pelvic inflammatory disease, which can lead to sterility. Herpes is another one that is hard to see—especially during viral shedding prior to an outbreak. Some people will go years without knowing they have herpes. As for HPV, college-age people are the most at-risk group, especially women. So if you are sexually

HPV Fast Facts

- Genital HPV is spread through skin-to-skin contact.
- Genital HPV cannot be entirely prevented by condom use.
- This virus is often asymptomatic—people usually do not know they have it.
- At least 50 percent of sexually active men and women acquire genital HPV at some point in their lives.
- HPV can be contracted from one partner, remain dormant, and then later be unknowingly transmitted to another sexual partner, including a spouse.
- Some types of HPV cause cervical cancer.
- Although smoking does not cause HPV, it increases the risk of getting an HPV infection by three times because the body is less able to fight the infection.

—BACCHUS Sexual Responsibility Week 2010 Campaign, www.BACCHUS Network.org/sexual-responsibility-week.html active, get tested and screened at your campus health center at least once a year. You might also want to look into the HPV vaccine (HPV can be a precursor to cervical cancer). Most campuses offer testing (including Pap smears—for women, not men) that are low-cost (a great holiday gift). If your health center doesn't have screening on campus, the staff can direct you to another center off campus. There are home kits available to test for HIV, herpes, HPV, chlamydia, gonorrhea, trichomoniasis, and hepatitis.

The following is a list of sexually transmitted infections available on your college campus (and yes, quantities are unlimited). Should you find yourself with a sore, an itch, or a bump that can't be explained, the following can help point you in the right direction—the direction of the health center.

A Guide to the Most Common STIs You Might Meet in College

Source: www.CDC.gov

Genital Herpes

According to the Centers for Disease Control and Prevention, one of every six teenagers and adults in the United States is infected with genital herpes. Women are more commonly infected than men, and it is estimated that one of every four women has herpes. The incurable viral herpes infections are caused by herpes simplex virus (HSV).

The major symptoms of herpes infection are painful blisters or open sores in the genital area. These may be preceded by a tingling or burning sensation in the legs, buttocks, or genital region. The herpes sores usually disappear within two to three weeks, but the virus remains in the body for life and the lesions may recur from time to time. Severe or frequently recurrent genital herpes is treated with one of several antiviral drugs that are available by prescription. These drugs help control the symptoms but do not eliminate the herpes virus from the body. Suppressive antiviral therapy can be used to prevent occurrences and perhaps transmission. Women who have genital herpes during pregnancy can transmit the virus to their babies. Untreated HSV infection in newborns can result in mental retardation and death. It is possible that a person may not experience a "first episode" until years after the infection is acquired. Condoms can help prevent infection, but can't eliminate the risk. Once infected, the virus is always present.

Genital HPV Infection

About 79 million Americans are currently infected with HPV. About 14 million people become newly infected each year. HPV is so common that most sexually active men and women will get at least one type of HPV at some point in their lives. Some of these viruses are called high-risk types, and may cause abnormal Pap smears (for women). They may also lead to cancer of the cervix, vulva, anus, or penis.

Genital warts (also called venereal warts or condylomata acuminata) are caused by human papilloma virus, a virus related to the virus that causes common skin warts. Genital warts usually first appear as small, hard painless bumps in the vaginal area, on the penis, or around the anus. If untreated, they may grow and develop a fleshy, cauliflower-like appearance. In addition to genital warts, certain high-risk types of HPV cause cervical cancer and other genital cancers. Genital warts are treated with a topical drug (applied to the skin), by freezing, or if they recur, with injections of a type of interferon. If the warts are very large, they can be removed by surgery.

Chlamydial Infection

This infection is now the most common of all bacterial STIs. Chlamydia can be transmitted during vaginal, anal, or oral sex. It's often referred to as a "silent" STI because symptoms can be mild or absent. In both men and women, chlamydia may cause an abnormal genital discharge and burning with urination.

> "A buddy at another college got diagnosed with chlamydia. He didn't know it, but his girlfriend got diagnosed. They gave him some horse pills just to be safe."
>
> —junior,
> Western New England University

In 2012, 1,422,976 cases of chlamydia were reported to the CDC from 50 states and the District of Columbia, but an estimated 2.86 million infections occur annually. A large number of cases are not reported because most people with chlamydia are asymptomatic and do not seek testing. In women, untreated chlamydia may lead to pelvic inflammatory disease (PID), one of the most common causes of ectopic pregnancy and infertility in women. Many people with chlamydia, however, have few or no symptoms of infection. Sexually

Chlamydia Fact

In 2012, women aged 20–24 years had the highest rate of chlamydia (3,695.5 cases per 100,000 females) compared with any other age or sex group. Chlamydia rates for women in this age group increased 1.8 percent during 2011–2012.

Source: www.cdc.gov/std/stats12/surv2012.pdf

active females 25 years old and younger need testing every year. Chlamydia can be easily treated and cured with anti-biotics. A single dose of azithromycin or a week of doxycy-cline (twice daily) are the most commonly used treatments.

HIV Infection and AIDS

HIV is the human immunodeficiency virus. It is the virus that can lead to acquired immune deficiency syndrome, or AIDS. In 2012, the CDC estimated 47,989 new diag-noses of HIV infection in the United States. AIDS was first reported in the United States in 1981. The HIV virus destroys the body's ability to fight off infection. People who have AIDS are very susceptible to many life-threatening diseases, called opportunistic infections, and to certain forms of cancer. Transmission of the virus primarily occurs during unprotected sexual activity and by sharing needles used to inject intravenous drugs. Having multiple sex partners or the presence of other sexually transmitted diseases can increase the risk of infection dur-ing sex. Unprotected oral sex can also be a risk for HIV transmission, but it is a much lower risk than vaginal or anal sex. If you have any questions about HIV infection or AIDS, you can call the AIDS Hotline confidential toll-free number: 1-800-342-AIDS.

Gonorrhea

The CDC estimates that, annually, 820,000 people in the United States get new gonorrheal infections, and less than half of these infections are detected and reported to the CDC. The CDC estimates that 570,000 of them were among young people 15–24 years of age. In 2012,

334,826 cases of gonorrhea were reported to CDC. The most common symptoms of gonorrhea are a discharge from the vagina or penis and painful or difficult urination. The most common and serious complications occur in women, and, as with chlamydial infection, these complications include PID, ectopic pregnancy, and infertility. Historically, penicillin has been used to treat gonorrhea, but in the last decade four types of antibiotic-resistant strains have emerged. New antibiotics or combinations of drugs must be used to treat these resistant strains.

Syphilis

During 2012, there were 49,903 reported new cases of syphilis. The CDC estimates that, annually, 55,400 people in the United States get new syphilis infections. The first symptoms of syphilis may go undetected because they are very mild and disappear spontaneously. The initial symptom is a chancre; it is a painless open sore that usually appears on the penis or around or in the vagina. It can also occur near the mouth, anus, or on the hands. If untreated, syphilis may go on to more advanced stages, including a transient rash and, eventually, serious involvement of the heart and central nervous system. The full course of the disease can take years. Penicillin remains the most effective drug to treat people with syphilis.

Other STDs/STIs

Other diseases that may be sexually transmitted include trichomoniasis, bacterial vaginosis, cytomegalo-virus infections, scabies, and pubic lice. STDs/STIs in pregnant women are associated with a number of adverse outcomes, including spontaneous abortion and infection in the new-born. Low birth weight and prematurity appear to be associated with STDs/STIs, including chlamydial infection and trichomoniasis. Congenital or perinatal infection (infection that occurs around the time of birth) occurs in 30 to 70 percent of infants born to infected mothers, and complications may include pneumonia, eye infections, and permanent neurological damage.

Bottom Line

If you want to find a sexually transmitted disease, college is the most convenient place in the world to get what you want. Get tested before getting into bed. With the new HIV tests, all it takes is a mouth swab—no needles. Make it a rule—no test, no getting in your pants.

Tip #71
The U of Birth Control

The Tip
Free condoms are all over the place. Never pay for a condom again.

The Story
I can't remember the last time I paid for a condom. I get my condoms all over campus. The people in the health office are great. They have a wide selection. I've also picked up free condoms at campus health fairs. They are all shapes, sizes, and flavors. I've even grabbed some glow-in-the-dark ones. It's better than a store. Stock up on free condoms. Buying them can run you about ten bucks a pack or more. I'm a poor college student. Stock up. If you don't see them in the health center, ask. They're available. I went to a party at my friend's school and a guy dressed up as a condom man was walking around the bar handing out free condoms. I never leave home without one. If you don't use a condom, you're just dumb. There's no reason not to.

> "I overheard my dad tell my brother, 'Don't be a fool—wrap your tool!'"
> —senior, Alfred College

—junior, Western Kentucky University

* * *

Some people graduate with honors, some with a new job, and some with a new child. Few people expect to leave with a new member of the family—but it happens. If this isn't your plan, then plan accordingly when you're having sex.

Birth Control in College

There couldn't be an easier place or time to find birth control. Most college campuses offer many accessible and affordable birth control options. This includes both prescription and over-the-counter choices through the health center. In addition, such services as pelvic exams, Pap smears, STD/STI testing, and counseling are also available. If your campus health center doesn't offer these services or cannot prescribe birth control, they can typically offer you a referral to resources off campus. If they won't offer you a referral, talk to your family physician, visit a local Planned Parenthood office, or look up "family planning" in your local phone book. To help in your birth control education, I've listed the following birth control options from the FDA's website (visit www.FDA.gov/ForConsumers/ByAudience /ForWomen for more information on birth control). The first one (no sex) is my addition to their list. Here's the list:

No Sex

What is it? No vaginal intercourse. How do I use it? Keep your pants on.

Possibility of getting pregnant? 0 out of 100 women report getting pregnant when avoiding sex (but there can be immaculate circumstances).

Some risks: You will get to know your sexual partner very well before having sex.

Does it protect me from sexually transmitted infections (STIs)? 100 percent (this includes no oral or anal sex).

Male Condom, Latex/Polyurethane

What is it? A thin film sheath placed over the erect penis to stop sperm from reaching the egg.

How do I use it? Put it on immediately before intercourse. Use only once and then discard. Pull out before the penis softens, and hold the condom against the base of the penis before you pull out.

How do I get it? You can buy it over the counter.

Possibility of getting pregnant? Out of 100 women who use this method for one year, 11–16 may get pregnant. The most important thing is that you use a condom every time you have sex.

Some risks: Irritation and allergic reactions. Polyurethane condoms are available for those with latex sensitivity.

Does it protect me from STIs? Except for abstinence, latex condoms are the best protection against HIV/AIDS and other sexually transmitted diseases. Condoms are the only contraceptive product that may protect against most STIs. Note: Condoms made from lambskin are available for those with latex sensitivity, but latex condoms are best at preventing pregnancy and protecting against STIs.

Birth Control Fun Facts

Scary Thought:

30.3 percent of females and 27.4 percent of males reported using withdrawal as their birth control method.

A Less Scary Thought:

About half of students are using two methods of birth control. Approximately 46 percent of women and 51 percent of males reported using a male condom plus another method of birth control.

—ACHA-NCHA-II Executive Summary Spring 2014

Female Condom

What is it? A lubricated, thin polyurethane pouch that is put into the vagina.

How do I use it? Put the female condom into the vagina right before sex. Use it only once and then throw it away. You need a new female condom each time you have sex.

How do I get it? You do not need a prescription. You can buy it over the counter.

Possibility of getting pregnant? Out of 100 women who use this method for one year, about 20 may get pregnant.

Some risks: Irritation, allergic reactions.

Does it protect me from STIs? May give some protection against STIs. Not as effective as latex condoms. More research into its effectiveness is needed.

Diaphragm with Spermicide

What is it? A dome-shaped flexible disk with a flexible rim made from latex rubber or silicone. It covers the cervix so that sperm cannot reach the egg.

How do I use it? Put spermicidal jelly on the inside of the diaphragm before putting it into the vagina. Put the diaphragm into the vagina before having sex. You must leave the diaphragm in place for at least 6 hours after having sex. It can be left in place for up to 24 hours. You need to use more spermicide every time you have sex.

How do I get it? You need a prescription. A doctor or nurse will need to do an exam to find the right size diaphragm for you. You should have the diaphragm checked after childbirth or if you lose more than 15 pounds; you might need a different size.

Possibility of getting pregnant? Out of 100 women who use this method for one year, about 15 may get pregnant.

Some risks: Irritation, allergic reactions, and urinary tract infection. If you keep it in place longer than 24 hours, there is a risk of toxic shock syndrome. Toxic shock is a rare but serious infection.

Does it protect me from STIs? No.

Sponge with Spermicide

What is it? A disk-shaped polyurethane device with the spermicide nonoxynol-9.

How do I use it? Put it into the vagina before you have sex. Protects for up to 24 hours. You do not need to use more spermicide each time you have sex.

You must leave the sponge in place for at least 6 hours after having sex. You must take the sponge out within 30 hours after you put it in. Throw it away after you use it. How do I get it? You do not need a prescription. You can buy it over the counter.

Possibility of getting pregnant? Out of 100 women who use this method for one year, 16–32 may get pregnant. It may not work as well for women who have given birth. Childbirth stretches the vagina and cervix and the sponge may not fit as well.

Some risks: Irritation and allergic reactions. Some women may have a hard time taking the sponge out. If you keep it in place longer than 24–30 hours, there is a risk of toxic shock syndrome. Toxic shock is a rare but serious infection.

Does it protect me from STIs? No.

Cervical Cap with Spermicide

What is it? A soft latex or silicone cup with a round rim, which fits snugly around the cervix. It covers the cervix so that sperm cannot reach the egg.

How do I use it? Put spermicidal jelly inside the cap before you use it. Put the cap in the vagina before you have sex. You may find it hard to put in. You must leave the cap in place for at least 6 hours after having sex. You may leave the cap in for up to 48 hours. You do not need to use more spermicide each time you have sex.

How do I get it? You need a prescription.

Possibility of getting pregnant? Out of 100 women who use this method for one year, about 17–23 may get pregnant. It may not work as well for women who have given birth. Childbirth stretches the vagina and cervix and the cap may not fit as well.

Some risks: Irritation, allergic reactions, and abnormal Pap tests. If you keep it in place longer than 48 hours, there is a risk of toxic shock syndrome. Toxic shock is a rare but serious infection.

Does it protect me from STIs? No.

> ### Want to Get Tested Right Now (or in a few minutes)?
>
> Contact your campus health center. Visit www.PlannedParenthood.org and search for a local health center. Visit; www STDTest Express.com and speak to a live consultant to help answer your questions and help you find a place to get tested.

Spermicide Alone

What is it? A foam, cream, jelly, film, or tablet that kills sperm.

How do I use it? Instructions can be different for each type of spermicide. Read the label before you use it. You need to put spermicide into the vagina between 5 and 90 minutes before you have sex. You usually need to leave it in place at least 6 to 8 hours after; do not douche or rinse the vagina for at least 6 hours after sex.

How do I get it? You do not need a prescription. You can buy it over the counter.

Possibility of getting pregnant? Out of 100 women who use this method for one year, about 30 may get pregnant. Different studies show different rates of effectiveness.

Some risks: Irritation, allergic reactions, and urinary tract infections. If you are also using a medicine for a vaginal yeast infection, the spermicide might not work as well.

Does it protect me from STIs? No.

Oral Contraceptives—Combined Pill ("The Pill")

What is it? A pill that uses hormones (estrogen and progestin) to stop the ovaries from releasing eggs in most women. It also thickens the cervical mucus, which keeps the sperm from joining with the egg.

How do I use it? You should swallow the pill at the same time every day, whether or not you have sex.

How do I get it? You need a prescription.

Possibility of getting pregnant? Out of 100 women who use this method for one year, about 5 may get pregnant. Some risks: Dizziness, nausea, changes in your menstrual cycle, changes in mood, and weight gain. It is not common, but some women who take the pill develop high blood pressure. It is rare, but some women will have blood clots, heart attacks, or strokes.

Does it protect me from STIs? No.

Oral Contraceptives—Progestin-Only ("The Pill")

What is it? A pill that has only the hormone progestin. It thickens the cervical mucus, which keeps sperm from joining with an egg. Less often, it stops the ovaries from releasing eggs.

How do I use it? You should swallow the pill at the same time every day, whether or not you have sex.

How do I get it? You need a prescription.

Possibility of getting pregnant? Out of 100 women who use this method for one year, about 5 may get pregnant. Some risks: Irregular bleeding, weight gain, and breast tenderness. Less protection against ectopic pregnancy (pregnancy in the fallopian tubes) than the combined pill.

Does it protect me from STIs? No.

"I get my pills at the health center. My doctor at home gave me a prescription and I fill it at school, but my friend got examined by the nurse and then got her prescription. It's so inexpensive, too. If your college doesn't offer them (some don't) then you can try a local clinic. My friend goes to Planned Parenthood."
—junior, Northwestern University

Oral Contraceptives—Extended/Continuous Use ("The Pill")

What is it? A pill that uses hormones (estrogen and progestin) to stop the ovaries from releasing eggs in most women. It also thickens the cervical mucus, which keeps the sperm from joining with the egg. These pills are designed so women have fewer or no periods.

How do I use it? You should swallow the pill at the same time every day, whether or not you have sex.

How do I get it? You need a prescription.

Possibility of getting pregnant? Out of 100 women who use this method for one year, about 5 may get pregnant.

Some risks: Risks are similar to other oral contraceptives. You may have fewer planned periods. If you miss a scheduled period, you may be pregnant. You will likely have more bleeding and spotting between periods than with other oral contraceptives.

Does it protect me from STIs? No.

Patch

What is it? A skin patch you can wear on the lower abdomen, buttocks, or upper body. It uses hormones (estrogen and progestin) to stop the ovaries from releasing eggs in most women. It also thickens the cervical mucus, which keeps the sperm from joining with the egg.

How do I use it? You put on a new patch and take off the old patch once a week for 3 weeks. During the fourth week, you do not wear a patch and you have a menstrual period.

How do I get it? You need a prescription.

Possibility of getting pregnant? Out of 100 women who use this method for one year, about 5 may get pregnant. The patch may be less effective for women who weigh more than 198 pounds.

Some risks: It will expose you to higher than average levels of estrogen than most oral contraceptives do. It is not known if serious risks, such as blood clots, are greater with the skin patch because of greater exposure to estrogen.

Does it protect me from STIs? No.

Vaginal Contraceptive Ring

What is it? A flexible ring that is about 2 inches around. You put it into the vagina and it releases hormones (progestin and estrogen) to stop the ovaries from releasing eggs in most women. It also thickens the cervical mucus, which keeps the sperm from joining with the egg.

How do I use it? You put the ring into the vagina yourself. You need to keep the ring in your vagina for 3 weeks, then take it out for 1 week. If the ring falls out and stays out for more than 3 hours, you need to use another kind of birth control method until the ring has been used for 7 days in a row.

How do I get it? You need a prescription.

Possibility of getting pregnant? Out of 100 women who use this method for one year, about 5 may get pregnant.

Some risks: Vaginal discharge, swelling of the vagina, and irritation. Other risks are similar to oral contraceptives (combined pill).

Does it protect me from STIs? No.

Shot/Injection

What is it? A shot of the hormone progestin that stops the ovaries from releasing eggs in most women. It also thickens the cervical mucus, which keeps the sperm from joining with the egg.

How do I use it? You need one shot every 3 months. How do I get it? You need a prescription.

Possibility of getting pregnant? Out of 100 women who use this method for one year, less than 1 may get pregnant.

Some risks: You may have bone loss if you get the shot for more than 2 years. Bleeding between periods, weight gain, breast tenderness, and headaches.

Does it protect me from STIs? No.

IUD—Intrauterine Device

What is it? A T-shaped device that is put into the uterus by a healthcare provider.

How do I use it? After a doctor or other healthcare provider puts in the IUD, it can stay in place for 5 to 10 years, depending on the type.

How do I get it? You need a prescription.

Possibility of getting pregnant? Out of 100 women who use this method for one year, less than 1 may get pregnant.

Some risks: Cramps, bleeding, pelvic inflammatory disease, infertility, and tear or hole in the uterus.

Does it protect me from STIs? No.

Implantable Rod

What is it? A thin, matchstick-sized rod that contains the hormone progestin. It thickens the cervical mucus, which keeps sperm from joining with the egg. Less often, it stops the ovaries from releasing eggs.

How do I use it? It is put under the skin on the inside of your upper arm. It lasts up to 3 years.

How do I get it? A doctor or nurse puts it under the skin of your arm. You will get a shot in the upper arm to make the skin numb, then the rod is placed just under the skin with a needle.

Possibility of getting pregnant? Out of 100 women who use this method for more than one year, less than 1 may get pregnant. It might not work as well for overweight or obese women. It might not work as well if you are taking certain medicines for things like tuberculosis (TB), seizures, depression, or HIV/AIDS. Tell your doctor if you are taking the herb St. John's Wort.

Some risks: Acne, weight gain, cysts of the ovaries, mood changes, depression, hair loss, headache, upset stomach, dizziness, lower interest in sexual activity, sore breasts, and changes in your periods.

Does it protect me from STIs? No.

Post-Coital Contraceptives ("Plan B"/"The Morning After Pill")

What is it? A pill with hormones (either progestin alone or progestin plus estrogen) that is similar to other oral contraceptives. It stops the ovaries from releasing an egg or stops sperm from joining with the egg.

How do I use it? You can use these after you have unprotected sex (did not use birth control). You can also use these if your birth control did not work (i.e., the condom broke). You must swallow the pills within 72 hours of having unprotected sex. For the best chance for it to work, you should start taking the pills as soon as possible after unprotected sex.

How do I get it? You can buy it over the counter if you are 18 years or older. If you are younger than 18, you need a prescription.

Possibility of getting pregnant? This method reduces the risk of pregnancy resulting from a single act of unprotected sex by almost 85 percent, if you take it within 72 hours.

Some risks: Nausea, vomiting, abdominal pain, fatigue, and headache.

Does it protect me from STIs? No.

Consult your doctor for additional birth control options.

Bottom Line

If you're sexually active and not looking to start a family, stay in control of your birth control. Otherwise, you might end up with a child, or two, or three. And there's not a lot of space in dorm rooms for cribs.

Tip #72
Possibly Pregnant

The Tip

If you think you might be pregnant, get help immediately.

The Story

It was January of my junior year; I had just come off of the pill in December. I was gaining too much weight from it. I was on my last pack. I didn't quite know when my cycle was because I had been on the pill for years. I was with my boyfriend one night. We were doing what we do. It ends up, the condom slipped off, but we didn't realize that until it was *all* over. When my boyfriend was looking for the condom after we finished, he couldn't find it anywhere. That freaked the hell out of us. We were looking everywhere. When I went to urinate the next day, I found it. It had slipped off and was inside of me. That next morning, I called my aunt who is a nurse. She has dealt with this sort of thing before. She guided me to seek help. I took a couple of pills that were prescribed for me. I told my boyfriend what happened. He was supportive. The next week was nerve-racking. I wasn't sure if it worked. I had some cramping and wasn't feeling so great, but I didn't get pregnant. Every time after that, we checked to make sure that the condom was still on. And we're still checking to this day! I don't want to be that 10 percent...

—junior, Florida International University

* * *

A condom breaks, a pill is forgotten, a drunken night ends and you realize, um, yeah, okay, we've got a big problem... If you think that you're pregnant, don't just sit there and panic. Contact your health center, doctor, or family physician and pick up an over-the-counter pregnancy test. If it's been within 120 hours of unprotected intercourse, ask your doctor or emergency room about emergency contraception. Help is all around you. Here is some helpful information on emergency contraception from the FDA:

> "The condom broke and it was too late. The next morning we went to the health center and she took the morning after pill. The next few days were horrible."
> —senior, Indiana University

- Emergency contraception, or emergency birth control, is used to keep a woman from getting pregnant when she has had unprotected vaginal intercourse.

"Unprotected" can mean that no method of birth control was used. It can also mean that a birth control method was used but did not work—like a condom breaking. Other things can happen as well that put a woman at risk for getting pregnant. A woman may have forgotten to take her birth control pills. Emergency contraception should never be used as a regular method of birth control.

- Emergency contraception keeps a woman from getting pregnant by stopping ovulation (stopping the ovaries from releasing eggs that can be fertilized), fertilization (stopping the egg from being fertilized by the sperm), or implantation (stopping a fertilized egg from attaching itself to the wall of the uterus).
- There are two types of emergency contraception available to women in the United States: emergency contraceptive pills (ECPs), and intrauterine devices (IUDs). In most states, you need to see a healthcare provider to get either type of emergency contraception. The healthcare provider may take your medical history and do a urine pregnancy test, and will talk with you about which type of emergency contraception is best for you. You should never take ECPs that belong to another family member or friend. It is very important to first talk with a healthcare provider.

If the scare is real, and you're pregnant, don't rush any decisions. Some people have babies while in college, some choose not to. Talk to all the people around you. Make sure that you have a strong support system and people you trust and love in your corner. Talk your parents (if possible), someone in the counseling office, a sibling, an extremely trusted friend, a spiritual leader, a therapist, or a family planning counselor. Then, move forward. And if you're a woman reading this tip, contact the dad. He's part of this, too.

Bottom Line
If you have a pregnancy scare, don't freak out. Get help (then freak out).

Harlan's Tip Sheet

Naked People, Places, and Resources

Campus Health Center
- Doctors are standing (and sitting) by. Most college health services offer free or extremely inexpensive screenings for sexually transmitted diseases, contraceptive consultation, and pregnancy counseling—start at your health center and counseling center. The people on campus will be able to direct you to local resources.

National Resources

- National Herpes Resource Center and Hotline
  1-919-361-8488 (9 a.m. to 7 p.m. Eastern Time,
  Monday through Friday)
  Website: www.ASHASTD.org/STD-STI/Herpes.html
- National STD and AIDS Hotline
  1-800-227-8922 or 1-800-342-2437 (twenty-four hours
  a day, seven days a week)
- National Institute of Allergy and Infectious Diseases
  Website: www.NIAID.NIH.gov
  Twitter: www.Twitter.com/NIAIDNews
- National Library of Medicine—MEDLINEplus
  1-800-338-7657
  Website: www.MEDLINEplus.gov
  Twitter: www.Twitter.com/MEDLINEplus4You
- Centers for Disease Control and Prevention
  1-888-232-3228
  Website: www.CDC.gov
  Facebook: www.Facebook.com/CDC
  Twitter: www.Twitter.com/CDCgov
- The Alan Guttmacher Institute
  Website: www.Guttmacher.org
  Facebook: www.Facebook.com/Guttmacher
  Twitter: www.Twitter.com/Guttmacher
- The BACCHUS Network
  Website: www.SmarterSex.org
- The American College of Obstetricians and
  Gynecologists
  1-202-863-2518
  Website: www.ACOG.org

- The National Women's Health Information Center (NWHIC)
  1-800-994-WOMAN (1-800-994-9662)
  Website: www.WomensHealth.gov
  Facebook: www.Facebook.com/HHSOWH
  Twitter: www.Twitter.com/WomensHealth
- Emergency Contraception Hotline
  1-888-668-2528
  Website: EC.Princeton.edu
- Planned Parenthood Federation of America
  1-800-230-7526, 1-800-669-0156 (to order materials)
  Website: www.PlannedParenthood.org
- Sex Addicts Anonymous:
  Website: www.SAA-Recovery.org
- *The Naked Roommate*
  Website: www.NakedRoommate.com
  Facebook: www.Facebook.com/NakedRoommate
  Twitter: www.Twitter.com/NakedRoommate
- Help Me, Harlan!
  Website: www.HelpMeHarlan.com
  Facebook: www.Facebook.com/HelpMeHarlan
  Twitter: www.Twitter.com/HarlanCohen

Want to Get Tested?

- Contact your campus health center
- Contact your local hospital or caregiver
- Ask the pharmacist at your local drug store for over-the-counter options
- Visit: www.PlannedParenthood.org
- Visit: www.STDTestExpress.com

Drinking on Campus

10

Tapping the Keg of Truth

Dear Harlan,

I'm a nineteen-year-old college freshman. I have several very good friends that I've known for a long time, some since middle school. Even now, we seem to get along most of the time, but there is one thing that always sets me aside from them: I don't drink.

I don't criticize them for drinking. I just don't join in. When I become legal, I will drink socially, but I don't see a point in drinking just to get drunk. Lately, two of them, whom I consider my best friends, have been excluding me. When I ask them why, they tell me that they feel bad that I'm not drinking and they are. How do I let them know that I'm not judging them?

I've thought about just giving in and getting drunk with them, but alcoholism runs in my family and I want to be the exception to that disease. I realize that by drinking every once in a while, I will not become an alcoholic, but I think there are better ways to spend my nights than drinking and spending the whole next day hungover. Am I just being too conservative?

—Sober

Dear Sober,

Too conservative would be walking into their rooms when they drink and grabbing their beer, then pouring it on them while screaming at the top of your lungs, "Too drunk to get an umbrellaaaaa?!"

Your friends' excluding you just sucks for them—not only do they lose a friend, but also a designated driver. The colder the winter, the more they'll miss you and your sobriety.

Thank them for their concern, but tell them that it makes you more concerned to be excluded. Remind them that you don't care if they get drunk, and they shouldn't care if you don't. If anything, they have someone to drive them around, watch their back, and bail them out should they do something stupid. You're a great friend to have.

Make sure they also know that you honestly don't mind hanging out and drinking something nonalcoholic. Should they still exclude you, don't worry, you'll find other friends. Not everyone drinks on campus (or gets so drunk that other people who aren't drunk are a problem). If you find they're just too insecure and stupid, use your free time to get involved with clubs, activities, sports, organizations, religion, or anything to help you meet people.

It's sad that this is what's happening, but friends can grow apart. Don't become a drunk just to keep your friends.

Tip #73
Drinking on Campus

The Tip
If you can't handle drinking and going to school, then you're not responsible enough to do both. Accept the fact that you're not and pick one.

The Story
My future is really important to me. I wanted to party, but I also wanted to go to class. The further I went into my major, the more I realized that college is the most important thing to me. I've had friends that have had really low GPAs and quit because they partied too much. My one friend was only sober two days a week. She had to move back home to Wisconsin.

Time to Party, Or Not

Hours per week spent partying:

None: 33.4 percent

Less than 1 hour: 12.5 percent

1–2 hours: 15.1 percent

3–5 hours: 21.3 percent

6–10 hours: 12.3 percent

11–15 hours: 3.3 percent

16–20 hours: 1.1 percent

21–30 hours: 1 percent

Most of us are mature enough and figured it out—that you have to do your homework and go to classes to stay here. Your job is to go to classes. There are mornings when I wish I didn't have to go to school but I need to. I just can't live my life drinking. We'll be in the library in our going-out clothes, and I don't go out unless my homework is done. I go to all my classes, even if I'm hungover. If you're going to do it, then you have suffer the consequences.

Our rules for drinking:

- No skirts at parties—you can get violated too easily.
- Tequila makes us psycho—my friend got into a bar fight after drinking tequila.
- No drunken dials—it always leads to a call to an ex and making an ass out of yourself, so we take away the cell phones.
- No friends with benefits—you hook up after drinking and then have sex. We try to keep that rule, but sometimes we break it.

—junior, University of Nevada–Las Vegas

∗ ∗ ∗

If you're using this book as a beer coaster, you might have a drinking problem...

Some students drink a lot, some drink a little (wine with Ramen), others don't drink at all. Alcohol is available and accessible on college campuses. Whether a campus is wet (allows booze) or dry (no booze for you), you can find it if you want it. Yes, it's illegal if you're under twenty-one, but people find it. Unlike high school, your parents will not know what you do (unless you get so stupid you break into a bread delivery truck, pass out on a baguette, and need to beg them to bail you out of jail).

Let me shock you—most students don't get stupid drunk. More than you think don't drink at all. First-year students have this idea that college is a drunken free-for-all where everyone is wasted. As a result, new students come to college and start drinking to fit in. But the truth, according to the American College Health Association's 2014 report, is that 20 percent of students have never used alcohol. And another 13 percent of students had not consumed alcohol in the thirty days prior to taking the survey. This means that ONE-THIRD of students had NO alcohol within

> ## What Is Defined as a Drink:
> One beer—12-ounce beer
> (a 20-ounce beer is 1.75 drinks)
> One glass of wine—5 ounces of wine
> One shot of alcohol—1.25 ounces of 80 proof distilled spirits

the past thirty days. When students were asked how many of their peers have NEVER consumed alcohol, students guessed 3.2 percent were totally sober, when in reality, 20.1 percent had NEVER consumed alcohol. What students think is happening is NOT happening. It's a fact. When asked to estimate how many students had used alcohol in the last thirty days, respondents thought 94.9 percent of their peers were drinking, when the actual percentage was only 66.8 percent. Yes, some college students drink, but most college students don't drink to the point of being completely stupid. How much you decide to drink or not drink is up to you (assuming you're of age).

Reasons Why New Students Drink

- *It's a group thing.* Drinking is typically pretty social, and it's easy to hang out with people who are drinking. The way you are included is if you drink.
- *It's a social crutch.* A lot of people have a hard time talking to strangers while sober. They call it shy. I call it afraid of being judged.
- *It's a hookup thing.* While you can't talk to that guy or girl in class while sober, you can simulate having sex in 15 different positions on the dance floor.
- *It's an emotional crutch.* Going to college is a dramatic change, and big changes are naturally uncomfortable. Put people in an uncomfortable situation and give them the chance to drink, and they'll drink. But they don't need to drink to accomplish these same things.
- *It's an addiction thing.* Social drinking can become antisocial drinking, which can become an addiction. Students with a family history need to be extra careful (yes, alcoholism has been proven to run in families).

Naked note: Most college students don't love getting

Who's Drinking?

58.7 percent of first-year students didn't have a sip of beer. Only 7.6 percent of beer drinkers categorize themselves as frequent drinkers.

—CIRP's 2014 Your First College Year survey

wasted, vomiting, and doing things they regret. Students drink too much because they can't say what they think and do what they feel while sober. They hate rejection and can't stand feeling uncomfortable (been there, done it). Want to have it all without having to get wasted? Find your people, find your places, and be patient. Focus on what you want (not being wanted). Create a world of options. The more people and places in your life, the less likely you'll be to buckle to pressure and do things that aren't in alignment with your values (e.g., drugs and alcohol). Follow the five steps in Tip #54 and apply them to all the other risks you'll take during your college experience. It works.

Bottom Line

Not as many people drink as you might think. If you can't do it sober, don't do it drunk.

Tip #74
Slow Down, Don't Drink Too Fast

The Tip

If you are not an experienced drinker, go slowly and figure out your limits.

The Story

I was not much of the partying type in high school. I was what you'd call inexperienced. I went to a party my first week of school and made the mistake of consuming a lot of alcohol on an empty stomach. I had whatever my friends were having. We had fun for a while, until things started spinning. About two hours into the night, I was on my hands and knees puking my guts out. I didn't quite make it into the bathroom, but no one saw me spill it. I was sick. I was the opposite of holding my liquor. I didn't know how much or how fast I could drink. My friends from my floor and a buddy from high school were there to make sure that I got home. This was the night before I had the worst hangover of my life. As for the hangover—water, drink lots of water. Never again did I partake in the brew without first eating the food.

—junior, Eastern Connecticut State University

* * *

There's no rush (unless you're running to pee). Should you decide to drink, pace yourself and know what the hell you're drinking.

A common recipe for party punch is a combination of grain alcohol, water, and sugary fruit punch mix. Grain alcohol is about 190 proof, or 95 percent pure alcohol. For the most part, it's odorless, tasteless, and potent. Because it doesn't have a lot of taste, it's extremely dangerous when consumed—even in small quantities. Someone who doesn't weigh much

Sobering Stats

Assault: More than 696,000 students between the ages of 18 and 24 are assaulted by another student who has been drinking.

Injury: 599,000 students between the ages of 18 and 24 are unintentionally injured under the influence of alcohol.

Death: 1,825 college students between the ages of 18 and 24 die each year from alcohol-related unintentional injuries, including motor vehicle crashes.

—According to the NIDA, www.CollegeDrinkingPrevention .gov/StatsSummaries /Snapshot.aspx and doesn't eat much doesn't need to drink much to get wasted, and get sick. It happens all the time. *Do not drink the punch*. If you do decide to accept some concoction that someone hands to you, then just hold it. Let it spill or pour some of it down a sink. If you do drink it (bad idea), don't drink much. Drinking too much too fast will make you sick and create serious problems.

Another relatively new way to get wasted quickly is to consume Alcoholic Energy Drinks or mix alcohol with an energy drink. This isn't just a bad idea, it's dangerous. DO NOT MIX ALCOHOL AND ENERGY DRINKS!!! Why? Alcohol is a depressant. Energy drinks are stimulants. The two combined can mask the effects of the alcohol until it's too late. This can cause people to drink too much too fast and get dehydrated very quickly (stimulants can cause you to pee more). This combo can make you go from sober to sick in a matter of minutes. As a rule, avoid all energy drinks when consuming alcohol.

When drinking alcohol, it's hard to say how much is too much. Factors like gender (the same amount of alcohol will always affect a woman more than a man), body weight, full/empty stomach, medications or other drugs, an individual's mood, what someone drinks, one's tolerance (the amount it takes to feel the effects of alcohol), and how fast someone drinks all contribute. Even if you know what you're drinking, you might not know how you'll react to it.

Another problem with so many new students is that they're also new drinkers. According to the Higher Education Research Institute at UCLA, more than half of all new college students never drank in high school. This means they don't know their limits. And they start figuring out their limits during the most important and unstable time in college.

Come to college with three places in mind where you'll find connections. Arrive with people in your corner who you can turn to while sober. If you do these things, you don't have to drink to feel connected and supported.

> "The key to any social situation where drinking is involved is to know your limit."
> —junior, Indiana Purdue–Fort Wayne

Drinking too much too soon can mess you up. You can oversleep, sleep around (and that can consume your thoughts), and sleep through classes (if you make it to classes). And a crappy GPA your first semester can end up burying you. So, if you choose to drink, pace yourself.

Bottom Line
Sip. Slow. Don't drink the punch!

Tip #75
Not Everyone Is Drinking

The Tip
A lot of people drink, but that doesn't mean you have to.

The Story
My first semester I was determined not to drink, and I didn't. I was worried about what my sorority sisters would think, but they were cool with that. You learn to hold an empty beer can after a while—the problem is when someone takes it from you and wants to get you a new one, I just tell them that I'm taking a break…like for the rest of the night. I still don't drink and none of my friends seem to care. A lot of my friends do things that I don't feel comfortable doing, and I don't say anything to them. I don't feel like I'm missing out on any part of college life. My boyfriend respects that I don't drink. There are a lot of things to do besides get drunk. It just doesn't interest me.

—junior, Western Illinois University

Bonus Sober Story
Freshman year, I went to my first college party. I've been to Catholic and private school my entire life, and the past four years had been an all girls' school experience. I didn't drink, I didn't smoke, and it was fun until about 2 a.m., when the sheer volume of people around me becoming more and more intoxicated and unaware of their surroundings was almost too much to bear. It did become too much when I saw a close

friend of mine do something I never imagined he was even capable of. I found some sober friends and left. My system was in a literal shock. I didn't go to sleep until the sun came up, and my mind was just reeling with what I'd experienced, even though somewhere in the depths of my brain I knew such behavior was kind of the college party norm. I decided to shower and take a walk. When I couldn't even write in my journal I decided to go for a walk-in counseling session at the Health Center. The woman was kind and inviting, and I got to let it all out. She helped me realize that even though what had gone on was normal to a lot of other people who were used to partying, it was good that I recognized that it wasn't normal for me, and good that I took steps to take care of myself (like leaving early and going to the health center). I also learned that people have a lot of different sides of themselves, and one of those sides is the intoxicated one. I realized that my friend is the still the awesome person that he is despite the thing he did when he was drunk, but I also realized that I didn't want to be around him when he was drunk, and that's okay. I've learned that the people I hang out with at night can be a little different from the people I hang out with during the day.

> "I see the weight they've put on due to their alcoholic binges. Alcohol is a sure way to gain the infamous freshman 15."
> —freshman, University of Florida

—freshman, Tisch School of the Arts,
New York University

* * *

Some people look like they're drinking, but really, it's all just a big illusion. That guy holding the beer? It's filled with Mountain Dew. That guy pouring drinks from the keg? He's totally sober and likes playing bartender so he has something to do. That girl with the mixed drink? It's cranberry and water. Not as many people as you think are drinking the alcohol. But sure, some are.

If you don't want to drink, then don't drink. If you don't want to tell people that you don't drink, just hold a drink and disguise it. You can pour out the beer and fill the container with something that looks like what you're supposed to be drinking (ginger ale looks like beer, coke looks like rum and coke, grape juice looks like cheap wine). If the problem is holding something, then you can hold a cup with 7UP and a lime. If you want to hold something and don't have a cup, you can just hold yourself. If you don't want to hold yourself then you can hold a small pet, like a ferret, guinea pig, or mouse (all great for making conversation).

If someone gives you a hard time about drinking, think to yourself, *Man, this person is so uncomfortable in his or her social thong* (if you don't understand this metaphor turn to the Naked Pause after Tip #3). Then smile and move on. If you choose to engage further, say that you just don't drink. If that's not enough of an answer, then say you have a medical condition or you're on antibiotics. If that still doesn't work, let him or her know that you don't drink because you tend to vomit uncontrollably in the person's room who pressures

> ### Cocktail Napkin Fun Fact:
>
> Only 35 percent of incoming students drank beer occasionally or frequently as high school seniors—half the peak values seen in the late 1970s.
>
> —Higher Education Research Institute at UCLA

you to drink (that should do it). The point is that if you're underage or uninterested, you have a choice.

Don't make the wrong friends. If all your new friends drink, you might feel like you don't have a choice. But you do. This is why you need people. If you design a world in college where you have options (a few groups of friends, for instance), you can have the power to say what you feel and do what you want to do without feeling pressured or trapped.

As a rule, if you only make friends with people who drink all the time, chances are you'll begin to drink sooner or later. If you have a few groups of friends, you can hang out with all types of people. It's all about options.

Bottom Line
To recap: if you don't want to drink, hold a cup, hold yourself, or hold a small animal.

Tip #76
The Social Lubricant

The Tip
It's easier to hook up and do stupid things when you're drinking.

The Story
During spring break of my senior year, I went to Cancun with some friends. We usually would go with a group of guys, but this time it was just the girls. When we are with

guys, they kind of protect us. This time it was different. When we went to bars everyone was all over us. It was

"free drinks for girls all night." I was already questioning my current relationship and whether it was still something I wanted to continue. I was going to graduate and we were going to be living far apart. My friends met up with a group of guys. The one I met knew I had a boyfriend, but was pretty persistent. He made a move on me at the bar. My friends tried to stop him, but I didn't. We made out that night. The next day I felt *so* guilty. My boyfriend found out. He asked me if I had ever cheated. I told him I didn't mean to do it. When I'm drinking, I tend to do things I wouldn't normally do.

One more thing people do when drinking—some of my friends are drunk dialers. These are people who call the people they haven't talked to in a while. They will literally go through their cell phones and delete numbers if they go out drinking so they're not tempted to

"If you can't call someone you've hooked up with twenty-four to forty-eight hours after you've exchanged bodily fluids, because you're afraid of being annoying, it should never have happened."
—an occasional drinker

call them when drunk. After a few drinks, it's easier to call an ex-boyfriend or someone you're interested in. Bad idea.

—graduate student, College of Wooster

* * *

FLASHBACK: Dating works like this—put a group of people in a room long enough and they will hook up. Put them in a room with alcohol, and it happens that much faster—not a good thing. But it's true. WE HATE REJECTION. Alcohol numbs our fears. Here's how alcohol acts as a social lubricant:

Most people can't talk to someone they like while sober because they're too afraid of taking risks—again, we hate rejection. When people drink, they find the courage to do and say things they could never say or do when sober. It's easier for some people to take risks after drinking because the more they drink, the less they fear being judged. People call it being "less inhibited," but I call it being less aware, more tolerant, and not as afraid of rejection (to take risks sober, see Tip #54).

Drinking Games

Beer Pong, Flip Cup, Power Hour, Quarters, Connections, Drunk Jenga, Beirut, Moose, Horse Races, Circle of Death, Sink the Biz: it's all good "fun" until someone vomits, blacks out, falls over, gets naked in public, gets arrested, gets photographed (naked), makes an ass of him or herself, or leaves the room in an ambulance after being declared the winner.

The problem with the drunken relationship is that when two people can only connect after drinking, once sober it can leave one or both feeling awkward, uncomfortable, confused, shy, paranoid, and afraid of making mistakes. That's when partners start getting controlling, jealous, and insecure. Assuming most of your life is spent sober, you'll probably want to be comfortable with someone while sober. That's why it's so much better to connect with someone while sober, assuming you want the connection to last longer than one night or a few hours or minutes (even if you don't, you still have to worry about if what you're doing is consensual).

Now, if you find that you can't find the courage to approach someone while sober, and instead you're drinking or doing a shot to find your courage, turn to Tip #54 and look into training for the sport of taking risks. You can also read more about this on my website. Drunk love typically turns into a sobering and sad reality with bad morning breath.

If you can't do it sober, don't do it. A relationship that's built on drunken hookups is a relationship built on a sloppy foundation that can fall apart at any moment. If you can't do it, say it, or feel it when sober, you shouldn't be doing it at all.

> ### Regrets: They Have a Few
>
> Fact: 29.5 percent of college students admitted to doing something they regretted as a result of drinking alcohol over the last twelve months.
>
> —American College Health Association, Spring 2014

Bottom Line
Drunk people say and do stupid things. Sober people say and do stupid things too, but drunk people say and do more stupid things.

Tip #77
~~Safer~~ Unsafe Sex and Alcohol

The Tip
Don't be so drunk that you bring home a random guy, don't use protection, and then freak out when you realize what happened.

The Story

We had had a party at our house. I drank way too much with my sorority sisters, to the point that I was blacking out. I then went to a bar with some close friends. I proceeded to drink even more. I don't remember anything, just snapshots of the night. You think you're taking in everything you see, but in reality, you're only taking in ten minutes of the night. While waiting for my friends outside, I bumped into some random guy. We started making out. I brought him home. We ended up having sex. My friends thought it was funny. Once you're not a virgin, your friends are not going to stop you. A few hours later, I just kind of snapped out of it and then freaked out. I kicked him out. I had some alone time where I just bawled. We didn't use a condom and I was freaking out. I went to the health center and got emergency contraception. The next day, everyone wanted to know what happened. I denied that it happened because I was so embarrassed. More than anything, I'm disappointed with myself. I let one night of intoxication almost ruin me.

—junior, Alfred University

Fact: Sex and Cocktails

22.3 percent of college men and 19.4 percent of college women reported having unprotected sex as a consequence of consuming alcohol in the last twelve months.

—ACHA-NCHA-II Executive Summary Spring 2014

* * *

If you're going to do it, then don't do it drunk. When you're drunk, you get sloppy and then you can mishandle the equipment. Let me explain...

It's a night where you meet that someone "special." You and the object of your affection find a cozy place to get more comfortable. You are in a deep kiss, bodies pressing, arms exploring, and hearts beating. You think to yourself, *Mmmm, this is oh-so-good, but…* This is the "but" that tells you that you have no clue who your partner has been with or what your partner may or may not have in his or her pants. I'm talking about herpes, genital warts, chlamydia, syphilis, gonorrhea, HIV…the list goes on and on. The action is too hot to stop and have your partner fill out a sexual résumé. Plus, you're too drunk to really care and it all feels "Mmmm, oh-so-good." You let it go. And you also let the rest of your clothing go. Now you're wearing nothing but each other's hands. Things start moving, churning, yearning, and grinding You decide that the moment is right to have sex. While you're drunk, you're not too drunk to remember to use a condom (assuming you can find a condom). But being so drunk, you and your partner fumble with the condom. First it goes on wrong, then it goes on right (but it could have sperm on it now). You forget to pinch the top of the condom to allow a reservoir for the ejaculate. While you're protected, you're not really all that protected. Besides, a condom can't protect you from exposure to some STDs/STIs. The sex happens, the sex ends, and the problems begin. One minute you're screaming, "Ohhh GOD," the next day you're screaming, "Help me, Harlan!" (No, I'm not the one in the bed, I'm the one people write to with their problems in the morning.) The condom broke, fell off, or disappeared.

According to the National Institute on Alcohol Abuse and Alcoholism, four hundred thousand students between the ages of eighteen and twenty-four have had unprotected sex, and more than one hundred thousand students between the ages of eighteen and twenty-four report having been too intoxicated to know if they consented to having sex. Those statistics are sobering (I know, I also hate it when people use that analogy when talking about alcohol, but it's true). This doesn't even factor in those who use protection and use it incorrectly, or use it correctly and still find themselves dealing with STDs/STIs. And emotionally, it's all so draining. When things go bad, you end up putting so much time and so much energy into these issues. Talk about time mismanagement. Save yourself the trouble and do it sober.

Bottom Line
When you drink it's easy to fumble a condom, go too far, or just get messy, leading you to possible sexual souvenirs or pregnancy scares.

Tip #78
Sexual Assault and Alcohol

The Tip
Watch out when you go drinking; you never know who is watching and what they may put in your drink.

The Story
The first night I actually got to go out and drink, I thought I knew the guys I was with, but I didn't. One of the guys put something in my drink. Usually, you can't taste roofies

or other date rape drugs—I sure didn't. I didn't remember the night—my friends told me the next day how I acted and who I left with. But I do remember the next morning. I woke up and I knew what had happened. I went to class and couldn't concentrate—all I could do was cry. I am so thankful to have friends that would listen. If it ever happens to you, most colleges have student health centers and they really helped me out.

—freshman,
University of Tennessee

* * *

FACT· Drunk people can't legally consent.

Women (and some men) often write to me or come up to me after a speaking event to say that they are survivors of sexual assault. Rape and attempted rape happens. Women share their stories with me all the time (men too). They tell me about the secrets, the shame, the confusion. Some think it's their fault that it happened. Some think that they did something to bring it on. No. Never. It's just not true.

> **Tragic Fact:**
> More than 97,000 students between the ages of 18 and 25 are victims of alcohol-related sexual assault or date rape.
>
> —National Institute on
Drug and Alcohol Abuse
>
> The National College Women Sexual Victimization Study estimated that between 1 in 4 and 1 in 5 college women experience completed or attempted rape during their college years. For more info on sexual assault, see Tip #101.

No survivor of rape, whether sober or drunk, is ever at fault. Never, never, never. It's not your fault! Please don't feel ashamed.

The ugly reality is that approximately one in four to one in five college women will be the victim of attempted rape or rape by the time they graduate (just as ugly, men are also victims, though at a lower rate). Most survivors know their attacker.

When people drink, they become less inhibited. They can be bad listeners. They can become aggressive, and far more dangerous. And they don't always take no for an answer. Sadly, you can't give anyone the benefit of the doubt when that person has been drinking. The reality is that **90 percent of sexual assaults involve alcohol, and 84 percent of the time, the assailant is someone the victim already knows. It's one night that can change your life forever**.

The National College Women Sexual Victimization Study estimated that between 1 in 4 and 1 in 5 college women experience completed or attempted rape during their college years. I know I keep mentioning this stat, but it's something you need to remember. And for the men reading this, yes, you can be survivors of sexual assault

Sexual Assault Facts

- Over 90 percent of all sexual assaults involve alcohol.
- 84 percent of victims know their assailants.
- 90 percent of sexual assault victims are female; 10 percent are male.
- Sexual assault also occurs in gay and lesbian relationships. The stigma of being gay or lesbian makes it even harder for these victims to come forward.

—U.S. Department of Justice

Bystander Intervention: Just Stop It, Now!

When you see a potentially dangerous situation unfolding before your eyes, intervene. Get your friends involved. Get campus police involved. Just get involved. YOU can prevent sexual assault before it happens. More on this in Tip #101.

too. For more info on sexual assault, see Tip #101.

Please be careful. Watch out for your friends. Watch out for yourself. If you're drinking, never drink from an open beverage that you have not prepared and had your eye on the entire night. Hang on to your drinks, even if you go the bathroom (a great time for someone to slip roofies in drinks) I've had several people tell me stories about this during my research for this book.

As for going home with hookups, one girl on a campus I visited told me the rule that she and her friends follow—no one goes home with anyone who has been drinking. They live by it. For the men and women who are aggressors—if you're with someone who is not sober enough to consent to sex, it's not consensual sex. If someone says no, listen. If you don't, it's called rape. It doesn't matter what *you* call it.

For those who are survivors of sexual assault—get help immediately. Call your local police, a campus sexual assault hotline, the Rape, Abuse, and Incest National

"Two months into their relationship, my best friend and her boyfriend went to a party and she got really drunk, so drunk that she could barely walk and he had to carry her back to the dorm. Instead of bringing her to her room or the common area, he brought her to his room and locked the door. She was uncomfortable but kept saying to herself, 'He won't do anything.' He did... She started experiencing PTSD symptoms. She was obsessed about keeping the door locked, and she couldn't sleep. She revealed to me what had happened to her two days later...I called the emergency mental health counselor that moment, and skipped all my classes the next day to be with her for her checkup and initial counseling...All that mattered was making her feel safe. It's been a month and she's still recovering, but I know she's doing much better than she would have if she had waited to talk to someone. I couldn't have handled it on my own."

—freshman, Tufts University

Network (RAINN) hotline (there's now online crisis support available at www.RAINN.org), or go directly to the emergency room after the assault. Tell the nurse and doctor what happened. They can collect evidence using a rape kit that you can use later, should you decide to take legal action. And again, please never think it's your fault. And you're definitely not alone.

FACT: Having sex with someone who is too drunk to say yes or no can be considered rape, whether you think it's rape or not.

More than seventy thousand students between the ages of eighteen and twenty-four are victims of alcohol-related sexual assault or date rape. And that stat only reflects reported incidents—who knows what the real numbers are. As a result, the government has started to take action and help college students.

Check out www.NotAlone.gov to find resources and support services. Not Alone was launched in connection with the White House Task Force to Protect Students from Sexual Assault. The Task Force was established on January 22, 2014. The Not Alone website is a place to learn your rights, get help, read stories, and know that you're never alone.

Bottom Line

There's a 100 percent chance that someone reading this will be (or has already been) a victim of sexual assault. Please, know that you're never alone, and please get help.

Tip #79
Don't Be So Stupid That You Accidentally Kill Yourself

The Tip
If you drink, at least make sure there is someone sober around.

The Story
My freshman year in college, a bunch of us went out to a party sometime in the first couple of weeks. This one guy, who was one of our friends, was drunk out of his mind—just belligerent. He was screaming at everyone and being really ignorant. Everyone got mad at him. A couple of us were designated drivers. He didn't want to leave the party and freaked out when we drove him home and got back to the dorms. He was screaming at everyone, and throwing punches. We took him back up to his room. He went inside and closed the door. We thought he'd be fine. A half hour later, someone was on my floor talking about how he was in the hallway screaming again, but went back into his room and passed

> "The first week of school I found out that my friend was diabetic. He played soccer with me and was always monitoring his insulin levels during practice. One night, he drank heavily and wasn't paying attention to his insulin level at all. When I got back home, I found out that he was passed out in the middle of the hallway and I called the paramedics. When they got there we informed them that he was diabetic. They asked what his insulin level should be—for some reason I remembered what it was supposed to be. They used the information to save his life."
> —sophomore, Carthage College

out. When I heard this, I went to see if he was all right. I opened the door and saw him lying on his back with vomit all over his mouth. He had thrown up and had passed out. It was all in his mouth and he was definitely not breathing. I started screaming for anyone to come and get help. I then stuck my hand in his mouth and was pulling out the vomit. It was so disgusting. I turned him over onto his stomach and was retching while trying to clear it all away. He then came to and started choking. The paramedics arrived and took him to the hospital where he had his stomach pumped. When he was well enough to leave, they arrested him. The judge near our school is hard when it comes to underage drinking. The guy had to spend the night in jail to sober up. We bailed him out the next morning. He was so embarrassed. Since then I have never seen him that drunk again.

—senior, Valparaiso University

***

My roommate during my junior year of college almost died. You've never heard about him. There's no reason for you to know. Unless he died on campus, incidents like this don't make the headlines. Thankfully, he survived.

It all started after a party one Friday night. He had consumed just enough alcohol to make him vomit in the middle of the night and throw up blood. He didn't think much of it because this had happened to him once before. As the day progressed, he looked worse and worse and worse. When we saw him in the afternoon, he looked green. He said that he wanted to take a nap and sleep it off. My friend and I didn't think that was a good idea. That's when we told him, either we drive you to the hospital or we call an ambulance. At first he resisted, but then he backed down and was taken to the hospital. Upon arrival, he started to pass out. He was then rushed into the emergency room for an emergency surgery. It turns out that he had ruptured his esophagus when he vomited and had been hemorrhaging throughout the night and day. He almost died. Luckily, he made it through surgery and was back at school a few days later. His parents were very appreciative. They bought me a shirt from the Gap to thank me. He survived, and I got a new shirt—a happy ending for everyone.

Do whatever you want to do, but be smart about being stupid. Don't accidentally kill yourself or stand by quietly while a friend kills himself or herself. If you're vomiting and you see blood, go to the doctor. If you're feeling sick beyond sick—get help. If you see that your friend is unconscious, call the paramedics. They can tell you what to look for to see if it's a true emergency. Just call them. Take care of yourself and then take care of the people around you. If you see that your friend is drunk and wants to drive home, stop him or her. If your friend won't listen, call the police and anonymously report him or her. If your friend is mixing drugs and alcohol, stop him or her. If you see that your friend is drunk and drinking a fifth of vodka from a beer bong, stop him or her. When a friend is too drunk and starts being

> **Fact: Every Year Students Die as a Result of Alcohol and Drug Abuse**
>
> In 2014, college students died as a result of bar fights, drunk driving accidents, alcohol-related hazing, drowning, drug overdoses, shootings, and being left by friends to "sleep it off." Take care of yourself and take care of one another.

stupid, you need to be the smart one, or your friend might end up the dead one or the one in the emergency room. If a friend won't listen to you, enlist other friends, parents, professionals, and even the police. Don't stop until the friend stops.

Bottom Line

If you're going to be stupid, don't be so stupid that you accidentally kill yourself or me or someone reading this. If your friends are going to be stupid, don't let them be so stupid they accidentally kill themselves.

Tip #80
Drinking and Driving

The Tip

Even one or two beers can screw you up and follow you around. It can also cost you a lot of money. I've seen this happen to many people.

The Story

A couple of friends and I went to a bar. They were having dinner. It was five miles from my school. I drove there with two twenty-one-year-olds. I had three beers in a little over an hour. So, you know, they all had the same beer. I thought I was fine to drive. So, I got in the car and was driving back home. To get to Elon, you have to cross over a railroad track. Of course, there was a train. To my left was a municipal building and there was a side road. It didn't seem like a good idea to cut through a police station after drinking a couple of beers, but I did. Of course, there were two police officers standing in front of the building. One motioned for me to stop. He said, "Are you lost, son?" I said, "No, sir, I'm just cutting through." Then he asked if I'd been drinking. Then I said, "Yes, sir." I didn't think I could lie. He asked if I was twenty-one years old. I told him I was twenty. Before I knew it I was out of the car and he had me by the arm guiding me into the police station. He unlocked the door and put me inside. My heart was beating out of my chest. He sat me down and gave me a Breathalyzer. The first time, I blew .03. I did it again ten minutes later and it was the same exact thing. Since I was drinking and I was underage, he could have taken my license and put me in jail. We would have never been caught had we not tried to take a short-cut. Since I was cooperating, he didn't arrest me, but he gave me a DUI (the same charge that would have gotten me arrested). Two years later, it still hasn't been resolved. It cost me about $1,000 for a lawyer, and I've been to court eight times. Now I'm twenty-one years old, I have a job, and I still have this unresolved issue that shows up everywhere I go. The employer did a report for an internship—have you ever pled guilty or been convicted of a misdemeanor—I thought that I wasn't convicted. A couple weeks later I was called and this was discussed. I need to disclose it. You never want this to happen again—it never goes away.

—sophomore, Elon University

* * *

You are stupid, selfish, and deserve to go to jail. When people tell me they drive drunk, I want to yell at them. I have to bite my lip (usually it's during a professional situation). I despise sharing the road with you. You might kill me, a loved one, friends, family, or your passengers. You might injure, maim, or kill yourself. And buzzed and high driving is just as dumb. Please, just don't drive at all if you're going to party. I beg of you, my family pleads with you, and all the people you might hurt, injure, or kill ask you. And no, I'm not being dramatic. We all know someone who has been impacted by drunk driving. We can stop it.

As for you people letting someone drunk drive you around—I know—it's so much easier not to bother asking the person driving you how much they've had to drink. I know—it's only a few blocks. I know—it seems so much easier to assume it will all be fine. But it's not easier, because should you run a stop sign, hit someone, get hit, swerve into oncoming traffic, brake too late, react too slowly, hit some ice, run into a tree, or just be lucky enough to only get pulled over and arrested, it will be hell. That's what can happen in a few blocks. A few blocks and a lifetime filled with regret.

The truth is that most college students do not drive after having even one sip of alcohol—to be exact, the ACHA-NHSA 2014 survey indicated that 78.8 percent hadn't driven under the influence of any alcohol in the previous 30 days. And really, there isn't any reason to drive drunk. Between buses, taxis, Uber, campus shuttle services, walking, and sober friends who can do the driving, there's no reason to drive drunk. Besides the safety issues, a felony charge for drinking and driving can follow you around for the rest of your life. Drinking and driving is one of those things that you wish you could go back in time and never let yourself do.

Assuming you're not reading this while awaiting trial for DUI, this is your chance to not get into a situation where you know you'll be filled with terrible regret and possibly do time in prison. I meant it when I mentioned it in the tip before—if you're in a situation where someone drives drunk, don't just look the other way. Call the police and report them. Wait

a few minutes and then drive by your friend pulled over on the road to see if there's anything you can do to help. A true friend will not ignore drunk driving.

And really, you can still get where you want to go without driving. A lot of campuses have free driving services that pick up students and drop them off—no questions asked. The idea is to provide a safe place to live and go to classes.

Bottom Line

Before driving drunk, think about the people you could possibly kill on the road and their families (that could include your grieving family), then think about jail time if you survive. It's so much easier to walk or to call for a ride.

Tip #81
Still Hungover...

The Tip
Drink water and rehydrate. It's cheap and it works.

The Story
As an expert in the art of the hangover, I'd say don't drink more just to drink more. Switch to water before the room spins. If not, you'll fall over the edge and pay for it the next day. Me, I have the worst hangovers. It's a sandwich of nausea. I can't eat. I barely keep my head up. It hits me in the morning or afternoon,

> **"I never found a hangover cure. I was miserable. I drank tons of water."**
> **—grad, Northwestern University**

depending on when I wake. Coffee doesn't work. The caffeine makes me urinate and lose liquid. The secret is hydration. I've found sports drinks to be helpful. I've tried protein shakes, but the consistency makes me gag. The best attempt to cure the hangover is sleep and water. Actually, that would be water and then sleep. I drink a glass of water before I go to bed. If I'm sick when I wake up, I drink another glass of water and then keep sleeping. I try to eat. If I'm not too sick, I'll stay up. The better advice is to not drink so much that you get a hangover in the first place. Drinking bad, very bad.

—senior, University of Southern California

* * *

A hangover is the headache, nausea, and aftereffect of drinking too much beer or liquor.

When it comes to curing the college hangover, a lot of people will tell you a lot of different things. Everyone has a "magic cure." There are even entire websites that share ways to move beyond the pain that comes after the party—from treatment with Borscht (beet juice) to a tuna hoagie to dill pickles to hot chamomile to cold milk. Whatever concoction you try is a waste of time, because time (again, not to be confused with the spice thyme) is the only magic cure that will help your hangover. Should you drink and find yourself feeling not so great when the buzz becomes a banging headache, drink some water (to help dehydration) and watch the clock. That said, if you're feeling lower than low and not getting any better, don't hesitate to call your doctor or take a trip to the emergency room.

If you get really desperate and start frantically searching for one of those miracle cures for your hangover, make sure that you read the fine print on the page. On two websites that claim to cure hangovers, the fine print (below) says it all (but really, most people are too drunk to focus on the fine print).

THESE STATEMENTS HAVE NOT BEEN EVALUATED BY THE FOOD AND DRUG ADMINISTRATION. THIS PRODUCT IS NOT INTENDED TO DIAGNOSE, TREAT, CURE, OR PREVENT ANY DISEASE.

If you're reading this, thinking, *Listen, the only way to cure a hangover is to drink some more alcohol*, you should put down your cocktail and jump over to Tip #82. You, my friend, are someone who is in serious need of some help.

Bottom Line
Drink too much and you'll pay and pray later (when people are sick, they tend to turn to a higher power for healing).

Tip #82
You Might Be an Alcoholic If...

The Tip
It's hard to know how bad your drinking problem is because there are so many times where everyone is drinking. Listen to your friends. They see what you're doing when you're too drunk to remember.

The Story
I have friends who I think have drinking problems. They seriously drink every night. They can go for hours. On a home game weekend, they're pretty much wasted or close to it for two days straight. They think it's not a problem because there are other people who are drunk with them. It's not like they're sitting in a room alone taking shots. I've mentioned something to them and then they say I'm the one with the problem. They think because they pass all of their classes, there isn't any problem, but it's possible to pass classes and still have an addiction. One of them has even told me that alcoholism runs in his family.

The problem I've seen is that college is filled with so many people who drink and party regularly that it's a part of life for them, and it's hard to tell when it's really a problem. Other than passing their classes, they're unreliable, irresponsible, they get in fights, and have a different girl every week. They drink all night to get wasted and miss at least a class a week. They say it's normal. I call it being in denial.

—senior, University of Georgia

***

If you are reading this particular tip while sipping a beer after promising yourself that you are done drinking, you might have a problem. If you're reading this in the morning while craving alcohol, you might have a problem (that means no vodka in your morning coffee). If you're reading while drinking several alcoholic beverages because your tolerance has increased, you might have a problem. If you find that you drink more than you plan on drinking, can't seem to control yourself, drink to relieve symptoms of nausea, sweating, shakiness, and anxiety, then you have a problem. If you find yourself falling into any of the above categories while reading this tip, you might be alcohol dependent. You can deny it all you want, but denial is a sure sign that you're in trouble. If your friends think

> ### Alcohol Abuse and Dependence
>
> 31 percent of college students met criteria for a diagnosis of alcohol abuse and 6 percent for a diagnosis of alcohol dependence in the past twelve months, according to questionnaire-based self-reports about their drinking.
>
> —ACHA-NCHA II Executive Summary Spring 2012

there's a problem, there's a good chance they're right. So, if you do have a problem, and can admit you have a problem, you can do one of two things. You keep drinking, or you can get help.

As for figuring out when you or someone you know has a problem, answering the following seven questions can help you find out:

○ Have you ever felt you should cut down on your drinking?

○ Have people annoyed you by criticizing your drinking?

○ Do you need to drink more to get drunk or feel the desired effect?

○ Have you ever felt bad or guilty about your drinking?

○ Have you ever had a drink first thing in the morning to steady your nerves or to get rid of a hangover?

○ Do you ever drive when you've been drinking?

○ Have you ever missed class or work because of your drinking?

One "yes" = possible alcohol problem.
More than one "yes" = highly likely that a problem exists.
If you want to get help, there is so much available. Most colleges have alcohol treatment counselors. If your campus doesn't have a counselor, the counselors in the health center

can refer you. The best part about being an alcoholic is that there is so much help and support available to help control your alcoholism. There is counseling. There are support groups. There is even medication.

And in case you didn't know, alcoholism runs in families. If you have family that has a history, you might be a part of family history about to repeat itself.

Bottom Line

College offers lots of opportunities. Unfortunately, one is to become an alcoholic.

Harlan's Tip Sheet

Naked People, Places, and Resources

Resources on or Near Campus

- Campus Health Center
- Alcohol counselors on campus
- Local hospital

Resources and Websites

- Alcoholics Anonymous
  Website: www.AA.org
- Al-Anon/Alateen

Call 1-888-4AL-ANON, Monday through Friday, 8 a.m. to 6 p.m. ET for meeting information.
Website: www.AL-ANON-ALATeen.org
- National Sexual Assault Hotline
1-800-656-HOPE (1-800-656-4673)
Website: www.RAINN.org
Facebook: www.Facebook.com/RAINN01
Twitter: www.Twitter.com/RAINN01
- National Domestic Violence Hotline
1-800-799-SAFE (1-800-799-7233)
Website: www.thehotline.org
Facebook: www.Facebook.com/NationalDomestic ViolenceHotline
Twitter: www.Twitter.com/NDVH
- The Rape Abuse & Incest National Network, 24-Hour Online Hotline
1-800-656-HOPE (1-800-656-4673)
Website: www.RAINN.org
Facebook: www.Facebook.com/RAINN01
Twitter: www.Twitter.com/RAINN01
- The BACCHUS Network
Website: www.SmarterSex.org
Website: www.FriendsDriveSober.org
Facebook: www.Facebook.com/TheBACCHUSNetwork
Twitter: www.Twitter.com/BACCHUSNetwork
- Centers for Disease Control and Prevention
Website: www.CDC.gov
Facebook: www.Facebook.com/CDC
Twitter: www.Twitter.com/CDCgov
- National Institutes on Alcohol Abuse and Alcoholism
Website: www.CollegeDrinkingPrevention.gov

- Substance Abuse and Mental Health Services Administration
  Website: www.SAMHSA.gov
  Facebook: www.Facebook.com/SAMHSA
  Twitter: www.Twitter.com/SAMHSAgov

You can find a list of additional resources at www.HelpMeHarlan.com and www.NakedRoommate.com.

Drugs on Campus ⑪

The Smoking, Snorting, and Pill-Popping Truth

Dear Harlan,

In November, my friends and I were heading back to campus at 1:30 in the morning after a night out. We were pulled over. We were immediately taken out of the car and searched. Unfortunately, I had a joint in my pocket and was whisked away to the police department.

I'm now two months into my one-year probation, but my parole officer informed me that my arrest might not clear my record by the time I apply for a job. It is sad that my future may be affected by such a meaningless and harmless crime, but it can happen to anyone. Word to the wise: if you are in a car and you have drugs, you are in danger. You do not have any rights, because a determined cop will always find what you have in your pocket.

—F. Justice

Dear F. Justice,

I appreciate the word to the wise, but I don't think the wise would have joints in their pockets. It should be a word to the really high people who get stupid and forget things...

This isn't about a determined cop. It's about a careless guy (you) packing a joint, taking a risk, and getting busted. This doesn't just happen in cars; it happens at parties, on the way to parties, in residence halls—all over. Getting arrested is the ultimate in coming down. Thanks for the note.

Tip #83
About Drugs on Campus

The Tip
If your closest friends smoke pot, chances are you'll cave in and smoke, too.

The Story
I'm not a smoker or a drinker—never have been one. I had a roommate I knew from high school. She was so against smoking pot when she got to college. I think in high school she was even in organizations against smoking tobacco. So this girl from high school, she met someone at orientation who smoked pot. She was like, "I'll never be in the room with her." She vowed to never smoke. The next year, I moved out. She then moved in with her friend from orientation (the one

who smokes). That's when we started drifting apart. Last I heard she started smoking pot, too. I was shocked when I found out. I didn't think she would smoke. I was just shocked. I know her whole family. I'm sure they have no idea. That's all I know. I really don't talk to her anymore.

—junior, Florida Gulf Coast University

* * *

BIG NEWS since the last edition: recreational use of marijuana has become legal in several states. MORE BIG NEWS: pot can still get you expelled and arrested on campus. Federal laws rule college campuses. I know you're thinking, "But I have a medical marijuana card!" Think again. Most campuses still don't allow it (but check with your school).

When I visit college campuses to speak, I ask students about drugs on campus. It's not the first question I ask (that would be weird, especially if my follow-up question were, "Just curious, where can I find some?").

The students typically fall into two categories—those students who haven't seen any drugs on campus, and those who see it on occasion. It's not like anyone is forcing anyone to do it, but it's around if you're looking. Generally, pot is the most common drug

"It is a creed amongst smokers that pot should be shared and enjoyed amongst others; it is a very communal thing. Some may say that marijuana is harmful, some may say that it is harmless, but I say it is beneficial, although I think that moderation is important."

—recent grad, Rutgers University

(although alcohol is used most commonly on college campuses and is technically a drug). Now cocaine and meth are popping up a lot. I'm also hearing about Molly and students sharing, selling, or buying their own personal prescription drugs—Adderall tends to be the most common.

No one will force you to use drugs, but people might invite you.

Oh and all this can kill you. Mixing Aderall and alcohol is way too common, and it's not safe. Whether you accept the invitation or hang with people who use drugs is your call, but if you hang out with them, there's a great chance you'll end up using, too. And if you think that you'll never use, even if you hang out with people who do, you're probably wrong.

The typical drug story is: you go to college vowing never to do drugs. Then you have a roommate or some new friends or a friend from high school who start partying a little bit. Let's say it's smoking marijuana. You don't agree with it. You don't like it. You are still never going to do it. No one pressures you, but the more you hang out with your friend and the people who are using, the less it starts to bother you. It might be a month, a year, maybe two years or three years—over time, you become desensitized. Like sitting in the middle of the manure factory, the smell and lifestyle choices become the norm. And then, one day, you decide to try it. It's not a big deal. You like it. Then you try it again. You then become a recreational user. Another year goes by and you've started to wake and bake (smoking up in the morning) and progressed to trying harder drugs. By then it's no big deal to do a little cocaine, ecstacy, or meth (yes, college students do meth). Other times, you just end up dating someone who does harder drugs and then pulls you into the experiences. Some people can manage their lives and stay in control, but even if you think you're in control of your drug use, you open yourself up to getting arrested, hurt, or expelled—risks that can mess up your life (it's not pretty having to check the "Have you ever been convicted of a felony?" box "Yes"). Oh, and you can accidentally die too.

Bottom Line

You can choose to do drugs or not to be around drugs. If you find that drugs choose to be around you, then you're probably on drugs, because drugs can't really make choices.

Tip #84
How to Avoid Them

The Tip

If you stay away from the people who do drugs, drugs will not be a problem.

The Story

No one has ever forced me to get high or roll (take ecstasy). My friends ask me if I want a bong hit and I'll just say, "Nah." They're just like, "Cool, more for me." When my friends party, and not all of them do, I'll sometimes hang out. When the bong, pipe, joint, or

> **Drug Fact:**
>
> Once you sell drugs, even if it's 0.1 ounce of marijuana to a friend, you will forever be a drug dealer.
>
> —anonymous

apparatus they've designed comes by me, I'll wave it off or just pass it along. I don't feel like I need to get high because it's there. I just don't like it. I also have a job where drug testing is done and I'm not about to let that get me in trouble. Sometimes I'll have a beer or two if I'm hanging out. In my college career, I've never seen anyone I've been around forced to do drugs. Everyone I've ever seen is an extremely eager and willing participant. If someone wants to avoid drugs they just have to pass it along or say no. Most of the people offering it end up too high to care what anyone else does or doesn't do.

—senior, University of Southern California

* * *

Drugs can typically be found in Colombia, Jamaica, and the shoe box in the closet under the dirty clothes of the guys who sell them on campus to make a few extra bucks. Once in a while, you might stumble across them. If you want to find them, you can ask around, and people will tell you where they're hiding. But you have to make an effort.

If you're someone who doesn't want to do drugs, then avoid asking people where you can find drugs and avoid hanging out with friends who do drugs. If that's just not possible, then at least avoid your friends while they're using drugs, because if you hang around people who do drugs all the time, you'll most likely end up doing them too. It's like going to the national buffalo wing tournament—it's hard not to sample some of the wings when that's all anyone is eating. And really, even if you don't end up using, then you'll end up being in places where a lot of people are using. You might end up at a party in a dorm room or in a car where someone is using. You could end up in a situation where people are in possession of or trafficking drugs. Then if the party gets busted, and if you're near the drugs, your life goes to hell. The best way to avoid drugs is to avoid the people who do them or sell them.

> ### Prevalence of Various Drugs for Twelfth Graders (cont'd.)
>
> - Inhalants: 2.5 percent used in past year; 6.9 percent used in lifetime
> - MDMA: 4 percent used in the past year; 7.1 percent used in lifetime
> - LSD: 2.2 percent used in past year; 3.9 percent used in lifetime
>
> —National Institute on Drug Abuse, 2013 (http://www.DrugAbuse.gov/Trends-Statistics/Monitoring-Future/Monitoring-Future-Study-Trends-in-Prevalence-Various-Drugs)

The first few months of college can be unstable at times—the temptation to experiment with drugs can be stronger when things aren't the most stable. Bonding over a bong or shared joint could seem alluring. It's tempting to want to party with people who invite you to hang out. It's hard to say no, especially when you don't have a lot of friends on campus and want to be included. But if you start hanging out with these kinds of people, this is what you'll do together. Getting wasted will become part of what you do. If you don't want to use, but you still want to be friends with these people, then meet up with them after they're done partying. And make sure they're going to a place where drugs won't be the main attraction (and that you're not in the car or close to the drugs if the cops show up).

Bottom Line
Avoid drugs by avoiding the people who do drugs, and avoid traveling to the countries where they grow drugs (a summer internship at a Colombian cocaine farm—extremely bad idea). Oh, and for the guy from Colombia who wrote to me upset that I mentioned Colombia and drugs, it's also not a good idea to spend the summer interning with a Mexican drug cartel or on an opium ranch in Afghanistan (better, right?).

Tip #85
Why Not to Do Drugs

The Tip
Drugs take up too much time—there's finding them, doing them, talking about them, and then recovering from them the next day.

The Story
I don't have the time to waste by doing drugs. I don't have the time to get high and then to come down. I don't

have time to worry about random drug testing. I don't get enough out of it to make it worth it. I'd rather be sober. I'm trying to get a decent GPA, plus I'm also working twenty hours a week to help pay for school, and I'm in a relationship that's better than any drug I've tried. I only see him a few times a week. He's not a real "drug." I've been finding that my friends who are into drugs really waste a lot of their time doing them, talking about them, and then worrying about what they did while on them. I'm as happy as my drug friends—even happier, I think. It's never interested me. From what I've seen, drugs are for boring people who don't have much else to do. There are so many other things I'd rather do with my time. Maybe that's just me.

> "My girlfriend dumped me because of my obsessive pot smoking habit and the fact that I pawned some of her stuff for pot."
> —senior, University of Portland

—junior, New York University

* * *

The two most honest reasons why I never got into drugs in college:

Smoking pot makes you hungry and it makes you eat a lot of carbs late at night. As an over-weight kid my first two years of high school (I was 5 feet 2 inches tall and 192 pounds in high school), I hated being overweight. It would always put me in a terrible mood. My pants got tight and then I was miserable.

> "Guys who do drugs are boring. It's sad that they have nothing better to do than waste their time, energy, and money on something that's so draining and lacks meaning. I have a weird issue with drug users."
> —recent grad, University of Missouri

Pot might have zero calories, but everything consumed after you smoke is packed with flavor. Getting high makes you eat. Usually it's eating late at night and you get tired and go to sleep. The more you eat late at night, the easier it is to pack on the pounds.

The other reason I never got into drugs was a fear of dying. Seriously, I was afraid I'd try cocaine and die the first time. I thought I might get some bad ecstasy and possibly freak out and die (I've had friends who have had bad trips from bad pills). The big problem with dying from experimenting (it happens) is that it puts my parents in an awkward position. They then have to explain that Harlan was only experimenting when he overdosed. They'd have to tell friends and family, "It was his first time, really it was." Of course, no one would believe that I was just experimenting. They'd think I was a junkie. My parents would then have to keep explaining to everyone that I was honestly just experimenting—clearly a tough sell that no parent should have to deal with. Besides, I like living. And really, the world is messed up enough without having to do drugs.

The other reason not to do drugs is that there are better things to do. If life is so horrible for you that you feel like you need to escape, then get some help. Because one day, when you do stop doing drugs to escape from the life that you find to be so hellish,

"I never smelled pot before—it smelled like burnt oranges."
—college student in Florida

you'll still need help. Most college campuses offer free counseling and unbelievable support services. But again, it's your decision. Just know what you're getting into if you decide to get into drugs.

Bottom Line
(no pun intended...okay, maybe a little)
I've never done a line because there's always a chance of dying the first time. And sure, you can die crossing the street, but it's much more dangerous crossing the street high on the way to visit your drug dealer.

Tip #86
Just Don't Accidentally Die

The Tip
Drugs are bad, mmmkay?

The Story
In November, I visited a good friend of mine. There were five of us crammed into his tiny apartment. I bought three ecstasy pills to share between my three friends and myself. Since I am very small, a half a pill can get me really high. (P.S.—this was not my first time tripping on E, this would be my fourth.) So, the drug takes its effect, and I'm loving it. I am feeling so happy, so loving, so wanting to tell everybody how much I loved them. Everything was going so well. I "peaked" (when the drug is most intense) and I crashed very gradually. My friend asked if I wanted to take a hit of pot on a bong while I was crashing. Sure, why not? I took a huge hit and immediately I started to feel odd. My head was swimming and my body felt shaky. I went into the bathroom and lay on the floor, completely fixated on a

small piece of lint on the bathtub. I was staring and concentrating so hard, I started drooling. My friend asked me what was wrong, but his voice was an echo. And it kept on happening, over and over. I would slip out of reality, hear echoes, see really crazy stuff, and then be fine. I thought I could control myself and the hallucinations, but in the end, I started screaming for my friend and I was convinced I was going to die. I wanted to jump out the four-story window in the room. I had never been so scared in my life that I was not going to come off an E trip alive. Finally, the pot wore off and I was fine. Everybody sounded normal, everything was okay, and I felt better. The next day I drove all the way back to my old college (about two hours) and slept for a good twelve hours. I have not been the same since that trip. I would get high (off pot) and get the same loopy "fading in and out" feeling. It has gotten better, but recently, I took a sleeping pill my doctor prescribed, and I started hallucinating badly. I don't know what brought it on, but I'm sure it has something to do with my nasty experience.

—college student, campus unknown

> "Ever wonder why six people come pouring out of the bathroom, wide-eyed and giddy while you are waiting to take a leak? Most of the time, it's because the bathroom becomes the playing field for blowing lines. It's no big deal, right? What happens when someone does too many lines and it becomes their last? Or what about the holder of an eightball before it gets cut up? Federal prison? Death? What makes it worth it? I see cocaine all the time."
> —junior, Frostburg State University

* * *

It would really be bad to do drugs and accidentally die (understatement of the book). The best idea is not to do them. But if you're going to do something stupid, again, don't be so stupid that you accidentally kill yourself doing it. I've seen a girl pass out at a fraternity party. I've seen a friend think that he was having a heart attack and go to the emergency room (he didn't really have a heart attack, he just freaked himself out and got scared). I've seen a guy almost fall into an empty swimming pool because he was too high to see that there wasn't any water in the pool. I heard about bad ecstasy trips where it

> **MOLLY "SAFE" SITES:**
>
> When using a site like dancesafe.org, make sure you cross-reference any information. Check with a doctor, drug counselor, or qualified expert. Do not blindly trust online guides and resources.

was a near-death experience. Then there was the student who shroomed and then came home, sprayed the fire extinguisher in the hall, and grabbed a girl's breasts (then he was arrested). There was the ex of a friend who did another line of cocaine and was found dead. Every year, students accidentally die from drug-related incidents. And sadly, it will happen again this year.

Of course, you shouldn't do drugs. But should you do them, keep the following in mind:

- Know where the stuff you're doing is from. It's hard to be sure that what you're doing isn't going to kill you. At least don't be the first to do it. Wait for other people and see how they react. Then decide whether or not to partake.
- Don't leave home while doing it. If you're going to be doing something stupid, make sure that you're in a place where you won't get arrested. Don't drive.

Don't be a public nuisance. Don't do things to draw attention to yourself.

- Do it in a "safe" place. A safe place is with people you know. Surrounding yourself with strangers is just stupid, especially if you're doing something for the first time. It's hard to know how your body will react. It's also hard to know how others around you will react. Drugs alter judgment and reasoning. Strangers who you think are safe people can turn out to be dangerous.
- Make sure you have trusted friends with you. If something unexpected should happen, you need friends to make sure you're taken care of. Trusted friends will take care of you; temporary friends might not.
- Don't mix alcohol and drugs. It's hard to know how your body will react to drugs alone. Add alcohol and you can go on a crazy trip, or just end up dead. It happens. Avoid drinking and drug use.
- If you're freaking out, seek medical attention. Some people just think that it will all pass. But that's dumb. If you or your friend is in a bad way, then get some medical attention. The object is not to die.
- If busted, get a lawyer and talk to your parents. No one wants to deal with the expense of an attorney and the hassle of parents, but if you make the wrong moves, this can haunt you for the rest of your life. Laws vary from state to state, and the right representation can help you make the best of a terrible situation.
- Legal in the eyes of the state may not be legal in the eyes of the school. Federal laws rule college campuses. In other words: getting high on or off campus can get you busted.

⚠ Sixth Edition Alert:

Prescription Drug Use/Abuse

* *

If I could make this blink or flash, I would (I'll work on that for the digital version). College students are finding new ways to get high and abuse drugs (congrats, you're all very creative). Molly is not your old aunt (I have an Aunt Molly), it's MDMA. And it can be incredibly dangerous. The other game is sharing, buying, and taking other people's prescription drugs. It's reported that 15.8 percent of college men and 13.8 percent of college women have used prescription drugs that didn't belong to them in the last twelve months (source: ACHA-NCHA II Spring 2014 Executive Summary). It might not seem like a big deal to some people, but it's not safe and it's kind of stupid—no, it's really stupid. It can hurt you, get you arrested, or kill you. Campuses are now cracking down and making it harder to refill prescriptions at the health center. And this is only the beginning of the crackdown. Expect to see and hear more.

> "My ex-boyfriend kept blacking out from doing drugs. He did everything. He shroomed. He smoked weed. He did coke. You name it, he was on it."
>
> —junior, University of Nevada–Las Vegas

One of the most frequently abused drugs is Adderall, a drug commonly prescribed to help with Attention Deficit Hyperactivity Disorder. Students will often use Adderall nonmedically to help them study and hyper-focus. While this might seem harmless, think again. You probably didn't know this, but research from the Substance Abuse and Mental Health Services Administration has indicated that nearly 90 percent of full-time college students who used Adderall nonmedically had engaged in binge drinking in the past month, and half were heavy alcohol users. Nonmedical users of Adderall were also more likely to smoke marijuana, use cocaine, use nonmedical prescription tranquilizers, and use nonmedical prescription pain relievers. Basically, if you're abusing prescription drugs like Adderall, it means you have a lot of things to deal with. So whatever you think about abusing prescription drugs, think again—that is, once you sober up and can think clearly.

Common Drugs Found on College Campuses

The following is a list of drugs and what they can do to you from the National Institute on Drug Abuse. One thing worth mentioning—it's a fact that on rare occasions doing cocaine for the first time can kill you. MDMA can kill you too (overheating and dehydration are common causes). Mixing Adderall and alcohol can kill you. And yes, meth can kill you, too. Now that list...

Marijuana

Other Names: pot, blunt, herb, ganja, weed, grass, boom, skunk, Mary Jane, gangster, chronic. There are more than two hundred slang terms for marijuana. Hashish ("hash" for short) and hash oil are stronger forms of marijuana.

Method Delivered: smoked, ingested.

Health Effects and Risks: cough; frequent respiratory infections; impaired memory and learning; increased heart rate; euphoria; slowed thinking and reaction time; confusion; impaired balance and coordination; anxiety; panic attacks; tolerance; addiction. Recent research findings also indicate that long-term use of marijuana produces changes in the brain similar to those seen after long-term use of other major illicit drugs. People who smoke marijuana often develop the same kinds of breathing problems that cigarette smokers have, like coughing and wheezing. They tend to have more chest colds than nonusers. They are also at greater risk of getting lung infections like pneumonia.

Cocaine

Other Names: blow, bump, C, candy, Charlie, coke, crack, flake, rock, snow, toot.

Method Delivered: injected, smoked, snorted.

Health Effects and Risks: increased heart rate, blood pressure, and metabolism; feelings of exhilaration; energy; increased mental alertness; feelings of restlessness, irritability, and anxiety; increased temperature; rapid or irregular heartbeat; reduced appetite; weight loss; heart and respiratory failure; chest and abdominal pain; nausea; strokes; seizures; headaches; malnutrition. In rare instances, sudden death can occur on the first use of cocaine or unexpectedly thereafter. However, there is no way to determine who is prone to sudden death. Once having tried highly addictive cocaine, an individual cannot predict or control the extent to which he or she will continue to use the drug. An appreciable tolerance to the high may be developed, and many addicts report that they seek but fail to achieve as much pleasure as they did from their first exposure. High doses of cocaine and/ or prolonged use can trigger paranoia. Prolonged cocaine snorting can result in ulceration of the mucous membrane of the nose and can damage the nasal septum enough to cause it to collapse. Cocaine-related deaths are often a result of cardiac arrest or seizures followed by respiratory arrest.

Added danger: cocaethylene. When people mix cocaine and alcohol, they are compounding the danger each drug poses and unknowingly forming a chemical experiment within their bodies. NIDA-funded researches have found that the human liver combines cocaine and alcohol and manufactures a third substance, cocaethylene, that intensifies cocaine's euphoric effects while possibly increasing the risk of sudden death.

MDMA (methylenedioxy-methamphetamine)
Other Names: Adam, clarity, ecstasy, Eve, lover's speed, peace, STP, X, XTC.

Method Delivered: swallowed, snorted, injected.

Health Effects and Risks: mild hallucinogenic effects; increased tactile sensitivity; empathic feelings; confusion; depression; sleep problems; drug craving; severe anxiety; impaired memory and learning; hyperthermia; cardiac and liver toxicity; renal failure; increased heart rate and blood pressure; muscle tension; involuntary teeth clenching;

nausea; blurred vision; faintness; chills; sweating. In high doses, MDMA can interfere with the body's ability to regulate temperature. This can lead to a sharp increase in body temperature (hyperthermia), resulting in liver, kidney, and cardiovascular system failure. Other drugs chemically similar to MDMA are sometimes sold as ecstasy. These drugs can be neurotoxic or create additional health risks to the user. Ecstasy tablets may contain other substances in addition to MDMA. The combination of MDMA with one or more of these drugs may be inherently dangerous. Users might also combine them with substances such as marijuana and alcohol, putting themselves at further physical risk.

More about Molly (Crystal MDMA): Molly (3,4-methy-lenedioxy-methamphetamine) is a synthetic, psychoactive drug that has similarities to both the stimulant amphetamine and the hallucinogen mescaline. It produces feelings of increased energy, euphoria, emotional warmth and empathy toward others, and distortions in sensory and time perception. The popular term Molly (slang for "molecular") refers to the pure crystalline powder form of MDMA, usually sold in capsules. The drug's effects last approximately 3 to 6 hours, although it is not uncommon for users to take a second dose of the drug as the effects of the first dose begin to fade. It is commonly taken in combination with other drugs. MDMA acts by increasing the activity of three neurotransmitters: serotonin, dopamine, and norepinephrine. The emotional and pro-social effects of MDMA are likely caused directly or indirectly by the release of large amounts of serotonin, which influences mood (as well as other functions such as appetite and sleep). Serotonin also triggers the release of the hormones oxytocin and vasopressin, which play important roles in love, trust, sexual arousal, and other social experiences. The surge of serotonin caused by taking MDMA depletes the brain of this important chemical, however, causing negative aftereffects—including confusion, depression, sleep problems, drug craving, and anxiety—that may occur soon after taking the drug or during the days or even weeks thereafter.

Some heavy MDMA users experience long-lasting confusion, depression, sleep abnormalities, and problems with attention and memory, although it is possible that some of these effects may be due to the use of other drugs in combination with MDMA (especially marijuana).

Methamphetamine
Other Names: Desoxyn, chalk, crank, crystal meth, fire, glass, go fast, ice, meth.

Method Delivered: injected, swallowed, smoked, snorted.

Health Effects and Risks: in the short term, meth causes mind and mood changes such as anxiety, euphoria, and depression. Meth may be as addictive as crack and more powerful. An overdose of meth can result in heart failure. Long-term physical effects such as liver, kidney, and lung damage may also kill you.

Long-term methamphetamine abuse has many negative health consequences, including extreme weight loss, severe dental problems ("meth mouth"), confusion, insomnia, chronic fatigue, mood disturbances, and violent behavior. Chronic meth abusers can also display a number of psychotic symptoms, including paranoia, visual and auditory hallucinations, and delusions (for example, the sensation of insects crawling under the skin). Meth abuse may also worsen the progression of HIV/AIDS and its consequences.

LSD

Other Names: lysergic acid diethylamide, acid, blotter, boomers, cubes, microdot, yellow sunshine, blue heaven.

Method Delivered: swallowed, absorbed through mouth tissues.

Health Effects and Risks: altered states of perception and feeling; nausea; increased body temperature, heart rate, and blood pressure; loss of appetite; sleeplessness; numbness; weakness; tremors; chronic mental disorders; persisting perception disorder (flashbacks). Effects of LSD are unpredictable. They depend on the amount taken; the user's personality, mood, and expectations; and the surroundings in which the drug is used. Usually, the user feels the first effects of the drug thirty to ninety minutes after taking it. The physical effects include dilated pupils, higher body temperature, increased heart rate and blood pressure, sweating, loss of appetite, sleeplessness, dry mouth, and tremors.

LSD is not considered an addictive drug, since it does not produce compulsive drug-seeking behavior. LSD does produce tolerance, however, so some users who take the drug repeatedly must take progressively higher doses to achieve the state of intoxication that they had previously achieved. This is an extremely dangerous practice, given the unpredictability of the drug. In addition, cross-tolerance between LSD and other hallucinogens has been reported.

Rohypnol

Other Names: forget-me pill, Mexican Valium, R2, Roche, roofies, roofinol, rope, rophies.

Method Delivered: swallowed, snorted.

Health Effects and Risks: visual and gastrointestinal disturbances; urinary retention; memory loss for the time under the drug's effects. Rohypnol is sometimes used to commit sexual assaults (also known as "date rape," "drug rape," "acquaintance rape," or "drug-assisted assault") because of its production of anterograde amnesia and its ability to sedate and incapacitate unsuspecting victims, preventing them from resisting sexual assault.

GHB—Gamma-Hydroxybutyrate

Other Names: G, Georgia home boy, grievous bodily harm, liquid ecstasy, soap, scoop, goop.

Method Delivered: swallowed.

Health Effects and Risks: drowsiness; nausea/vomiting; headache; loss of consciousness; loss of reflexes; seizures; coma; death. Repeated use of GHB may lead to withdrawal effects, including insomnia, anxiety, tremors, and sweating. Severe withdrawal reactions have been reported among patients presenting from an overdose of GHB or related compounds, especially if other drugs or alcohol are involved.

Ketamine

Other Names: SV, cat Valiums, K, Special K, vitamin K.

Method Delivered: injected, snorted, smoked.

Health Effects and Risks: increased heart rate and blood pressure; impaired motor function/memory loss; numbness; nausea/vomiting. For ketamine at high doses: delirium; depression; respiratory depression and arrest. Low-dose intoxication results in impaired attention, learning ability, and memory. At higher doses, ketamine can cause dreamlike states and hallucinations, impaired motor function, high blood pressure, and potentially fatal respiratory problems; and at still higher doses, ketamine can cause delirium and amnesia.

Psilocybin
Other Names: magic mushroom, purple passion, shrooms.

Method Delivered: swallowed.

Health Effects and Risks: nervousness, paranoia, muscle relaxation or weakness, ataxia, excessive pupil dilation, nausea, vomiting, and drowsiness. There is also a risk of poisoning and death, if one of many existing varieties of poisonous mushrooms is incorrectly identified as a psilocybin mushroom. The psychological consequences of psilocybin use include hallucinations, an altered perception of time, and an inability to discern fantasy from reality. Panic reactions and psychosis may also occur, particularly if a user ingests a large dose. Long-term effects such as flashbacks, risk of psychiatric illness, impaired memory, and tolerance have been described in case reports.

Codeine
Other Names: Empirin with codeine, Fiorinal with codeine, Robitussin A-C, Tylenol with codeine, Captain Cody, Cody, schoolboy, (with glutethimide) doors and fours, loads, pancakes and syrup.

Method Delivered: injected, swallowed.

Health Effects and Risks: pain relief; euphoria; drowsiness; nausea; constipation; confusion; sedation; respiratory depression and arrest; tolerance; addiction; unconsciousness; coma; death. Repeated exposure causes the body to adapt, sometimes resulting in tolerance (that is, more of the drug is needed to achieve the desired effect compared with when it was first prescribed) and withdrawal symptoms upon abruptly stopping drug use. Symptoms of withdrawal can include restlessness, muscle and bone pain, insomnia, diarrhea, vomiting, cold flashes with goose bumps ("cold turkey"), and involuntary leg movements.

Amphetamine (Dexedrine, Adderall, Ritalin, and Concerta)

Other Names: bennies, black beauties, crosses, hearts, LA turnaround, speed, truck drivers, uppers.

Method Delivered: injected, swallowed, smoked, snorted.

Health Effects and Risks: increased heart rate, blood pressure, and metabolism; feelings of exhilaration; energy; increased mental alertness; rapid or irregular heartbeat; reduced appetite; weight loss; heart failure; nervousness; insomnia; rapid breathing/tremors; loss of coordination; irritability; anxiousness; restlessness; delirium; panic; paranoia; impulsive behavior; aggressiveness; tolerance; addiction; psychosis.

Bath Salts, Spice, and Salvia

For information, visit www.DrugAbuse.gov/Drugs-Abuse /Emerging-Drugs.

The information preceding is from the National Institute on Drug Abuse. To learn more, check out www.DrugAbuse.gov.

Bottom Line

Be smart about being stupid. If you do drugs, don't die.

Tip #87
College Smoking Butts

The Tip

Smoking in college isn't as exciting as in high school. It's no longer forbidden. It's not as cool. You don't need to smoke to stand out.

The Story

I smoked from seventh grade all through high school. In high school it was like the rebel thing to sit around and smoke cigarettes—but when I got college, it all just wasn't fun anymore. The thrill was gone. I no longer had to steal cigarettes from my mom. I could buy them. Once I got to college, I just stopped smoking. It got really disgusting. I started to smell like it; my roommates didn't like it. Cigarettes became a nuisance. We used to have a smoke bubble to encase the smokers on campus. We got rid of it. The ceiling was discolored and the windows were tinted yellow. I was just repulsed. Besides losing the thrill, I've noticed that a lot of guys are disgusted by it, too. It's not so glamorous. In the words of a close guy friend of mine, "She can be the hottest girl, but once she lights up, I turn around and walk away."

—sophomore, Wilkes University

* * *

To help with research for this tip, I went into a busy bar near my place (a bar where people can smoke). I wanted to see what it was like to actually kiss an ashtray. So, one busy Saturday night during a playoff game, I looked for an ashtray to kiss. I started with small talk, and when the time was right, I made my move.

As expected, it was really disgusting.

While it's proven that cigarette smoking causes cancer and other serious health risks, it also makes you stink like an ashtray and costs you a lot of money to support your habit—I can't believe cigarettes cost six and a half bucks a pack. Three packs a week is over $1,000 a year. Save your money and buy a new laptop or tablet at the end of your sophomore year! Smokers are all over campus. Usually they're hanging outside, a good 15 feet from the door. If you're not planning on smoking, be prepared to see people lighting up around you. Then don't start—not even socially when you're drinking.

Who Really Smokes

Perceived Use: Students think 76.9 percent of fellow students on campus used cigarettes within the last 30 days.

Actual Use: Only 12.2 percent of college students actually reported using cigarettes in the last 30 days.

—ACHA-NCHA-II Executive Summary Spring 2014

The social smoker is an interesting phenomenon. One of my good friends started off as a social smoker. He'd only smoke when drinking. Ten years later he's still smoking. He smokes in the morning, when he takes a break at work, after he eats dinner, and on the toilet (he says it helps him go). Basically, it's whenever he's awake. It's the social smokers who become regular smokers. It's not like people start smoking and say, "From now on, I'm going to smoke every day for the next twenty years." It's a gradual process.

The best way to avoid it is to not start. It's tempting

to want to stand around and bond, and it gives you something to hold (for more things to hold, see Tip #75). But the smoke only lasts about five minutes. Then it's over.

If you should find that you are smoking and can't quit, see if your campus has a group to help smokers quit. Also, check into tobacco replacement systems via your campus health center. They have cheap drugs to help you kick the habit. If you want to quit, you can do it. But if you don't start, then you won't have to quit.

Bottom Line
Just appreciate that the casual smoker becomes the regular smoker. Instead of smoking, don't start. Please note: you can still stand around with the smokers and breathe secondhand smoke. They're cool with that.

Harlan's Tip Sheet

Naked People, Places, and Resources

Hotlines and Websites
- Alcohol/Drug Abuse Referral Hotline—twenty-four-hour hotline provides referrals to treatment facilities 1-800-ALCOHOL (1-800-252-6465)

- National Clearinghouse for Alcohol and Drug Information
  1-800-729-6686
  Website: www.Store.Samhsa.gov
  Facebook: www.Facebook.com/SAMHSA
  Twitter: www.Twitter.com/SAMHSAgov
- National Council on Alcoholism & Drug Dependence (NCADD)—provides information on counseling services for alcohol or drug abuse
  1-800-NCA-CALL (1-800-622-2255)
  Website: www.NCADD.org
- U.S. Department of Health and Human Services National Drug and Alcohol Treatment and Referral Routing Service—get confidential information on and referrals for drug or alcohol abuse.
  1-800-662-4357
- National Hotline Cocaine Information and Help
  1-800-COCAINE (1-800-262-2463)
- National Institute on Drug Abuse
  Website: www.DrugAbuse.gov
- Club Drugs—a service of the National Institute on Drug Abuse (ecstasy and other club drugs)
  1-301-443-1124
  Website: www.ClubDrugs.gov
- The National Youth Anti-Drug Media Campaign
  Hotline: 1-800-788-2800
  Website: www.AbovetheInfluence.com
  Facebook: www.Facebook.com/AbovetheInfluence
- Drug Free America—information and a diary of people who have lost loved ones to drugs
  Website: www.DrugFree.org

Facebook: www.Facebook.com/PartnershipDrugFree
Twitter: www.Twitter.com/DrugNews
- The BACCHUS Network
Website: www.SmarterSex.org
Website: www.TobaccoFreeU.org
Facebook: www.Facebook.com/TheBACCHUSNetwork
Twitter: www.Twitter.com/BACCHUSNetwork
- Crystal Meth Anonymous
Website: www.CrystalMeth.org

Money, Laundry, and Cheap Eats

12

Assuming You Have Enough Money to Eat and Do Laundry

Hey Harlan!
How hard is it to make it financially at an out-of-state college without my parents' support? Is this possible?
—Short on Cash

Hey Short on Cash!
Here's something to make you smile:

According to the College Board, "The average net price in the public four-year sector reached an estimated $3,030 in 2014–15, compared to a published price of $9,139." In other words, most students do not pay the sticker price. While in-state and out-of-state tuition will vary, investigate all the possibilities.

Going to the college of your dreams—in state or out of state—might be easier than you think. Get in touch. Pick up the phone and get connected with the financial aid counselors at the schools that interest you. Speak with an advisor. Explain your situation. See if the advisor on the other end can give you a general idea of the type of aid available. Ask about academic and need-based assistance. There are grants, loans, scholarships, and work-study programs that can help you pay for college. You won't be able to get exact figures, but you could get a rough idea. Then apply and see what happens.

The next step is to get familiar with scholarships. Become familiar now and continue to apply as you go through college (use the free online scholarship searches). Once in school, you'll come across even more scholarships through the department of your major, service organizations, religious organizations, parents' place of work, professional organizations, national fraternities, and national sororities.

If your financial aid counselor can't show you the money—keep looking. It's there. And should you want to take out loans, you can always do it that way. It would be nice to have your parents' support, but if you don't, you can still get to where you want to go.

Tip #88
Loans, Grants, Scholarships, and Loose Change

The Tip
There's money out there if you go after it.

The Story
I have found in my experiences that people are always willing to give money outside of the resources available in the financial aid office. I went to a professional website for occupational therapists and read about scholarships available. I had to write an essay about why I wanted to be an OT and why I should receive the scholarship. So, I wrote the letter, sent in my transcript, got a letter of recommendation, and sent it in. A few months later, I got a check for $1,000 for books and expenses. I didn't think that I was going to get jack. I thought thousands of people would send in letters. If more people took the time to write the essay, get a copy of their transcript, and send it in, they would get a lot of money. They said the most you can get is $1,000, and the least is $250. I would have gotten something just for doing the work. These foundations raise money and set it aside for scholarships. It's the same in a lot of fields. I didn't hear about this through my advisor—I just searched on a scholarship website. www .Fastweb.com is the best one I've seen. When a grant or scholarship comes up, they email me a notice. It doesn't get much easier than that. I used it in undergrad and I use

it now. It's as easy as writing an essay and then it's boom, bang, you send it out. The money is so there.

—graduate student, Touro College

***

According to the College Board, the average cost (including tuition and fees, room and board, books and supplies, transportation, and other expenses) at a private four-year school is $42,419. If you're going to a public four-year school and live in state, you're looking at $18,943. If you're out of state, make it $32,762. If you're paying in loose change, that would be 424,190 dimes, 189,430 dimes, or 327,620 dimes. But wait—breathe. Most students will NOT pay this price. What you pay varies from campus to campus. Most students get some kind of financial aid. Aid is money in the form of student loans, grants, scholarships, and jobs that can help cut costs. Visit your financial advising office and connect with a financial aid counselor to guide you along the process (see the next tip).

> **STUDENT DEBT DEFAULT:**
>
> Do NOT default. Defaulting is NOT making a payment on your student loans within 270 days of the due date. Consequences can include fees, penalties, garnished wages, lawsuits, ineligibility for other programs, and other negative consequences. Don't default, get help. Visit: studentaid.ed.gov /repay-loans/default/avoid.

One piece of advice that I wanted to make sure to include in this edition of the book—understand the money part of college. You need to understand the FAFSA forms, Pell Grants, and the different types of Direct Loans (see answer here: www.StudentAid.ed.gov

/Types/Loans). Not only will understanding the financial part of the experience help you secure money to pay for college, but you understand the paying-it-back part and work to find more money (free money is the best). You'll also learn more than you ever imagined. For example, a college student who is convicted of a felony drug offense is ineligible for federal aid and can be forced to repay any grant money received (sucks, I know). The more you understand, the less stressful this will be. Lean

on the experts on campus who can help. If your parents are helping with the costs, still, get involved. Make sure you understand what you're committing. Who knows, you might be the one who has to pay these loans back in the future. Here's a brief overview to get you familiar with each part of financial aid. If you already know, this will be a quick refresher. Another invaluable tip—find other students who have received loans and grants. Get them in your corner. If you can get advice from the people who got the money, you'll be set up for success. If you don't know of anyone, ask your advisor to introduce you. You can also ask your high school counselor or post a note on the Naked Roommate's Facebook wall.

Grants and Scholarships

This is money that doesn't have to be repaid and that you don't have to work to get. Grants come from federal and state governments and from the particular institution you're attending. Scholarships are usually awarded based on achievement inside and outside the classroom. Use the free online scholarship searches to see what's available (see Tip Sheet for websites). Also, inquire about available scholarships within the college by talking to professors and advisors in your department. If you're in a fraternity or sorority, look into scholarships awarded through the national office. Scholarships can also be available through churches and religious organizations, your parents' place of work, community organizations, the athletics department or academic departments, and by being the right application at the right time. Unbelievably, millions of dollars for scholarships go unawarded every year.

Loans

The federal government offers and sponsors loans—most are low-interest loans awarded based on students' financial need. Because the government subsidizes loans, there is no interest charged until the student graduates. Once you max out your federal loans, you can apply for private loans. Talk to your financial aid advisor to understand the various types of loan options. DO NOT take more than you need. The new digital surround-sound stereo system, forty-two-inch plasma TVs, and designer clothes are phenomenal now, but that will quickly end when the loan payments begin.

Know What It Will Cost Before Spending It!

Calculate how much your loans will cost you once you graduate. Visit www.CollegeAnswer.com/Tools/Loan-Repayment-Calculator.

Work-Study

Work-study programs are part-time jobs that are offered as part of the financial aid packages. It's money students work to earn to help with extra expenses like books, fees, and other costs (like food). It's also a way for student workers to gain experience and help serve the community and campus. If you see someone at the campus info desk studying or napping when not dispensing info, there's a good chance he or she is part of work-study program.

When paying for college, the best tip is to talk to upperclassmen and your financial aid counselor—see the next tip. It's the people who have been through the process and know the process who can share lessons learned. Use the people around you. Each college has its own way of navigating the system. Do not be afraid to ask!

Bottom Line

Look for money during all four years. Talk to people who have been there. And if anyone tells you to take out a bigger loan so that you can buy a plasma TV, assume that the person is just dumb, or working on commission at an electronics store.

Tip #89
Your Financial Aid Advisor: Money, Money, Money, Monnnnneeey

The Tip
Find an advisor you feel comfortable with and trust, and stay with that advisor the whole four years. Take the advisor's card and build a relationship. It will make future visits so much easier.

The Story
It's so annoying to have to meet with a new advisor each time you go and explain your story from the beginning. This means having to start over every time. When I got to school, I found an advisor who got to know me and my family's financial situation. I met with other advisors when he wasn't available, and it wasn't comfortable at all. I learned to call ahead and to make an appointment with him. Even if I had to wait a day or two for my answer, I'd wait. He helped us find as many loans as possible and looked over my parents' financial documents every year to help us get as many government loans as available.

FAFSA Forms:
The government forms that you need to fill out to apply for financial aid (www.FAFSA.ed.gov).

My grades weren't good enough for scholarships, but he was familiar with them. Make sure that your advisor is someone you like and someone with whom you have a positive rapport. Really, it makes it so much better. Going to the same person made something totally foreign to me easier to understand. Having a great relationship has even helped me after graduation. Whenever I have questions on loan statements, I call him and fax over what's confusing and he's still there for me.

Another tip that I'd love to go back and tell myself is to apply for loans early, because the sooner you get your financial aid forms in, the more money that is available. That's something that not a lot of people told me.

—senior, University of Delaware

* * *

It's like having your own personal money advisor in your corner—a coach to help you beat, or at least navigate, the system. There is money out there—you just have to go after it and know the people who can show you where to get it.

Before even setting foot on campus, contact your college's financial aid office and get hooked up with an advisor (no, not like the hookup in Tip #55). Advisors should be happy to talk to you. They encourage calls. Their job is to help you pay for college. Between Direct Loans, Perkins Loans, Pell Grants, filling out those FAFSA forms (the only thing worse is filling out the forms while getting your teeth pulled), making deadlines,

> ## Loan Resources and Info
>
> Sallie Mae (www.SallieMae .com)
>
> Fastweb (www.FastWeb.com)
>
> Citiassist (www.StudentLoan .com)
>
> FAFSA (www.FAFSA.ed.gov)
>
> The College Board (www.CollegeBoard.com)
>
> And never pay for a scholarship search service—check out the free services online.

and sorting through your financial aid package, it helps to have an expert in your corner who has seen it all before. And when your parents have questions, if they're the ones handling the paperwork, you can get the answers. That's what the advisor is paid to do.

If you're unhappy with your financial aid award package, see if your advisor can reconsider your award.

Your New Best Friend

Visit your financial aid advisor on a regular basis. Think of your advisor as your new best friend (with the keys to the bank safe).

Many times, what you're initially offered is largely part of a computer formula. Each situation is unique. There could be additional grants or scholarships available. Walk into the office, be polite, smile, and plead your case to the advisor (crying can help). A conversation can get you hundreds, if not thousands, of dollars more in free money. It's happened to my friends. Make sure you stop by and visit with your financial aid advisor before you have a financial crisis. Checking in on a regular basis will help you stay up to date on programs and opportunities to get more money. And should you ever face a financial crisis, it's nice to have the right kind of friends to lean on.

The biggest obstacle in getting the most financial aid is that most students don't care enough to make the added effort. Use your financial aid advisor. And as I mentioned in the previous tip, use the people who have just been through the system as your second, third, and fourth advisors. It was through a friend that a close friend of mine heard about a scholarship offered through a country club.

She was given thousands of dollars each year. There is money all over the place—ask around. Do not be shy. You might just win the college lottery!

Bottom Line
Take advantage of your financial aid office and find an advisor who can get to know you as an individual. Should this tip help you save money, please consider buying several hundred copies of this book with your saved cash.

Tip #90
Part-Time Jobs, Big-Time Benefits

The Tip
By becoming a Resident Assistant (RA), you can get free housing and/or food and a stipend! Not to mention help students on campus.

The Story
I became a summer RA after my freshman year so I could attend summer school and get free housing and food to boot! I met so many people, gained leadership experience, and got to stay near my boyfriend, too! Parents love the idea of having their child be an RA because it shows that you are responsible and it takes a huge financial burden off of

"Work a lot over the summers and save money. Once you are at school it goes so quickly!"
—senior, SUNY Cortland

the student and their family. As an RA, I met a diverse group of student leaders and I also became a knowledgeable person about the campus. Being an RA isn't for everyone, though. You have to be willing to enforce and follow all the rules, which can put a damper on the whole college experience!

—sophomore, University of Texas

* * *

I had few part-time jobs in college. I sold T-shirts to freshmen during orientation, going from room to room (it was kind of illegal to sell T-shirts, but people needed clothes, right?). I worked in the campus newspaper advertising office for a few months. I got paid commission and was given an "A" parking pass (it was so beautiful it made me want to cry). I also worked on the campus newspaper (that's how I started writing my advice column). I had a friend who made a ridiculous amount of money working as a computer lab student worker. My ex worked as a paid research lab assistant. A quiet friend worked in the library. A buddy of mine was a server at a sorority—second-best job to being a sorority houseboy.

One suggestion—if you need to get a job to help pay for college, then try to find a job that can help you figure out what you want to do with your life. If you're interested in going to medical school, get a job in the campus hospital or health center. If you're interested in going into the restau-

"Spring of my junior year, I got the opportunity to participate in the Disney College Program in Orlando, FL. Basically, you go to Disney World, and work there. I got a job in a merchandise role, working in one of the resorts. Disney also provides housing for the College Program students. I got to work and live with people [from] all over America, and all over the world. It was so much fun, getting to be in Disney World for four months. I felt like I was bleeding magic everywhere. There is also the opportunity to take classes with Disney professionals while you are there to learn about the company, and after the class I took, it definitely helped me narrow down what I wanted to do when I 'grow up.' I had learned about this program my freshman year, but always came up with excuses as to why I couldn't apply that semester. I finally realized I was running out of semesters to do the program, and I had to just go for it. Had I not, I would have missed out on one of the most memorable things I have ever done in my life."
—senior, Virginia Tech

rant business, get a job working as part of campus food service. If you want to go to law school, work in the law school or at a local law firm. If you want to go into psychology, find a job helping a professor in the lab. The best-case scenario is that you'll love what you do and find contacts who can help you get into grad school or get a job. The other best-case scenario is that you'll find out that you just don't love doing what you thought you wanted to do—and then you can do something else.

As for work-study jobs, these come highly recommended. These are jobs that the school makes available for students as part of their financial aid packages. Typically, they're jobs on campus that range from working in an academic office, working in a residence hall, and shelving books in the library, to putting brochures together in the admissions office. They can pay anywhere from minimum wage on up, but generally are pretty decent. I know one girl who was paid $8 an hour to make copies and answer phones. If you get a job in a department within your major, you can make money, make contacts, and build relationships that can help you when it comes to letters of recommendation and jobs. Ask upperclassmen what the cushiest jobs are. Working with the sports teams has huge benefits. If you're looking to make good money and have a flexible schedule, waiting tables is the best. I used to wait tables at home during breaks—I'd make about $100 on a good day.

Bottom Line
If someone offers you a job where they tell you the benefit is having keys to all the buildings on campus, the job probably comes with a broom, mop, and a shirt that reads, "Campus Custodial Services." But you would get to know the campus...

Tip #91
The Credit Card and the $600 Candy Bar

The Tip
Getting a credit card is so easy on campus. When you get one, don't skip town when the bills arrive. You'll pay for that free gift later.

The Story
I went to college and innocently signed up for a credit card. I was hungry and they were giving away food. It had a credit limit under $500, so I knew I wouldn't get into too much trouble with it—so I thought. I used the card a few times and then just kind of forgot about it. I left town for summer break and skipped out on the bills. I didn't think to have them forwarded. A collection agency tracked me down during the summer at home. My dad answered the phone and freaked out. They ended up bailing me out. It cost over $600 and my credit history is a mess. I don't even know if I can rent an apartment now.

> "My parents charge everything. They figured that they should put tuition charges on their credit card. They've gotten thousands of miles because of me."
> —senior, Indiana University

—junior, Savannah College of Art and Design

New Credit Card Rules
You might need a parent to get that plastic. Check out the Credit Card Accountability, Responsibility, and Disclosure (CARD) Act of 2009.

* * *

There used to be a time when you would find friendly people in the most populated areas on campus handing out things like candy, T-shirts, footballs, mugs, stuffed animals, bottled water, and other random crap that people tend to take and then put in a closet or throw away. As of 2009, you'll have to walk 1,001 feet off campus to find them (they aren't allowed to advertise within 1,000 feet of a college or university). These friendly folks aren't giving you something for free. They want

> "After receiving three cards in the mail, I figured that I would just use them for books and other school-related expenses. What I didn't realize was that when your books are about $500 a semester, there is no way that you can pay that off right away. To make a long story short, three years and several thousands of dollars in debt later, I'm still paying for that English 101 book."
> —junior, Northern Michigan University

you and they want you badly. It's kind of sexy. But they're not interested in your love or body, they just want to give you credit—that is, a credit card and a candy bar. And if you're under 21 and have a parent who can cosign the agreement or demonstrate that you have income to pay the minimum charges, you're in business.

> "The Internet, a credit card, and college don't mix. E-commerce bills run up fast. Make sure you have a way to check your account before they send a statement to school."
> —sophomore, Juniata College

Credit cards don't make people go into debt; people who use credit cards and don't have money will go into debt. The credit cards often get a bad rap because college students who don't have money tend to go into credit card debt. When it comes to credit

"The first time I used my credit card was to buy a pair of shoes. I knew I had the money in the bank and promised myself that I would pay the bill immediately. That was the beginning of the end. I started to use it for meals, for groceries, for spring break, airfares, clothing, and books. When I maxed out the first card I moved on to the second and third card in my drawer. I went wild. My balance was over $8,000 and I had a 17.9 percent interest rate."

—debt-free grad, Mesa State College

cards, it's only bad if you use them and can't afford to pay the bills immediately. That's where people run into problems.

As a rule, get your credit card and charge only what you have money for at that moment. Transfer the money (you can do it online) that same day. Use your credit card to establish credit (see Tip #92 for more info), in case of emergencies, and to get mileage awards or whatever reward you sign up for. One credit card is enough. Make sure there are no annual fees. Look for incentives. I qualified for free airfare to Europe or the equivalent in cash after using mine for four years. And be careful with online purchases. They can add up sooo fast. Whatever you do, if you do carry a balance, make sure you pay the minimum. If you can't afford the minimum, contact the credit card company and make arrangements. Never ignore bills. Doing so will haunt you and hurt your credit score (making it hard to buy a car, rent a house, or get a loan in the future).

Beware: it's easy to get carried away if you're not careful. And watch out for interest rates. If

Naked Tip: Earn Thousands of Rewards Points

If your parents are helping with costs, consider opening a credit card to charge tuition and books. Your parents charge it and pay it ASAP. Then you can earn thousands of rewards points and establish credit in your own name.

you're late paying, your interest rates can jump up to 29.99 percent or higher. Check out the little mock charge demo I put together to show you how quickly things can add up and get out of control (the following example is based on a credit card with a 17.5 percent interest rate and a 2 percent monthly minimum).

One Semester:

Spring Break	$1,500
Books	$225
Food/Restaurants	$125
Clothing	$150
Total Balance:	$2,000
Minimum Payment (2 Percent):	$40
Interest:	$1,600
Time to Pay Balance in Full:	**7.5 years**

Bottom Line

Credit cards, when used properly, can be used to open doors (no, this isn't a metaphor—I mean if you lock yourself out of your place you can unlock your door).

Tip #92
Bad Checks, Bad Credit, and Bad Ideas...

The Tip
When you can't pay the minimums, make arrangements with creditors.

The Story

I used my four credit cards and got in too deep. Three years later and thousands of dollars in debt, I couldn't make the minimum payments and pay rent, the cell phone bill, and the utility bills. I was working, but it was no longer enough to cover it all. I'd been late on bills before for the credit cards and as a result my interest rates were jacked up. I called to try to have it lowered, but no luck. I was transferring one balance to the other one, paying with those instant credit checks. It got to be too much, so I just stopped paying. I shut down. The accounts were suspended and then the companies started calling and calling. I eventually told my parents what was happening and they helped me out. I'm now working to pay off my bills and trying to figure out how I can fix the damage. They say it can take seven years to repair credit. Had I at least called and made payment arrangements, the companies wouldn't have been so aggressive.

> "Don't write bum checks. I would write bad checks for food and groceries when I got to college. I didn't care. My credit is pretty much screwed. I shouldn't have done that."
> —sophomore, Eastern New Mexico University

—senior, College of Charleston

* * *

For every action, there is a reaction. If you skip classes, you risk failing out of school. Have unprotected sex, and you risk getting a sexually transmitted infection/disease. Write bad checks, and you risk establishing a terrible credit history that can follow you around for years and years and haunt you when you least expect it.

How Your Credit Score Works

Credit scoring is a system creditors use to help determine whether to give you credit. Information about you and your credit experiences, such as your bill-paying history, the number and type of accounts you have, late payments, collection actions, outstanding debt, and the age of your accounts is collected from your credit application and your credit report. Using a statistical program, creditors compare this information to the credit performance of consumers with similar profiles. A credit scoring system awards points for each factor that helps predict who is most likely to repay a debt. A total number of points—a credit score—helps predict how creditworthy you are; that is, how likely it is that you will repay a loan and make the payments when due.

—Federal Trade Commission Website (www.FTC.gov)

Now, you might be thinking that it's not a big deal to blow off a payment here and there. But it becomes a big deal when you want to take advantage of the zero percent interest financing for that new car, only to find out that you don't qualify because your credit rating from college is a disaster. It doesn't seem like a big deal now, but it will when you fill out an application to rent a place and the landlord runs a credit report that comes up "NO WAY IN HELL" and refuses to rent to you (and no, NO WAY IN HELL is not an actual credit rating). Messing up your credit doesn't seem like a big deal until you try to buy a home and can't secure a mortgage because your lender ran a credit report and your credit rating was abysmal. It's fun to pass bad checks, not pay bills, and pay late, but once you start living life beyond college, your terrible payment habits will become a huge problem. And by the way, passing bad checks is a crime.

In case you're not familiar with how credit works, lenders, landlords, and other credit card companies look at your credit rating to determine how much of a risk you are to do business with. The worse your history is, the bigger a risk you are. Things like paying bills late, not paying bills at all, opening too many lines of credit, overdrawing your checking account, and having a history of companies reporting you to one of the three big credit bureaus reduce your credit rating. The lower the rating, the worse your chances are of being someone people want to do business with (see the sidebar on the previous page for the FTC explanation of your credit score).

Want a Free Credit Report?

Visit www.AnnualCredit Report.com for your free annual report, in accordance with the Fair and Accurate Credit Transaction Act (FACT Act).

Do it the right way and save yourself all of the aggravation. If not for yourself, then do it for your future. You'll thank yourself tomorrow for being responsible today.

Bottom Line

It can take seven seconds to write a bad check, but it takes seven years to repair your credit. (Note: does anyone actually write checks?)

Tip #93
Checking Out the College Checking Account

The Tip

Set a budget, use cash, and don't abuse the ATM/debit card.

The Story

I had an idea what college would cost, but I was way off. I would use my ATM debit card to handle costs that

"I paid for my book with my debit card and I was overdrawn by $90. Overdrawn fees are a bitch."
—junior, University of Southern Indiana

came up. I had it on an auto-billing service where there was an automatic deduction. I also used it for

an organization that didn't run the charges until after I thought the money was already gone. It was impossible to figure out where the money was going to and where it was coming from. I ended up getting overdrawn and paying over a hundred dollars of fees from all the times it happened. I had to close the account and start over. I now have an ATM card that is just an ATM card. I can

"Get overdraft protection in case it happens—and it can happen to responsible people like me."
—senior, Northwestern University

now track where and when the money moves. It also helps me to know what I'm spending. I do have a credit card, but I only use it for emergencies or when I need to purchase something over the phone. When I do, I transfer the money right away. The credit card and the bank are hooked up online, so it's easy to transfer money.

—senior, San Diego State University

* * *

This seems like kind of a boring tip, but it's an important one. If it will help, play some music for atmosphere. That song "Money Money Money, Monnnnneeey" will work, or something by 50 Cent is close enough (his name is currency). I was an idiot when it came to my checking account in college. I never wrote it all down. It was after bouncing a check and dealing with the wrath of my parents and paying ridiculous fees that I started paying more attention. It took me years to straighten myself out. Take the time to do things the right way now and you won't have to spend hours dealing with "idiot you" years down the line. I'm being vulnerable here. Please, don't be like me. Set up your finances and be responsible—it will help you throughout your entire life. Here's the plan to do it right.

> "Only take money out once a week. Take out an amount you know you'll need to get by easily with, but don't use an ATM for the rest of the week. You can't lose what you don't have on you to lose."
> —sophomore, York University

When you get to school, or even during a summer visit, establish an account at a local branch. Ask about student accounts. You want to avoid fees. This includes ATM fees, minimum balance fees, checking fees, and teller fees. They add up fast. If you do it all digitally, make sure you have an online management system like Quicken or Mint. If you do it with paper, get checks that come with carbons (it helps to know who you wrote checks to in case you don't record your checks in a ledger). Appreciate that banks are competitive and want college students as account holders. Don't be afraid to negotiate to get the best plan. Also, make sure that you have overdraft protection (in case you get overdrawn you won't

> "I'm overdrawn all the time. My bank charges me $32 each time. I recently received a note from them that said I was overdrawn at least ten times in a year. That means that I lost $320 and God knows what happened to my credit future."
> —fifth-year senior, UCLA

have all the ridiculous fees). And make sure you know how many ATM transactions you can perform a month without being charged. Check to make sure that there isn't an additional fee for transactions with a live teller—some banks charge teller fees (which I could understand if they were fortune tellers, too).

As for these debit/credit cards, they can be the devil. They are too much work to keep track of. It's hard to know when the transaction goes through and when the money leaves your account. Sometimes you'll find a certain vendor will hold money, just in case it needs it (hotels, car rental companies, and even gas stations will do this). The hold means that the money is no longer available to pay other bills. That's where it gets tricky. If you want to charge something, get a credit card separate from your checking account and make sure you only buy things that you can pay for immediately (unless you have so much money that you will never over-draw the account). If you can use your card and get mileage, reward points, or some other kind of bonus, there's nothing wrong with that. Just pay the balance immediately. If you're afraid of losing control, get a credit card with a small credit line or a credit card where you load cash on it. They now have these cards that work like gift certificates. You put on a certain amount and then once you run out of money, you have to recharge the card with cash. One more suggestion—include the names of your parents on the

Online Management Tools

Get Quicken, Mint, or an online money management tool that can help you stay up to date with your accounts. Balancing your checkbook can be one click away.

account. It helps so that they can transfer money into the account (and bail you out if you lose control).

Bottom Line
Look for the lowest fee checking account (like free) with online access. Handle debit/credit cards with care; it's too easy to get overdrawn—and that can be sad (see Tip #100 on depression).

Tip #94
Sorry, This Book Is Now "Used"

The Tip
Utilize the Internet—sites like www.Half.com and www.Amazon.com. They have the same books as the campus bookstore, and often for at least a third of the price. Plus, you can actually get money back when you sell your books.

The Story
Most college bookstores have a monopoly on the market (especially private college bookstores). They overcharge massively. For example, I bought a British history textbook that was $70 new in the bookstore, but was on www.Amazon.com used for $6. Then I resold it for $22 (I printed a prepaid shipping label off the computer). The student bookstore was buying it back for $10. Also, make sure the book you're buying is the same edition

> "The only way I get books now is through the Internet."
> —student, University of Delaware

that the professor is using. That's the part of buying used books online that you have to be the most careful about.

—senior, Franklin College

A sadistic professor once made me buy a book on Russia for $50. I didn't even open it. When I went to sell it back, they offered to give me $5. I offered them a dirty look. I kept the book and used it as a doorstop—it was a nice doorstop. I hope you don't use this book as a doorstop. Actually, I don't mind. If you're not reading it, at least it can be useful while it's not being read. Hmm... now I'm kind of hoping you'll use it as a doorstop.

> "Try to find upperclassmen who had the same class and get books from them."
> —student, Manhattan College

When it comes to buying books, the best suggestion is to buy used or rent. Now you might think, *Harlan, I don't buy anything used or rent*. But this time, it's different. It's not like underwear, socks, or shoes. It's not a status symbol to have a new book—just a symbol that you throw away money. The average used book is dramatically less expensive than the new book and it has the same exact words (minus the doodles in the cover). The only difference is that you might deal with a little wear and tear. Some books have minimal wear and maximum savings. When coming across used books that have already been highlighted, they're

Buying Software

Take advantage of educational discounts. Students with an ID can get huge discounts (as much as 95 percent off). Buy online (search: educational software discounts) or buy on campus.

still good books. Just use a different color highlighter to represent your highlights. Do not depend on someone else's highlights. The owner of your previously owned book might have failed out or have been an artist who highlighted based on emotions, not the lecture notes.

Another way to get your textbooks is to rent them. Yes, renting is the newest textbook trend. You only pay for the time you use them (and no, you don't get money back if you avoid using them by blowing off your reading assignments). According to the National Association of College Stores, textbooks can be rented for about one-third of the cost of buying new books. So, investigate rental programs through your campus bookstore and search online. Make sure you understand the terms and conditions so you don't end up having to buy the books or paying other fees. Excessive highlighting (what?), writing in the books, missing pages, or damaged spines can mean getting charged to replace the book you rented (painful). If you don't want to rent a physical book or buy it, look into etextbooks. This can give you access to the digital version of the textbook for a specific amount of time (it's kind of like renting).

RENT BOOKS BY THE HOUR?!

Watch *Shark Tank*? On one episode, a group of students launched a new way to help you get textbooks when you need them. Mark Cuban bought in. Check out www.PackBackBooks.com. Rent books by the hour. (Now, if only students who sexile their roommates could rent rooms by the hour.)

"Don't buy books until you need them. Go to the library and check out textbooks. I rarely buy books."
—senior, Emerson College

Should you buy your books, then when the semester ends, chances are you'll want to sell them back. Most campus bookstores run the traditional, "We buy back your book and you feel as if you've been robbed in broad daylight" buyback options. Even the economics professors marvel at how the price of a textbook can drop 80 percent in three months. Before running to a bookstore, consider selling your books online, to a local bookstore, or through a campus book network. These mini-networks let students who finish a course list their books to sell to students beginning the course. Ask an upperclassman or your RA about your options. Make sure that the used book you're buying isn't a foreign version of the book (ask the seller if buying online).

> "Make sure if you shop online that you're getting the right edition of the book. I know a lot of people who thought they got a deal, but found that they were stuck with an old edition. Do not overlook the edition."
>
> —junior, Earlham College

One more book tip: when it comes to nonacademic books (like in English class), call your college library and then your local community library. There's a chance it might be in circulation so you won't have to buy it.

Bottom Line
If renting a textbook, avoid highlighting too much or you can be charged the full price of the book. Seriously? Huh? What? Are they kidding? How much is too much? Guess you'll have to ask the highlighting cop.

Tip #95
Cheap Strategies for Eating (or barely eating)

The Tip
If there is a Save-A-Lot or other similar discount grocery store around, go to it!

The Story
Ahh, you're finally in college. But the food is terrible, so what do you do? Find one of your close buds who has a car and drive to your nearest Save-A-Lot or other similar store. By going to a store and buying non-name brand foods, you're saving money that can be used for other items. As for me,

> "Work in the food services. I worked in catering on the weekends for three years and ate for free. I also got to bring home leftovers for my roommates."
> —senior, Northeastern University

$50 worth of food at Save-A-Lot will last me for up to two or three months. Or if you're really low on cash and want to go back, just sell the food items that you don't like to your friends. Someone will buy it from you, eventually.

—freshman, Xavier University

* * *

I tried to make this page edible and fruit-flavored, but publishing hasn't advanced that far yet. There's also the risk that you'd eat this entire book. Now, some strategies for eating more for less:

- Get a part-time job where you can get paid and eat well for free. Waiting tables at a sorority (a dream job for many), serving at a local restaurant, or working in catering can be a huge help. The best of these is the catering options. When the parties are all over, the people working the events can sometimes take the food home or it eat following the event. If you can work part-time on the weekends, you will save so much money. Typically, it's the weekends that cost the most. The reason—school cafeterias don't always serve all meals on the weekends. Ordering out can get expensive. Plus, you have the added expense of whatever you do on the weekends.
- Get a few friends together and shop at a warehouse club like Costco, Sam's Club, or BJ's Wholesale Club and split the bill. You can eat for weeks. In addition, there are canned foods, soups, pastas, and other nonrefrigerated items where all you have to do is add water.
- Always use coupons—there are so many deals out there if you take advantage of them. Search for them online. Sign up for www.Groupon.com and www.LivingSocial.com, look at Facebook Deals, and check out all the competing sites for discounts. You can find a book of coupons in the student union or a high-traffic area. Ask about student discounts or discount cards. If the coupon is a "buy one, get one free," find someone to go in with you or buy one and keep the other one for another meal.
- When your schedule doesn't allow you to get to the dining hall, a lot of times you can get meals to go.

Ask the dining hall director if the meal plan includes meals to go. Also, ask about late night and weekend options to cut costs.

- Take a little bit of food with you from the cafeteria. Just put a piece of fruit in your bag. If you don't have a bag, then put it in your pants. I'm not saying to steal food, but if you don't have time to sit and eat every meal in the cafeteria that day, rather than going hungry, take a bagel or Pop-Tarts as a snack. And chew slowly. That can help, too.
- Bring food from home. If your mom or dad is a good cook, bring back frozen food. Even if they're not good cooks, bring food. Pack pre-cooked frozen food in one-portion plastic bags. Keep them in your freezer (assuming you have one), and use it when you're on the run.
- Go to functions on campus where there is food. You don't need to stay for the event. Just go long enough to eat (if you're poor and hungry).
- Sign up at www.NakedRoommate.com. I'm always working to give away free stuff to college students. You can sign up on my website or via the tap on my Facebook page (www.Facebook.com/NakedRoommate).

If you find that you're too poor to eat and are going hungry, talk to the people in the dining hall or contact someone in financial aid. Explain the situation and see if you can get a meal plan. If it's a no go, see if you can get a job working in a cafeteria. And no, don't steal your roommate's food—not cool.

Bottom Line

If you're really strapped for nourishment, get a job in food services. The catering jobs tend to yield massive employee leftovers. Take it all home and freeze it.

Tip #96
Laundry Tips: This Page Is Not Fabric Softener

The Tip
Stock up on underwear.

The Story
The truth about college laundry is that doing it will be a rare event. Nowadays Febreze and that wrinkle spray stuff are amazing, and they are often decent substitutes in a jam when all the machines are being used, you don't have time, or you're just too lazy—decent for everything but underwear. My guy friends tell me this is not true and underwear can be worn far past its prime. Trust me, if you want anybody to come in contact with your underwear, or possibly remove it, this is not true. So make sure you have enough underwear to compensate for your laundry laziness. I only do my laundry about once a month—after I've worn each and every one of my thirty-four pairs of undies.

—freshman, University of Illinois at Chicago

* * *

If you're reading this and you're desperate for clean underwear, you can tie two strings to this page and use it as underwear. Better yet, you can use each page of this book as underwear, which should take you through two semesters, or three quarters (if you're on the quarter system).

For those who are actually looking for laundry tips, please follow these helpful suggestions and your whites will stay white, your darks will stay dark, and nothing and no one will bleed:

- Don't wash dark and light colors together. They will bleed and then you'll end up wearing mostly pink and gray clothing (not a problem if those happen to be your school's colors). And wash on permanent press (cold water works best).
- Check out concentrated laundry detergent. It takes up less space on your shelf and lasts a long time, plus it's better for the environment. It saves space when it comes to storage and is lighter and easier to carry than the 200-ounce jug of detergent.

- Find a Laundromat near campus if the washing machines in the residence halls aren't maintained well. Some Laundromats have food, music, and drinks. It's also a way to meet scantily clad people with no clean clothes to wear.

- Avoid shrinkage—read clothing labels carefully. When in doubt, don't toss it in the dryer. Hang-dry what might shrink. Fold clothes immediately.
- Never leave your clothes in the dryer unattended— clothes often get stolen if they sit in the dryer long enough. And if they get stolen, you're left looking over members of the same sex from head to toe—not because you're interested in them, but because you're wondering if that person is wearing your pants.

- Do laundry at slow times—not on the weekends.
- Laundry detergent pods. Absolutely genius.
- Don't overstuff the machine. If there's no room to agitate, your clothes won't get clean and you'll get agitated.
- Quarters are gold—save quarters, take quarters from home, give that extra three cents so you can get two quarters instead of forty-seven cents back (unless you have a laundry card that can be loaded with money and swiped to wash and dry).
- The laundry room is a great place to start a conversation with someone. The best lines: (1) Can I borrow your fabric softener? (2) Gee, that smells terrific! (3) Excuse me, is this your thong or mine?

Ways to avoid having to do laundry:
- Date someone who loves doing laundry.

- Take advantage of the inside-out method—this is the act of turning clothing inside out to get an extra wear (socks, underwear, T-shirts).
- Take your laundry home and just ask a parent to do it.
- Borrow a roommate's clothing.
- Bring your dirty clothes to a Laundromat that washes them for you and charges by the pound.
- Avoid working up a sweat or soiling your clothing (by keeping your body under control and wearing the same clothing dozens of times).

Bottom Line

When doing laundry, brush your teeth and fix your hair before heading to the laundry room. It might not seem romantic, but two people in a hot, steamy room for hours with the aroma of fabric softener sheets is a recipe for love.

Harlan's Tip Sheet

Naked People, Places, and Resources

Definitions

- *Financial aid office:* The office that handles student requests for financial assistance with tuition and college costs. This is the place that handles the money.

- *Financial aid advisor:* The individual who will help answer your questions regarding availability of money, loan options, and paperwork questions.
- *FAFSA:* Free Application for Federal Student Aid. This is the government form that must be filled out for financial aid. Contact your financial aid advisor with particular questions.
  Website: www.FAFSA.ed.gov

Financial Aid, Scholarships, Grants, and Loans

- Scholarship Searches—use free searches such as FastWeb.
  Website: www.FastWeb.com
  Facebook: www.Facebook.com/PayingforSchool
  Twitter: www.Twitter.com/PayingforSchool
- The College Board—information on aid and links to other resources.
  Website: www.CollegeBoard.com
- Sallie Mae
  Website: www.SallieMae.com
- Citibank
  Website: www.StudentLoan.com

Credit Information

- Free Credit Report
  To order, visit www.AnnualCreditReport.com, call 1-877-322-8228, or complete the Annual Credit Report Request Form and mail it to: Annual Credit Report Request Service, P.O. Box 105281, Atlanta, GA 30348-5281.

- Federal Trade Commission—helpful information on understanding credit and credit cards.
  Website:
  www.Consumer.FTC.gov/Topics/Money-Credit
  Facebook:
  www.Facebook.com/FederalTradeCommission

Additional Resources

- Buying or Renting Books
  Visit your local campus bookstore or search online. Do your own keyword search. There are several major online textbook services out there. The ones students mentioned most:
  Website: www.Half.com
  Website: www.BNCollege.com
  Website: www.Amazon.com
  Website: www.Chegg.com
  Website: www.ECampus.com
  Website: www.Textbooks.com
  Website: www.PackBackBooks.com
- Laundry Tips
  Never do laundry on the weekends (it's too busy).
  Don't leave your detergent or basket (I'll steal it).
  Get rolls of quarters at the grocery store service desk or at a bank.
- Educational Software Discounts
  Website: www.JourneyEd.com
  Facebook: www.Facebook.com/JourneyEd
- Academic Superstore
  Website: www.AcademicSuperstore.com

Note: Apple, Dell, and other retailers offer student discounts. Flash your ID before making your purchase.

- Coupon Codes
Search for online coupons. Visit my websites, Facebook, and Twitter pages for links to online deals.

Dear Harlan,

Does the freshman 15 really happen? I've heard many rumors about people going off to college and when they come back a few months after being a freshman, they've gained fifteen to twenty pounds. I want to know so I can be prepared when I start college to not start packing on the pounds!

—Fearing the Fifteen

Dear Fearing,

It's true. It happened to me. Actually, I still have my freshman 15. I keep it in a jar in the refrigerator as a constant reminder of just how easy it is for me to lose control. I haven't eaten pizza, wings, or subs past midnight since my freshman year in college (and no, it's not really in a jar—it's in Tupperware). See Tip #97 for more…

Dear Harlan,

I'm a sophomore in college in New Mexico. I recently came home after attending one semester at the University of Arizona because I felt like I did not fit in there. I was having trouble making friends, so I moved back in with my mom. Now, I regret the decision. I'm unhappy here. I do not know anyone. I am wondering if I should transfer somewhere else and give the whole college experience another chance or if it is too late.

—Stuck at Home

Dear Stuck,

The college brochures never tell you…but college can suck at times. No one tells you because then you wouldn't go to that college. But clearly, it can be a tough transition that takes work, time, and effort on your part. The problem with transferring after one semester is that when the problem isn't the college, the problem travels with you. You can transfer from college to college to college, but until you figure it out…see Tip #102 for more.

Tip #97
The Freshman 15...Or, Um, 45

The Tip
Remain active, be wary of the cafeteria buffet, and don't drink too much.

The Story
I was a ballet dancer for fourteen years. When I moved out of state for college I didn't realize that my dancing had kept me in shape all those years. I didn't participate in anything active besides walking to class or to the cafeteria, which by the way was a huge all-you-can-eat buffet every day! The partying was happening every night. I did not do too well in my classes my first year, and I also gained forty-five pounds. Try dealing with the humiliation of going home on vacation and hearing all of your old friends say, "Your face has filled out," "Are you pregnant?" etc. Now that I'm a fifth-year senior, I've lost most of the weight but I wish I had never gained it in the first place!

—senior, St. Cloud State University

* * *

I gained my freshman 15, lost it, and then kept it (it's in a jar in the freezer). Actually, I did gain and lose it, but I didn't keep it.

I have no idea how it happened, but eating breadsticks, wings, and pizza, drinking an occasional beverage at 3 a.m., and then sleeping resulted in the addition of a few pounds. On top of that, I frequently took advantage of the all-you-can-eat option available in the cafeteria. See, my mom never did a lot of cooking with a deep fryer, and those chicken fingers and french fries were tempting. We also didn't have a soft-serve ice cream/yogurt machine with ten different toppings next to the kitchen table.

Easy access to food combined with the lack of movement and all the changes that come with college make consuming calories easier than ever. So much of college is built around social calorie consumption. If it's not social, it's emotional eating. Craving comfort can easily lead to junk food. Had I not been overweight in high school and overly aware of my eating habits, I can only imagine the poundage I would have been packing.

It's easy to gain weight in college. BUT it's also easy to not gain weight. In fact, there are some students who will actually lose weight (more on this at the end of the tip). If you eat during normal hours, exercise regularly, and snack smart, then you don't have to worry about gaining weight. Most meal plans offer a healthy option (a trough of frozen yogurt is not a healthy breakfast), or at the least, a salad

"Always take the stairs if possible. Do not eat french fries every meal of the day. Take only one dessert."
—freshman, Radford University

bar is available. If you don't have a low-fat dressing option, use the oil and vinegar. (BYOB: bring your own balsamic.)

A new development is the listing of calories on food items in the dining hall. Some dining services have apps you can download to help you log calories (I'm a fan of MyFitnessPal). If you log calories, make sure you talk to your doctor to find out how many calories are appropriate for your weight, height, and activity level. Should you overindulge, take advantage of classes in the recreational center. There are often classes that you can join for free (spin, cardioboxing, martial arts) Even better—become an instructor. Then you have to go.

> "Exercise regularly to avoid the freshman fifteen, the sophomore seventeen, the junior twenty...Eating late at night, drinking, and eating too much helped me put on a few."
> —senior, University of Pittsburgh

Another way to stay active is through sports (this does not include bowling on the Wii). If you find that you're having a hard time managing your weight, don't just ignore it. Rapid weight gain or weight loss can often be a sign of something more than just eating too much and not exercising. It's one of the common signs of depression and other mental health issues. If you find that you're gaining too much weight or losing too much weight, don't wait to get help (I hope the weight word play wasn't too annoying here, it just seemed to work, ya know?). As I mentioned in the box on page 450, if you're coming to

> "Stock your dorm room with food. My food is what is keeping me from the freshman fifteen! I always have healthy snack foods like fruit and nuts in my room to bring to class with me and eat while doing homework. Instead of eating pizza, I'll eat some dried fruit."
> —freshman, University of North Carolina–Chapel Hill

campus with a history of weight loss or weight gain or have a history of an eating disorder, have a plan for how you'll manage your weight before there's a problem. This can include seeing a nutritionist on campus, having the name of a therapist with you before you need help, going to Weight Watchers meetings (if you're on maintenance this is helpful), or finding a support group—have the info handy, just in case.

Bottom Line
Eating a large pizza, a dozen breadsticks, fifteen wings, a bag of chips, a pound of chocolate-covered peanuts, a bag of dried fruit (to be healthy), and drinking a six-pack of thick malted beer before bedtime will make your pants tight.

Tip #98
The Student Body Image

The Tip
Hang out with people who are obsessed with their bodies, and you will become obsessed with yours.

The Story
When I was in high school I didn't worry as much about what people thought. When I got to college, it was all I thought about. It had a lot to do with the people I'd hang around with. They were obsessed with how they looked. It started to affect what I did and how I thought. Like, they

said that they were going to the gym every day—I'm like, "I have to go." Then they eat nothing and I'm like, "I have to eat nothing." It's hard to eat when no one else is eating. What I learned is that I had to find a way to get away from it, if even for a short period of time. I found another group of friends through campus organizations and in classes. I learned that it's all about how I feel about myself, not how they feel about me. It's important to have a wide variety of friends. If you don't, you start acting like the group you hang out with. It becomes easy to get obsessed or lose yourself in the process.

—junior, University of Connecticut

Bonus Tip

Even a small compliment can turn someone's day in a new direction. It's ok for those compliments to come from ourselves!

The Story

I hate it when I am in a locker room or bathroom and there is a group of girls standing in front of a mirror bashing their bodies. "My nose is crooked," or "My thighs are so fat, I hate them," or even "My chest is so small, I need to get implants someday." It seriously makes me sick. In the past, I have left the room, gone home, and tried to erase from my mind what I observed. But recently I decided to speak to a group of these body-bashing girls; I gave each of them compliments on different aspects of their physical appearances—"I think you have a great smile. And I think you have beautiful shoulders. And I think your calves are fabulous." Then I saw something amazing happen. I watched their eyes brighten, their posture straighten, as if they had never really seen themselves before. It was clear that the girls were no longer focused on what they disliked about themselves, but they acknowledged other beautiful parts of their bodies. Before I left, I shared with them that whenever I am having a bad day, I think about what I love about myself and what my best friends love about me. I love that I am healthy and natural, and to me that is what makes me beautiful. And living with the knowledge that I am beautiful feeds my confidence and self-esteem. I am comfortable with who I am, and I wake up every day feeling as though I can conquer the world.

—freshman, UC Davis

* * *

I have ears that protrude (please see photo on back cover). Several years ago, a reader wrote to me suggesting that I would be far more handsome if I surgically pinned my ears back. I ran the letter from "Doris in Dallas." My reply went something like this:

Dear Doris,

Yes, I'm aware that my ears stick out. And when I forget about them, there's occasionally someone to offer a friendly reminder, suggesting that I have them surgically stitched closer to my head (the same people who offer comments regarding other people's weight, hair, and wrinkles). Thank you, but I don't want to change. If someone doesn't like me because of my ears, it's not a loss. As for women, I've had extremely attractive women find me (and my ears) extremely attractive—and not

just women with ear fetishes (are there such women?). Some
even tell me that my ears are fun to play with.

And for those flat-eared people looking to change,
there's no surgery I know of to have your ears pushed out.
I appreciate your letter, and I love that you enjoy the col-
umn. Maybe, one day, you'll love my ears, too. I do.

It's taken me a while to see, but my ears are an asset.
They separate me from all the flat-eared men of the world.
They're attractive. At least that's what people have told
me. Following my reply, I was flooded with ear-adoring
mail from men and women around the country. Some sent
their pictures. Some shared stories of what they wanted to
do with me and my protruding ears (don't imagine) I even
had a man in Dallas offer to host me in his hot tub if I was
in town (never took him up on that one).

I've seen and heard firsthand that other people will
love those things that we don't necessary love. It's not just
ears; it happens with
butts, boobs, noses,
hair, lack of hair—
whatever it is that you
don't think is attrac-
tive, can be. The only catch is that you have to believe it's
attractive (which can be a tough sell to yourself).

"There are two mints you should always take: breath mints and compliments."
—sophomore,
University of Massachusetts–Dartmouth

When it comes to body image, we are our own worst
enemy. Most of us have a skewed image. And most of
the time, it's not the most flattering image. If you want
to reflect an image that will make you attractive, here's
how you can do it. Stand in front of the mirror wearing
the tightest thong possible. Don't look away. Commit to

working to change the things you don't love and learning to love the things you can't change. Trust that someone else will love them too. Until you can be comfortable with your reflection, it's hard to expect anyone else to be. If you find that you can't love or even like what you see and can't change it, then get help—a good therapist (or even a bad therapist) can help you change your focus and love the things that are hardest for you to embrace as just another part of you that makes you you. Until you can love your body and all its perfect imperfections, it will be too hard to take risks because you'll be too afraid that someone will discover what you've spent so much time hiding.

> "It's pretty hot when a girl is confident. The thing that bothered me about one of my past girlfriends was that she was so obsessed with her weight that it interfered with the relationship. When I told her that she was beautiful, she would never believe it—but it was true."
>
> —senior, Western New England College

Bottom Line

No matter the size of your bottom line, someone will want it.

Tip #99
Exposing the College Eating Disorder

The Tip

If you see someone who you think has an eating disorder, don't just look the other way or make comments. Help that person.

The Story

People have a tendency to get scared when they see someone they know suffering from an eating disorder. I never thought I would be someone who would become anorexic. My sophomore year, I was put into the hospital. I'm five feet, seven inches, and weighed close to ninety pounds—down from 124 pounds back when school started. When it was obvious that I was losing weight and getting way too thin, my friends in my sorority didn't help. They once put a flyer in the hallway that had information about eating disorders, or made flip comments, but that's as far as they went. No one really talked to me. I think they were too scared and didn't know what to do or how to help. If you see someone in trouble, tell that person. If they don't listen, then call that person's parents and alert people on campus—that person needs your help more than ever. After transferring to another college, I'm finally getting better. I hope my story can help others.

—junior, University of Missouri–Kansas City

* * *

You're in good company. I still struggle with my body and eating. Always have. In high school, I gained fifty pounds (I was five feet, two inches, and 192 pounds). I then lost it all, and more, my sophomore year and kept it off. In college, I gained a few pounds, but nothing too dramatic. I had a good idea that drinking beer, eating a pizza at three in the morning, and not working out would mean gaining weight. But for me, eating isn't about food. It's about emotions. It's how I cope. And when I get uncomfortable, I want to eat. I've learned how to manage my emotions and food—I have people and places to help me find balance.

BEWARE: the lack of control that's part of college, the constant pressure to look a certain way, and the abundance of all-you-can-eat, high-calorie foods make a dangerous recipe that can lead to an eating disorder (if you don't already have one). There are so many triggers. On top of that, spending so much time away from home (this includes commuter students) means that it's easy to hide an eating disorder from family or close friends (who can see you and stop you). It can get dangerous extremely fast.

Favorite App

MyFitnessPal is what I use to log my calories.

Rather than obsessing or worrying, get familiar with your campus's recreational center before leaving for college. Pick a sport or cardio class. Make "being active" part of your daily routine, so that you can eat a little more without seeing it, feeling it, or worrying about it. If you're coming to college with an eating disorder, find support on campus before setting foot on campus. If you're someone who develops an eating disorder, get help sooner than later. If you're forcing yourself to vomit, binging, not eating, or binging and then exercising excessively (bulimia doesn't always include vomiting), it's a sign that you're in trouble. Visit the counseling office and speak with a therapist. Explain your situation. And if you're someone who has a friend who develops an eating disorder, don't turn your head and look the other way. Be a good friend and get involved. Talk to the counselors at the health center. Talk to your friend's parents. Talk to your friend and make sure he or she gets help.

If you do gain weight, I'm a fan of Weight Watchers. It's just a great way to make lifelong changes. It teaches you how to eat for life. You can follow the program online or you can find a meeting near campus (sometimes they'll bring the meeting to you if there is a group of people interested). They didn't pay me to say this. It's just what I use to keep myself at a healthy weight.

If you're looking for support or want to share your stories, please post them in the Naked Roommate forums (www.NakedRoommate.com).

Bottom Line
It's way too easy to develop an eating disorder, or trigger an old one, in college. Be aware and get help before you're forced to get help.

Sixth Edition Bonus Tips

Bullying on Campus
College students are being bullied. It comes in the form of physical bullying, verbal bullying, and/or social bullying. The game—make other people feel like less so the bully can feel like more. But everyone loses.

- If you're being bullied, reach out to the people in your corner for help and support. If you find you are being bullied in class, online, in a club, in an organization, at work, or in other social situations—DO NOT put

What Is Bullying?

Bullying is unwanted, aggressive behavior among school-aged children that involves a real or perceived power imbalance. The behavior is repeated, or has the potential to be repeated, over time. Both kids who are bullied and kids who bully others may have serious, lasting problems.

In order to be considered bullying, the behavior must be aggressive and include:

- *An Imbalance of Power:* Kids who bully use their power—such as physical strength, access to embarrassing information, or popularity—to control or harm others. Power imbalances can change over time and in different situations, even if they involve the same people.

- *Repetition:* Bullying behaviors happen more than once or have the potential to happen more than once.

Bullying includes actions such as making threats, spreading rumors, attacking someone physically or verbally, and excluding someone from a group on purpose.

—www.StopBullying
.gov/what-is-bullying
/definition/index.html

up with it. There may be laws in your state or a code of conduct on campus to protect you. Campuses and universities are developing policies at this very moment to protect you.

- If you are the one doing the bullying (or part of a group that's bullying), STOP. Get help. Find new friends. Get the people doing the bullying help. People in pain inflict pain. There is NO WAY a bully is healthy and happy. Turn to the resources and support services on campus to help. And standing by while your friends are doing the bullying makes you a bully too. And now, the consequences of bullying are more severe than ever. Beyond laws and rules that can get you arrested or expelled, if someone you bully hurts him- or herself or other people, you may be responsible.

- If you witness someone being bullied, be a friend and/or alert people who can help. Turn to the people, places, and resources on campus and make it clear what you saw or heard.

Getting Sick on Campus

Getting sick sucks. It's the worst. Some of you might get sick on campus. WARNING: It can be one of the loneliest times on campus. It's when you get really homesick. Even the students with the hardest shells like a little tender loving college care. The best advice is to leave for campus prepared. Take all the stuff you'll need in case you get sick. Bring a sick bucket filled with acetaminophen (Tylenol), naproxen (Aleve), ibuprofen (Advil), something for your stomach, and anything else you might need. Walk down the aisle of a drug store and imagine everything you might need and bring medications. When you get sick, instead of being a hero, go to the health center sooner rather than later. If you need medication, take a cab to a local drug store. If you don't know what to take, talk to the pharmacist (instead of calling home). If you feel like garbage and can't make it to the store, see if you can get the meds delivered. NEVER take anyone else's prescription medications.

Students with Disabilities

There are more students than ever going to campus with documented disabilities, from ADHD to depression and everything in between. There are two types of students: the ones who embrace their issues and the ones who fight them. The ones who fight them go off their meds because they are at school and want a "fresh start." These are the ones who make a HUGE mistake. Then there are those who embrace what they have and consult a doctor when making dramatic changes and decisions. Whatever you do, don't go off your meds. There's nothing smart or fresh about denying who you are and opening yourself up to setbacks and risks. If you want to cut back, then talk to a doctor and do so under the care of a medical professional.

As for registering with the Office for Students with Disabilities, make that a priority. Even if you think you've beaten it, having the relationship with the office and being able to take advantage of special accommodations is a gift. You don't have to use the resources, but at least you have access to them, just in case.

A Heartfelt Letter to Depressed Students from Me (Harlan)

Hi, It's me...

Should you need this page, rip it out, keep it with you, remember these words.

I can never understand your pain. I'll never know your darkness. I can't grasp the heaviness bearing down on you. But I do know one thing with absolute certainty—ending your life is not the answer. It gets better—so much better. Reach out. Let one person inside. Trust the people who can guide you. Trust the people who have faced this hell and survived it. The shame, the pain, and the fear will pass. On the other side of darkness is light. Compassion is around you. Friends, family, and loved ones you've yet to meet want to hold you, love you, and support you. I promise with all my being—it gets so much better. You have lost hope in the darkness, but help will light your path. Call this number (1-800-SUICIDE). Contact a parent, grandparent, brother, or sister. Talk to a trusted friend. Call 911 now—reach out. Keep breathing. Stay here. When you do reach light, please write me. I want to hear your words. I want to share your story. Together, we can save lives, but it starts with you saving your own. Please get help. Now.

Love,
Harlan

Tip #100
Depression and Other Major Mental Health Issues

The Tip
Asking for a little help does not make you weak.

The Story
I have been told by many that I am a very strong person. I'm nineteen and living in what seems to be more like a soap opera than real life. I never wanted to admit that I could have depression. Then, the beginning of this semester, I started to notice behavior I could not ignore. I would often overreact (often hysterically) to everyday stressful situations. I was sleeping—a lot—planning to wake up at 7 a.m., but often missing entire days of classes and increasing my homework and adding stress. I was eating all the time and gaining weight. I didn't want to do the things that made me happy.

Depression Screening

National Depression Screening occurs in October of every year. Here's the URL for the website: www.MentalHealthScreening.org

All I wanted to do was sit in my room and sleep, or sometimes just stare and think. I decided it was time to take action. As a resident advisor, I was aware of all the resources on campus for people in "my situation," never thinking I would be one of them in need. Frantic and stressed, I did something that was extremely hard for my hard-headed, independent personality: I called the counseling center with the words "I believe I have depression, and I am ready to seek help." Now, with my depression medication and weekly counseling sessions, I feel like my old self again. My motivation is back, I am not unnecessarily emotional, I am happy. Although I am

still dealing with the hole I've dug myself into due to my class absences, late assignments, and missed tests, I am looking forward to the future, as I can feel myself getting better and better each day. It takes courage to admit you have a problem, and to be serious about wanting to fix it. I now feel stronger than ever.

junior, Bowling Green State University

* * *

I promise, even though this tip includes information about depression, it will not be depressing. I also promise to work my best to hold your attention during the ADHD part of this tip. That reminds me, let's play some music to make this tip as upbeat and happy as possible. There's Neil Diamond's "Sweet Caroline," Mika's "Love Today," Pharrell's "Happy," and Harlan Cohen's "The Syphilis Song."

So, you might get depressed. If you do, give it voice. No secrets. Tell family, friends, and a therapist. I wish we were all born with a therapist because we can all use one. An objective expert listener is good medicine. Never before have there been more resources, treatments, information,

Who Feels Overwhelmed?

- 77.0 percent of male students reported that they felt overwhelmed by all they had to do any time within the last twelve months.

- 91.6 percent of female students reported that they felt overwhelmed by all they had to do any time within the last twelve months.

Who Feels Hopeless?

- 39.3 percent of male students reported that they felt things were hopeless any time within the last twelve months.

- 50.0 percent of female students reported that they felt things were hopeless any time within the last twelve months.

—ACHA-NCHA-II Executive Summary Spring 2014

and support available for you. On most campuses, there is at least one full-time therapist, and therapy is often covered by your health insurance.

If you didn't already know it, a lot of students are dealing with mental health issues. According to the ACHA-NCHA-II Fall 2014 Executive Summary, 27.8 percent of men and 34.9 percent of women felt so depressed it was difficult to function. New friendships, relationships, living arrangements, financial burdens, classroom stress, temptations, and emotions can be the ingredients that trigger depression. And a lot of the time, it starts in your late teens and early twenties. Factor in that your support system for the past eighteen years is either far away or not what it used to be, and some students will be sent spiraling to a bad place. The problem is that it's easy to pretend to be happy without anyone else knowing something is deeply wrong. And the people who know you best aren't close enough to see you're in trouble and save you.

The first step in overcoming depression is recognizing it. It's normal to have some signs of depression some of the time, but five or more symptoms for two weeks or longer, or noticeable changes in usual functioning, are factors that should be evaluated by a health or mental health professional. (Also worth mentioning—people who are depressed may not be thinking clearly and need help to get help.)

The following are symptoms of depression:

- Sadness, anxiety, or empty feelings
- Decreased energy, fatigue, being "slowed down"
- Loss of interest or pleasure in usual activities
- Sleep disturbances (insomnia, oversleeping, or waking much earlier than usual)
- Appetite and weight changes (either loss or gain)
- Feelings of hopelessness, guilt, and worthlessness
- Thoughts of death or suicide, or suicide attempts
- Difficulty concentrating, making decisions, or remembering
- Irritability or excessive crying
- Chronic aches and pains not explained by another physical condition

"No one has it all together. I finally realized that everyone is flawed. The idea that no one is expected to be perfect in all situations has been one of the most valuable concepts for me."
—sophomore, Brandeis University

About Suicide

Be patient. Get help. Find answers. Suicide is never the answer. It gets better. If you're having thoughts of suicide or death, I'm begging you (seriously, and I haven't begged you in this entire book) to get help. What's so tragic about suicide is that things always get better over time. I know I keep saying it, but it's true. There's help, support, therapy, and medication. If you think that you're going to do something terrible to yourself or others, get help. Contact the counselors on campus, call your local hospital, contact a crisis hotline (1-800-SUICIDE), and get some help. Your family and friends want to help you—not grieve for you.

> "My ex-boyfriend has been calling me crying. He's at a school where he really didn't want to go. He's been hanging out with friends from home. I've told him that he really needs to get some help."
>
> —freshman, Indiana University

If you have a friend that you think might be depressed, contact the people I just mentioned and find out the best way to approach your friend. I've talked to so many survivors of attempted suicide—every single one is so thankful to still be here. Their families are thankful. Their friends are thankful. The dark cloud that hangs over you today will clear up in the near future—BUT YOU NEED TO BE HERE to see the clouds part and the sun shine. PLEASE, PLEASE, PLEASE, get help. Your friends, family, and the world need you.

A Few Words about Addiction

Never before has it been easier to develop an addiction in college. There are so many "exciting" ones to choose from: drinking, drugs, sex, video gaming, gambling, overeating, porn, and the list goes on and on. Addiction is often linked to depression and other mental health issues. And it makes complete sense that someone might self-medicate rather than turn to a therapist or doctor to get some help. Drugs and alcohol can help numb the pain and provide a temporary escape. Then there's sex addiction (online porn, masturbation, risky sexual encounters)—it's not about intimacy; it's about masking the other underlying emotions. There's gambling addiction—it seems harmless, but it can cost students their savings and future. I was recently at a campus where the president of the sophomore class robbed a bank at gunpoint to pay for his online gambling debt. Another student killed his roommates rather than pay gambling debts. Online gambling, casinos near campuses, and poker games down the hall are habits that can turn into a serious addiction (see the hotlines at the end of this chapter). Other addictions include video game addictions, Facebook and texting addictions (not yet clinically recognized), and other Internet addictions (be careful of The Fifth Wall).

> ## Suicide
>
> Suicidal feelings, thoughts, impulses, or behaviors always should be taken seriously. If you are thinking about hurting or killing yourself, SEEK HELP IMMEDIATELY. Contact someone you trust to help you: a good friend, academic or resident advisor, or
>
> - staff at the student health or counseling center
> - a professor, coach, or advisor
> - a local suicide or emergency hotline: 1-800-SUICIDE (1-800-273-8255)
> - a hospital emergency room
> - 911
>
> No matter how bad you might feel, no matter how hopeless it might appear, it's all temporary—it can and will get better. But suicide is forever.

If you miss class because you've been drinking too

much, gambling into the morning, having sex, masturbating, creepin' on Facebook, or playing video games, it's a problem. When you miss class (the equivalent of work), that's a big problem. In the following pages you'll find a list of mental health issues. If you're reading this list thinking, "I want to find out what's causing me to do this or that," it's a sign you need help. Please get some.

Other Common Mental Health Issues

Some of you might be coming to campus with these mental health issues, some of you might be diagnosed with one, and some of you will have friends with one. I hope this list can help you find support and learn how to support the people who need it. And it's worth mentioning, the onset for many mental health issues is in your early twenties. Meaning, be aware, take care of you, and get help before you need it.

Bipolar Disorder (Manic Depression)

Bipolar disorder is a type of depressive illness that involves mood swings that go from periods of depression to periods of being overly "up" and irritable. Sometimes the mood swings are dramatic or rapid, but most often they occur gradually, over several weeks. The "up" or manic phase can include increased energy and activity, insomnia, grandiose notions, and impulsive or reckless behavior, including sexual promiscuity. Medication usually is effective in controlling manic symptoms and preventing the recurrence of both manic and depressive episodes.

—National Institute of Mental Health

Symptoms of Bipolar Disorder

People with bipolar disorder experience unusually intense emotional states that occur in distinct periods called "mood episodes." An overly joyful or overexcited state is called a manic episode, and an extremely sad or hopeless state is called a depressive episode. Sometimes a mood episode includes symptoms of both mania and depression. This is called a mixed state. People with bipolar disorder also may be explosive and irritable during a mood episode. Extreme changes in energy, activity, sleep, and behavior go along with these changes in mood. It is possible for someone with bipolar disorder to experience a long-lasting period of unstable moods rather than discrete episodes of depression or mania. A person may be having an episode of bipolar disorder if he or she has a number of manic or depressive symptoms for most of the day, nearly every day, for at least one or two weeks. Sometimes symptoms are so severe that the person cannot function normally at work, school, or home.

(Source: www.NIMH.NIH.gov/Health)

Symptoms of Generalized Anxiety Disorder

People with generalized anxiety disorder (GAD) go through the day filled with exaggerated worry and tension, even though there is little or nothing to provoke it. They anticipate disaster and are overly concerned about health issues, money, family problems, or difficulties at work. Sometimes just the thought of getting through the day produces anxiety. GAD is diagnosed when a person worries excessively about a variety of everyday problems for at least six months. People with GAD can't seem to get rid of their concerns, even though they usually realize that their anxiety is more intense than the situation warrants. They can't relax, startle easily, and have difficulty concentrating. Often they have trouble falling asleep or staying asleep.

Physical symptoms that often accompany the anxiety include fatigue, headaches, muscle tension, muscle aches, difficulty swallowing, trembling, twitching, irritability, sweating, nausea, lightheadedness, having to go to the bathroom frequently, feeling out of breath, and hot flashes.

(Source: www.NIMH.NIH.gov /Health)

Symptoms of Attention Deficit Hyperactivity Disorder

Inattention, hyperactivity, and impulsivity are the key behaviors of ADHD. It is normal for all children to be inattentive, hyperactive, or impulsive sometimes, but for children and young adults with ADHD, these behaviors are more severe and occur more often. To be diagnosed with the disorder, a person must have symptoms for six or more months and to a degree that is greater than others of the same age. Students who have symptoms of inattention may:

- Be easily distracted, miss details, forget things, and frequently switch from one activity to another
- Have difficulty focusing on one thing
- Become bored with a task after only a few minutes, unless they are doing something enjoyable

- Have difficulty focusing attention on organizing and completing a task or learning something new
- Have trouble completing or turning in homework assignments, often losing things (e.g., pencils, assignments) needed to complete tasks or activities
- Not seem to listen when spoken to
- Daydream, become easily confused, and move slowly
- Have difficulty processing information as quickly and accurately as others
- Struggle to follow instructions

(Source: www.NIMH.NIH.gov/Health)

About Self-Injurers

Every year I get flooded with mail from students who hurt themselves. They cut, puncture, and cause physical self-harm. The intense physical pain can cover up the emotional pain of feeling lonely, angry, hopeless, unloved, or excluded. Self-injurers may also have an eating disorder or an alcohol or drug problem, or may have been victims of abuse. While most self-injurers don't want to commit suicide, sometimes the injuries can lead to illness or accidental death. Here are signs that a friend might be self-injuring:

- Cuts or scars on the arms or legs
- Hiding cuts or scars by wearing long-sleeved shirts or pants, even in hot weather
- Making poor excuses about how the injuries happened

(Source: www.NIMH.NIH.gov/Health)

Bottom Line

The happy news about depression and other serious mental health issues: there's more help than ever before to help you manage and get beyond these issues. It's confidential, part of tuition, and can help you the rest of your life.

Tip #101
Sexual Assault

The Tip
Tell someone.

The Story
I was a victim of sexual assault one year ago. I cannot stress enough that you must seek help immediately, because it is vital to your state of being. I didn't tell my parents for a year, and it was my biggest regret. In short, I went crazy and spiraled into a deep depression. I needed help, but I was too afraid to ask. Do not make the mistakes that I made. Do not wait for months to go to therapy and build back everything that was taken away from you. Do not become a victim, become a survivor. Be strong and tell someone. Just one person. Trust me, it changes everything.

—sophomore, college withheld

> You Are
> Never Alone
> Visit www.NotAlone.gov

* * *

I'm not trying to freak you out, but bad things can happen on college campuses. The National College Women Sexual Victimization Study estimated that between one in four and one in five college women experience completed or attempted rape during their college years. Most of the time, it's with someone the victim knows. Some of the time, alcohol is involved. Whatever the circumstances are, it's never the victim's fault. It's never, never, never your fault (see Tip #78 for more on this).

> ### Beware
> **Acquaintance Rape**
> 84 percent of sexual assault victims know their assailants.
>
> **Alcohol and Sexual Assault**
> Over 90 percent of all sexual assaults involve alcohol.
>
> —U.S. Department of Justice

While there are things you can do to minimize your risk, sometimes it just happens. Still, these are some things to keep in mind:

- Never go home with a stranger.
- Never take open cups or drinks from a stranger.
- Never let your friends go home with a stranger. Watch out for your friends and do not let them do something with someone that you think is unsafe.

> "When going out with friends to bars or parties, never leave without everybody you came in with, and keep track of each other throughout the evening."
>
> —college withheld

- Never walk home alone (even on a safe, small campus).
- Never ignore your gut feeling.
- Never be afraid to defend yourself.
- Never be afraid of insulting someone or being rude if you sense danger.

If someone you know has been sexually assaulted, or if you've been sexually assaulted, go to the hospital and get examined. You can decide to pursue legal charges later, but first, get help. Call your local hospital, call a local crisis hotline, or call the RAINN hotline (in the U.S., call 1-800-656-HOPE). They have an online hotline too: www.RAINN.org.

A resource that comes highly recommended is the book *I Never Called It Rape* by Ellen Beattie. Find support, take time to heal, and then if you're strong enough, you can help other victims on their journey toward recovery. For those men who are victims of sexual assault—it happens to men too—get help and seek support.

If you are a victim or survivor, or helping someone in that situation, go to NotAlone.gov to get the resources and information you need. You can also call the National Sexual Assault Hotline at 1-800-656-HOPE.

Another way to prevent sexual assault is to be an active bystander. If you see or hear someone in a potentially dangerous situation, stop it before it happens. Think of the following 4 Ds (from Vassar College: savp.vassar.edu/prevention/bystander-intervention.html).

1. *Direct:* Step in and address the situation directly. This might look like saying, "That's not cool. Please stop." or "Hey, leave them alone." This technique tends to work better when the person that you're trying to stop is someone who knows and trusts you. It does not work well when drugs or alcohol are being used because someone's ability to have a conversation with you about what is going on may be impaired, and they are more likely to become defensive.

2. *Distract:* Distract either person in the situation to intervene. This might look like saying, "Hey, aren't you in my Spanish class?" or "Who wants to go get pizza at Bacios?" This technique is especially useful when drugs or alcohol are being used because people under the influence are more easily distracted than those who are sober.

3. *Delegate:* Find others who can help you to intervene

From the White House (cont'd.)

7. If you see someone who is too intoxicated to consent, enlist their friends to help them leave safely.

8. Recognize the potential danger of someone who talks about planning to target another person at a party.

9. Be aware if someone is deliberately trying to intoxicate, isolate, or corner someone else.

10. Get in the way by creating a distraction, drawing attention to the situation, or separating them.

11. Understand that if someone does not or cannot consent to sex, it's rape.

12. Never blame the victim.

—www.itsonus.org

in the situation. This might look like asking a friend to distract one person in the situation while you distract the other ("splitting" or "defensive split"), asking someone to go sit with them and talk, or going and starting a dance party right in the middle of their conversation. If you didn't know either person in the situation, you could also ask around to see if someone else does and check in with them. See if they can go talk to their friend, text their friend to check in, or intervene.

4. *Delay:* For many reasons, you may not be able to do something right in the moment. For example, if you're feeling unsafe or if you're unsure whether or not someone in the situation is feeling unsafe, you may just want to check in with the person. In this case, you can combine a distraction technique by asking the person to use the bathroom with you or go get a drink with you to separate them from the person that they are talking with. Then, this might look like asking them, "Are you okay?" or "How can I help you get out of this situation?" This could also look like texting the person, either in the situation or after you see them leave and asking, "Are you okay?" or "Do you need help?"

And to all those who are doing the assaulting—just stop. If you can't ask for consent, you can't have sex. If you've been drinking, you can't consent or ask for consent. When in doubt, don't do it. The burden of proof when it comes to sexual assault can be low on college campuses. For example, if you put your hands on a body part without asking first and he or she says NO—that can be assault. ALWAYS ask before touching. ALWAYS ask before kissing. ALWAYS ask before getting physical. Make it sexy and whisper in his or her ear, "Is it okay to put my hand here…" And wait for him or her to say or signal YES before putting it there. If you don't know the answer is clearly YES, you MUST stop. Otherwise, you can call it what you want, but the law calls it assault.

Bottom Line

Sadly, it can happen to you (men and women). Be aware. And should something bad happen, get help. And again, when it comes to sexual assault, I can't say it enough: it's NEVER, NEVER, NEVER the survivor's fault. Never.

Tip #102
To Transfer or Not to Transfer

The Tip
Try to make it work—you might be surprised what you discover.

The Story
I came to college ready to transfer, but found something great here. In high school, I was hoping to go to Ohio State University, but didn't get in. I was really depressed, but figured I'd go here and then transfer after a year.

This has been an awesome surprise. It's the opposite of what I thought I had wanted before leaving for college.

I've been so surprised how much I like the personal attention of a smaller college. It has helped me to develop close relationships with my professors. My religion professor has become a mentor and friend. I have dinner with his family. I tried to make it work, and I haven't left. I found what I was looking for here without ever knowing what it was that I wanted. It's important to try to make it work before giving up on a college.

—senior, Marian College

* * *

Take a good look around—according to ACT, Inc., about one in four students who start college will not return to the same school their sophomore year. Only about a quarter of students attending community colleges get their two-year degree within three years. Transferring or dropping out happens. I never planned on it happening to me, but it did. Like breaking up with a beautiful girl, I rejected my first college. It wasn't her, it was me.

> "I really wanted to transfer because I didn't really like any of the people I was meeting, but all of that changed when I met this sophomore guy in my dorm."
> —freshman, Bucknell University

No, that's not just a line. I mean it. It was the timing. I just never found my place. I knew what I needed. I knew what I wanted. I wanted and needed a fresh start. And with that, I transferred to Indiana University and began a relationship that hasn't stopped.

It wasn't until my second college experience that I learned how to get comfortable with the uncomfortable that is the college experience. I never knew. Had someone told me to be patient, find my places, and find people in my corner, I wouldn't have transferred. Had someone told me that college can naturally be uncomfortable at times and shared everything in these pages, would I have stayed put? Then again, if my experience never happened the way it did, there would be no *Naked Roommate*.

Before transferring, make sure that you're transferring for the right reasons. If you're patient, find your places, and find people in your corner and it's not the right fit—transferring might be the answer. If it's not the right fit socially, emotionally, physically, financially, or

"I transferred five times before finding what I finally wanted."
—junior, Clemson University

academically, figure out what isn't right and where you can thrive. Make sure you know exactly why you're leaving and what will be different at your next school. Identify your people and places on your next campus before leaving. Otherwise, like bad body odor, you risk having the same problems follow you from campus to campus. One student I spoke with at Clemson University who had transferred five times finally realized that the problem wasn't the college—the problem was her. She came to the conclusion that what she was looking for wasn't at one particular college—it was inside herself. Then again, you might find that college itself isn't the right fit. That's cool. It happens.

Avoid transferring to run from a problem or to run to a place because it's in your comfort zone. It takes time to make your current school comfortable. Also, make sure that you're transferring to a college that will accept your transfer hours. If the academic office at the college you're considering gives you a hard time, plead your case.

Transferring all your credit hours can be the difference between graduating in four, five, or six years.

Transferring to a new campus: when you arrive at your new school, take advantage of all the orientation and welcome events. Even if you've experienced them all once before during your first freshman year, do it again. The students and professionals you'll meet are the people who will make your new college home and, should you have a tough time adjusting, you'll know of people you can lean on along the way. A lot of transfer students have a hard time adjusting. One of the biggest complaints is that you feel old. You feel like everyone already has friends. You're not eighteen and feel out of place. My advice—get over yourself, get involved, and get comfortable with the uncomfortable. Reread the first chapter of this book and apply daily. Give your classmates permission to be younger and more immature, and give yourself permission to be older and wiser. Put yourself in rooms with upperclassmen and take on leadership positions. Get a job that can help you meet people. Use your age and wisdom to help guide and support other students. Give people time to get to know you, and be open to meeting new people. And do it all fast because, unlike other first-year students, you only have two years on campus.

Attention Transfer Students

You are smarter, more experienced, and wiser than the others. Get involved fast and give people time to get to know you. You are intimidating not because you're older, but because you know more and have more life experience.

Considering Transferring Because of...

- *Financial reasons?* Make sure that you've talked to the financial aid office and pleaded your case. Also, investigate scholarships, grants, and work-study programs.
- *Academic reasons?* Make sure you're really leaving to find a better program and that you're not just using it as an excuse to leave an uncomfortable situation. Also, make sure you know what academic credits can and cannot be taken with you (think five-year-plus plan).
- *Social reasons?* Make sure you find people who can support, guide, and help you. There are people you pay, people who volunteer, and people you ask. Make sure you have places where you can do things you love to do once you arrive on campus (for example, if you want to debate, shop around for the best debate program).
- *Emotional reasons?* Make sure you have a therapist, counselor, or professional in your corner. When you leave for your new college, make sure you know why it will be different and what you'll do differently once you get there.
- *Physical reasons?* Where you live, work, play, and pray can matter. If you need to be closer to home, make sure you still have your places and people on campus. Don't just go back to the life you lived in high school.

When Arriving on Campus after Transferring...

- *Get involved in all new student activities.* Don't think you're not included or too old to participate. Pretend you're a first-year student. Feel young again.
- *Use your academic advisor.* See if you can find academic clubs and activities on campus to help meet people and enrich your academics.
- *Meet your professors.* Get help before you need it. Considering that you're older and wiser, you should know that knowing your professors will help you succeed. And it can help you find mentors, jobs, and opportunities on campus.
- *Live in a residence hall.* If possible, choose to live in a living and learning community where you can live and learn with students. Be in the middle of the action.
- *Don't waste time.* You don't have as much time to find your place. Therefore, map out a path and follow it before you arrive on campus.
- *Consider getting a job on campus.* One of the best ways to meet people is to work with them. Work in a busy spot on campus and you will find yourself busy and involved.
- *Get over yourself.* Yes, you are older, but wiser. Use your age and experience as an asset. People might be intimidated by you because you're not as immature. Give them time to see that you can be just as immature at times too (I know you can).

Bottom Line

Know exactly why you're transferring. Otherwise, you might just transfer the problem to another campus, because the problem might just be you.

Tip #103
Safe, Schmafe

The Tip

Never walk home late at night alone.

The Story

After three years of walking around on my own, something happened. One night, after having one too many drinks and getting split up from my friends at a campus bar, I decided to walk home on my own. On the way through a not-very-good area, a man came out of nowhere (he had probably been visible the whole time, but I never noticed him), grabbed my arm, and tried to pull me off the street. Everything after that is kind of blurry. I know I ran and got away, but by the time I got home, I was sobbing and scared. This was an hour that I can't account for. All that happened is that some guy scared the hell out of me, but in the intoxicated state I was in, it could have been so much worse. No, I never walked home alone again. Now, I'll call a cab or cling to the people I'm with.

—senior, University of Minnesota–Twin Cities

✳ ✳ ✳

Suppose you were crazy (this assumes you're not crazy) and you were looking to catch people off guard. You might consider heading to a college campus. It's the place where most people walk around with a false sense of security, and often in a reduced state of alertness. And it's not psychos that are the main concern—consider the drunks and possible sex offenders who go to college. On campus, there is often the "it will never happen to me" mind-set, but it's going to happen to someone. Who's to say it's not going to be you? I'm not trying to make you paranoid, but don't give anyone the benefit of the doubt. Nice people are often not-so-nice people in disguise.

How Safe Is Your Campus? Look It Up and Get the Facts

All schools receive federal funding that requires them to list their crime stats. Look up your school by visiting OPE.ed.gov/Security.

While I'm a huge fan of technology, I do think there can be such a thing as TMA (too much access). See, I'm the guy who people write to for advice. I know what people are thinking and what they're doing while you're not watching. Always assume that there are people who are watching you (right now someone is watching you—look around, see, look again). When I say watching, I don't mean looking at you from across the room (although that might be happening too). I mean they are looking at your Facebook info, checking your Tweets, reading your blogs, seeing what you pin on Pinterest, watching where you are via some kind of social networking GPS service, or googling your name and finding pictures and mentions of you in blogs and other places. There are people who can see your schedule, relationship status, moods, pictures, videos, and movements without you EVER realizing it. Most of these

people are harmless, but some are up to no good. And that's enough reason to be vigilant. So, before you post personal info, think about the creepiest people on campus having access to it and using it for something that would make you uncomfortable. Yes, set your privacy settings. Sure, choose to be discreet. But posting "My roommate is out of town" or "I'm bored and alone" is just an invitation for the wrong people to find you.

If there is one class you should take in college, it's a self-defense class (for women and for men). A lot of campuses offer them as electives. Sometimes they're not affiliated with the college or university. You'll see them advertised on campus kiosks. (A great idea is to host a course as a residence hall program or sorority event.) I have friends who took part in one of these programs while at Northwestern University in Evanston, Illinois. It was the IMPACT program. Sessions take place over two weekends. Participants train and are involved in simulated attacks to test their skills. If you have the opportunity to take a self-defense class as an elective, take it. Another great resource is Girls Fight Back. There's a book, a website, and a training program (they can even come to your campus). I've known the founder, Erin Weed, for years, and she's amazing. Check it out: www.GirlsFightBack.com. The more difficult of a target you are to a potential assailant, the less desirable a victim you become. And please—AVOID fights. Every year I read stories about college students who get stabbed or shot in late-night fights. The way to win the fight is to walk away.

I never thought it would happen to me, but it did. I was mugged—at gunpoint. (Yes, it makes it so much more dramatic, but it's true, there was a gun.) I was walking through a safe college neighborhood with a friend one night. We were one block off of a busy street. A man walked by us and pretended to go into an apartment. He then started following us. We moved faster. He started to move faster. Being the helpful guy that I am, I turned around to ask him if he needed some help with something. That's when he pulled out a gun. He said, "This is a stickup." (Yes, he actually used that line, which indicated that he was not a very creative mugger, but I didn't mention this to him.) He appeared nervous, just a little less nervous than me. My friend was about ten steps ahead of me and kept walking. The guy told me to get on the ground. I was lying facedown on the cold concrete

Bad Things Happen Alone

Bad things tend to happen more often while walking alone. People who walk in groups tend to avoid problems. Don't walk alone. Do not walk home alone. Hey, no walking by yourself. What I'm saying is NEVER WALK HOME ALONE!!!!!!!

sidewalk. He ripped my chain off, took my wallet, and told me to shut the (insert expletive) up. Like a true amateur, he finished his mugging by directing me to count to one hundred. I started counting and heard a car pull up and a door close. He was gone. When I got to twenty-five, it was all over. I lost $28, my innocence, and a pair of underwear (I got nervous). Actually, I'm kidding about the underwear, but it did scare the crap out of me. I never thought it could happen to me. We never do.

Bottom Line
Yeah, it happens to people like us.

Tip #104
Commuting? Words to Take with You

The Tip
If you are a commuter student, make an effort to join a club or activity on campus. Also, make friends with people in the dorms; it gives you a place to crash for the night.

The Story
I don't feel excluded, but I need to branch out a little more. I'd like to have more friends in different disciplines. I get to campus at 7:30 a.m. and stay until 4:00 p.m. I joined choir even before getting there. I have a lot in common with the people in the music building. It's fun to get to know a lot of people. I'm taking all sorts of classes and I'm talking to all the people in my classes. I have so many people I can

say hi to. And one of my friends from high school lives in the dorms, so I can crash there. I have requested permission to do so and it was happily granted. I was hanging out there and the friend I know from high school's friend came by and we ended going to a party. And now when I see her on campus we talk a lot, and I talk to her friends (who happen to be in music). I also play pool in the pool room. That helps.

—freshman, Mesa State College

* * *

Commuting can go both ways—it has its perks, but it presents some unique challenges.

First, you have to get to and from campus. Then you need to study for classes (making it that much harder to study with other students in class). Then you need to figure out how to feel like you're a part of campus. Things like seeing a professor during office hours aren't always so simple. Getting involved in clubs, activities, and organizations needs to be planned. On top of that, a lot of commuters have other responsibilities—a job, children, or other people to take care of at home. College becomes more like a place to visit or work than a home away from home. Unlike students who live on campus, commuters need to go that extra mile (sometimes fifty miles a day) to get involved and feel connected to campus life. You must find your places and

> "Every time I'm in the student center, waiting for my mom to pick me up, I meet people. Commuting makes it harder to feel connected to campus. I haven't experienced the total college experience. I need my independence to grow."
>
> —sophomore, University of Houston

people on campus to make connections. Consider college like a job. Get there early and stay late. Make it your home away from home. Make getting involved outside the classroom mandatory. The longer you are physically on campus, the faster and better the chances you will find your connections. You might even find a friend who can let you crash on campus.

If possible, try one more time to explore ways to live on campus. Talk to an advisor in the financial aid office and see if you can find a way to make it work. You don't even need to live on campus every day and night. If grant money or scholarships are not available, and a student loan is out of the question, consider becoming a resident assistant (free room and board). Talk to whoever handles RAs in the residence life office. If living on campus just isn't going to happen, find out if there are any jobs on campus that can help with the expenses. If you have to work—and most commuters need to work—at least try to work on or close to campus.

> ### Parents and Commuting
>
> Share the section on commuting from *The Naked Roommate: For Parents Only*. This will help them see how they can support and encourage you to get involved on campus.

This way you can make friends with people who live on campus. They can be your connection to campus life and even offer you a place to crash. If a job isn't something that excites you, then make it a point to stay on campus as long as possible. Get on campus

"Commuters want to get involved, but don't always know how. They need to know their resources better than students who are living on campus do."
—Director of Commuter Affairs

early and stay all day. Treat it like a job. Make it required to get involved with at least one organization or activity.

One way to feel connected on campus is to seek out commuters. There is often a club or organization for them. By connecting with commuters, especially the upperclassmen, you can meet people with whom you have something in common and can map out strategies for how to get the most out of college life.

Attention First-Generation Students

First-generation students are students who are the first in their family to attend college. You guys and girls are often the most at risk of not making it to graduation (scary, I know). Whether you're commuting or living on campus, make sure you seek out people on campus who can help you and advise you during the college process. Because your family members haven't been there and done it, it's a MUST to seek out people on campus who can help you along the way. You can find mentors and assistance in the new-student office, multicultural centers (whatever your ethnic roots, there should be a group on campus), the counseling center, and in the classroom. You can also connect with other students in the Naked Roommate forums (www.NakedRoommate.com).

Bottom Line

Commuters have to go that extra mile (or one-hundred-plus miles) to get involved. If you must commute, try to go to class, work, and hang out on campus. Find a few good friends and find a place to crash.

Tip #104.1
Community College: A Smart and Less Expensive Road

The Tip
Never let anyone tell you community college is a waste of time.

The Story
I chose to attend community college for two years before I transferred to Michigan State University. I was in the honors program, ended up with a full scholarship, and got my associate's degree. I had a much easier time coming to a Big Ten school and actually understanding what was going on. I saved about $40,000 and have a degree to fall back on if I need to.

—junior, Michigan State University

* * *

Considering that more college students than ever before are going to community college (3.4 million 18–24-year-olds), you need to have a tip of your own. For some of you, attending community college is your first choice. For others, it's the only choice due to financial, family, or other reasons.

After talking to hundreds of community college students and professionals over the years, I can tell you with absolute confidence that community college can be the most surprising, worthwhile, financially rewarding,

Naked Tips on How to Have the Best Community College Experience

- Attend all orientation/new student events.
- Get to know your instructors the first few weeks.
- Stay on campus during the day.
- Work on campus if possible.
- Participate in at least two club activities or organizations.
- Do something on campus without your high school friends.
- Get a part-time job related to your studies.
- Meet with your financial aid advisor regularly.
- Save your money.
- Stay on campus and study.
- Form study groups in class and get together outside the classroom.
- Take public transportation (which makes it harder to leave campus, giving you more time to study and get involved).

and fulfilling experience of your academic career. It has a long list of perks. You will typically be in smaller classes, taught by teachers who are trained to teach (as opposed to researchers who are required to teach). You often have an easier time getting to know your instructors. You can get involved outside the classroom through athletics, clubs, organizations, band, leadership groups, honors divisions, student government, and academic opportunities. There are also part-time jobs and other opportunities that will shock you once you check into them. You have access to health services and professional services. You can get involved, find amazing professionals to help mentor you (who might also work in the community), and yes, you might even get to travel to conferences across the country for free. Most of the perks that I listed in chapters 5 and 7 are waiting for you if you want them. Another perk—there aren't as many people who get involved, so there are more opportunities for you to do so.

Because most students go to campus and go home, the few students who do get involved get to do a lot. The VERY best part: you can get all of this at a fraction of the cost. Then, once you complete your coursework, you can often be guaranteed entry into a four-year institution that you might never have been able to attend had you applied right out of college.

All that said, community college can have drawbacks. It can be like being in grades 13 and 14 of high school if you let it. It's way too easy to not get involved. It's simple to go to class, go home, and go to work. It's too easy to hang out with your high school friends. It can be way too comfortable. Unlike high school, you aren't required to stay on campus. And not being on campus as frequently means that opportunities to get involved in life beyond the classroom aren't as easy to find. Living at home can also be a challenge (for help with your parents, share the chapter on community colleges from *The Naked Roommate: For Parents Only* book with them). Between work, school, family obligations, friends, and relationships, it's easier to not get involved at a community college. Most students have NO CLUE just how many amazing opportunities are available.

> "My first year I didn't do anything and I hated it. My second year I got involved with the student ambassadors, student senate, work study, and student leadership academy. I've learned so much and traveled to Missouri and California. I'm going to be going to Mexico as part of a volunteer project."
> —sophomore, Ivy Tech Community College

Treat community college like a four-year school. Follow the tips in chapters 1 and 4. Check out *The Naked Roommate's First Year Survival Workbook*. Plan to arrive on campus in the morning and leave late at night. Treat school like a job. Pick two or three activities or organizations that interest you and get involved right away. Commit to them. Meet your instructors. Form study groups. Eat meals on campus. Find your people, find your places, and practice transitioning. Start with a positive attitude. Do all these things and you'll be shocked by what happens next. You'll have an awesome experience and be prepared to transfer to a four-year school. It all starts with being excited about this experience and taking advantage of life on campus.

> **Talk Money ASAP**
>
> Talk to your financial aid advisor ASAP. Discuss the master plan so you can use community college as a way to secure scholarships, grants, and the lowest interest loans.

Bottom Line
Treat your community college experience like a four-year institution, but only stick around for two years (three at the most).

Tip #105
Diversity: Sexual, Religious, Racial—It's All Good

The Tip
Have your own experiences before you pass judgment on other people based on their skin color, religion, or origin.

The Story

I had never met an Indian person before coming to college. I know that sounds weird, but it's true. I met her in Interpersonal Communication my freshman year. She sat next to me and we were assigned to work together on a group project. We got along well and became friends. A couple weeks later, she took me out to dinner to an Indian restaurant. It was so cool. She told me all about her culture. She had never met anyone who was Jewish before. After we went to dinner, she was like, "My parents don't really like Jewish people, but I'll tell them that I do." It was a little weird to hear that her parents wouldn't like me and didn't even know me—I've always been friends with everyone. I guess I can understand a little bit. I have a few friends who only hang out with white people. They're not rude. They just don't make an effort. They've grown up that way and are stuck in their ways. It's sad— it's really sad.

—freshman, Southern Indiana University–Evansville

***

Love who you are and love others. If you don't know who you are, figure out what you love and who you want to be. "Diversity" is a word thrown around college campuses. It can have a range of meanings. My definition is straightforward. It's appreciating differences and being open to learning about something unfamiliar. The problem with new students and diversity is that everything is so unfamiliar during the first year that it makes dealing with different people, lifestyles, religions, and cultures a little overwhelming at times. The knee-jerk reaction is to run the other way when faced with diversity issues. It's a normal and natural reaction. But try not to run away to your comfort zone. Instead, stand still. Take a good look at what you're faced with and then try to learn from it. Experience it firsthand.

> "It's not always like the brochures. It helps to seek diversity. It can be easy to stay in your own group of friends. At a big college, people tend to stick close to each other. Having a part-time job that puts me in the middle of campus has helped me to branch out and find different friends from different places."
> —junior,
> University of Wisconsin–Green Bay

Whoever you are and however you define yourself, make sure you find people who can support, guide, and love you. Find similar people who identify with you. Be supported and offer support. And then—this is the most important part—find people who are different from you. Give them time to get to know you, your culture, sexual orientation, identity, values, personality, and all the things that make you someone worth loving. If you're supported and have people in your corner, it will be easier to be patient and allow others time to get to know you.

Homecoming with an LGBTQ Twist

"October 26, 2012—Northern Arizona University shook up the traditional homecoming model for gender roles last weekend, when a woman was crowned king and a male, queen. That juxtaposition, designed to be more inclusive of diverse sexual identities, will be mirrored at Arizona State's homecoming customs this weekend."

—www.USAToday.com/story /news/nation/2012/10/26 /arizona-colleges-home coming-gender/1660689

If someone in your world chooses to be hateful, hurtful, or hostile—distance yourself. Quietly walk the other way. But don't stop meeting other people. Make an effort to get to know people who are different from you. Push your boundaries. Experience diversity. It's a chance to learn about things you never imagined. It's an opportunity to learn about yourself, and another person's culture, lifestyle, or religion. These conversations, experiences, and moments are lessons that leave a lifetime impression on you and the people you meet.

Bottom Line

When something makes you want to run, ask yourself what you're running from. If the answer is based on stereotypes and secondhand information, stop running. Experience it for yourself. When you do, you'll be shocked what you discover.

Harlan's Tip Sheet

Naked People, Places, and Resources

Campus Counseling Center

- Free counseling is often available for any of the issues mentioned here. It's confidential, and if you exceed the number of free sessions you're allotted (assuming there is a limit), you can usually get help on a sliding scale (which means you pay what you can afford).

From one-on-one counseling to group therapy, talk to the people who can help.

- Recreational Center/Gym/Field House
  Inquire about organized classes to help you stay in shape. If your school doesn't have a recreational center or gym, ask about student discounts at the gyms near campus.
- Sexual Assault Hotline or Counselor
  Check to see if your campus has counselors available. You can always dial 911 or call your local hospital.
- Nutritionist/Registered Dietician
  See if your health center has a nutritionist on campus to help with balancing your diet and managing your weight.

Addiction

- Alcoholics Anonymous
  Website: www.AA.org
- Gambling Anonymous
  Website: www.GamblersAnonymous.org
- Sex Addicts Anonymous
  Website: www.SAA-Recovery.org

Depression

- National Hopeline Network
  24-Hour Suicide Hotline: 1-800-SUICIDE (1-800-784-2433)
- Half of Us
  Website: www.HalfofUs.com
- National Mental Health Information Center
  Website: www.MentalHealth.gov (to more links)
  Facebook: www.Facebook.com/SAMHSA
  Twitter: www.Twitter.com/SAMHSAgov

- ULifeline
  Website: www.ULifeline.org
- The Jed Foundation
  Website: www.JedFoundation.org
  Facebook: www.Facebook.com/JedFoundation
  Twitter: www.Twitter.com/JedFoundation
- National Institute of Mental Health
  Website: www.NIMH.NIH.gov/Health
  Facebook: www.Facebook.com/NIMHgov
  Twitter: www.Twitter.com/NIMHgov

Sexual Assault

- RAINN—the Rape, Abuse & Incest National Network
  is the nation's largest anti–sexual assault organiza
  tion. There's now an online hotline too.
  Website: www.RAINN.org
  Facebook: www.Facebook.com/RAINN01
  Twitter: www.Twitter.com/RAINN01
- National Sexual Assault Hotline
  1-800-656-HOPE (1-800-656-4673)
- CDC Website with Links
  Website: www.CDC.gov
  Facebook: www.Facebook.com/CDC
  Twitter: www.Twitter.com/CDCgov
- National Domestic Violence Hotline and Website
  1-800-799-7233 or 1-800-787-3224 (TTY)
  Website: www.thehotline.org
  Facebook: www.Facebook.com/NationalDomestic
  ViolenceHotline
  Twitter: www.Twitter.com/NDVH

Anorexia/Bulimia/Eating Disorders

- The National Women's Health Organization
  Website: www.WomensHealth.gov
  Facebook: www.Facebook.com/HHSOWH
  Twitter: www.Twitter.com/WomensHealth
- National Eating Disorders Association
  Website: www.NationalEatingDisorders.org
- National Association of Anorexia and Associated Disorders
  Website: www.ANAD.org
  Facebook: www.Facebook.com/ANADHelp
- The Body Dysmorphic Disorder Foundation
  Website—a comprehensive site for victims of BDD
  Website: www.TheBDDFoundation.org

Safety on Campus

- Girls Fight Back
  Website: www.GirlsFightBack.com
  Facebook: www.Facebook.com/GirlsFightBack
  Twitter: www.Twitter.com/GirlsFightBack

Diversity Issues

- On campus, contact the office of the dean of students.
- ACLU: American Civil Liberties Union
  Website: www.ACLU.org
- PFLAG: Parents, Families and Friends of Lesbians and Gays
  Website: www.PFLAG.org
  Facebook: www.Facebook.com/PFLAG
  Twitter: www.Twitter.com/PFLAG

College: A Higher Education

It's Almost Time to Say Good-bye

Dear Harlan,

How is college? Is it fun like everyone says it is, or will I want to come back home? How was your first year in college? Was it hard? Were you scared to finally be on your own? Did you have a nice roommate? Did you have trouble getting to know people? Was it difficult to get around campus? How did you know if you picked the right school to go to? How will I know? As you can see I have a lot of questions on my mind. I would be grateful if you could help me out.

—Baby Love

Dear Baby Love,

I feel like I'm back in college during finals...

So, Baby Love, I think at this point in the book, I've covered most of your questions. The answer is that so many of these questions you ask can't be answered until you get to campus. I can tell you more about my experience, but my experience isn't going to be your experience. What was normal for me might not be normal for you. But when it comes to the big picture of what's to be expected, I think you can leave for school with a good sense of what's ahead of you. And what awaits you is a story yet to be written—a story filled with unexpected twists, wild turns, new emotions, new experiences, different kinds of people, laughs, tears, smiles, and memories that will last you a lifetime. I hope this book helped you, and I hope it will continue to help you during your college adventure. And then, I hope you'll share what you've learned with other students (see Tip #107).

ANSWER KEY:

- College is a once-in-a-lifetime experience.
- It's fun, but not always happy fun, if you know what I mean.
- My first year was hard, but that's what helped me to write this book.
- I was so scared, I tried to keep my long-distance girlfriend so I wouldn't be alone—until she dumped me.
- My roommate was nice (nicer when he was messed up), but we didn't connect.
- I had trouble really getting to know people, but that takes time.
- Getting around campus was easy, once I figured out how to get around campus.
- If you can't be true to yourself, then it's not the right college. That's the test.

Tip #106
The U of No Regrets

The Tip
As awful and painful as mistakes can be, they're the reason we grow to be better people. I wouldn't change a thing.

The Story
I sat for a long time trying to figure out what it is that I would do differently when looking back at my college life. If I were to change the past, and erase all the trials and tribulations that I've experienced in life, as nice as that would be, I wouldn't have turned out the way that I am today. When it comes down it, as painful as the past might have been at times, each experience has been necessary to help me grow into the person I am today. And that's not something I'd ever want to change.

—sophomore, Suffolk County Community College

* * *

I try to live my life by a thing I call The No-Regret Rule. Whenever I have to make a difficult decision, I ask myself the following question: "What is it that feels right for me right now, at this very moment in my life?" I ask myself that question because I know that I will change over the years, and there's a good chance that later in life I'll look back at a decision I made and think, *I should have done that differently…*

We all do it.

As your college journey is about to begin, or as it continues, you'll have a lot of tough choices to make—who will be your friends, how to get involved on campus, how to pay for school, how you deal with difficult roommates, what major to pick, to hook up or not to hook up, to get into to drugs or not, to remain a virgin or lose your virginity, to pledge a fraternity or sorority, to drink or not to drink, to get help if you're feeling down and depressed or not—the questions will swirl around your head day after day. And you're going to have to make decisions. When you do, this book will be here.

"Just chill—it will all come together."
—senior, Allegheny College

The purpose of *The Naked Roommate* is to help you to make the best decisions—no-regret decisions. I only hope the information throughout this book will help guide you to the best choices for you. I hope what I've written will help you. I hope the tips and stories shared from students will help you. I hope the resources, support services, facts, stats, websites, and hotlines will help you. The information in this book is all about helping you to get the most out of college life. It's the book I wish someone had given to me. Now you have it and more information than any college student has ever had as part of college life. So now, when faced with a new and uncomfortable situation, ask yourself the question, "Is this the right choice for me?" you'll know more than you ever wanted to know or needed to know to make the best choice throughout your college experience—and beyond.

Bottom Line

Be true to yourself. Be your personal best. If you don't know who you are or what is your best, figure it out. Do this and leave college with more than a degree—an understanding of what you love and what you don't love. Then you can spend the rest of your life doing what you love to do. There's nothing greater you can take with you from college than this—it's called passion.

Tip #107
Your Tip Goes Here

The Tip
Enter your tip here.

_____
_____
_____
_____

The Story
Enter your story here.

If your tip is already in the book, send me your story that corresponds to a current tip. Don't hold back any details! The more information, the better the tip and story.

_____
_____
_____
_____
_____
_____

_____

_____

_____

_____

As you go through your college experience, keep this space in mind. When something throws you, shocks you, depresses you, confuses you, scares you, makes you laugh, makes you smile, or makes you think, "I wish someone told me…", send the tip and story to me via email to harlan@helpmeharlan.com (subject: Naked Roommate Tip Seventh Edition). Thanks for sharing the nakedness!

The Naked Rear End

The Naked Roommate Online
www.NakedRoommate.com

Check out www.NakedRoommate.com and become a member of the "nicest" community for college students in the world. Seriously, if you're not a nice person, get some help, and come back later when you can be nice (I'm serious). This is a place where you can connect with other college students, ask questions, offer answers, or just read what everyone else is thinking. Once you start your college experience, you too can become a Naked Expert and offer advice to students looking for help. Please sign up and spread the word!

The Naked Roommate
www.NakedRoommate.com

The Naked Author
www.HarlanCohen.com

Naked Online Networking and Videos
Facebook, Twitter, YouTube, and Instagram

Facebook
www.Facebook.com/HelpMeHarlan
www.Facebook.com/NakedRoommate
www.Facebook.com/NakedRoommateForParents

Twitter
www.Twitter.com/NakedRoommate
www.Twitter.com/HarlanCohen
www.Twitter.com/NakedRoommateForParents

YouTube
www.YouTube.com/HarlanCohendotcom

Instagram
www.Instagram.com/HarlanCohen

The Naked Author Speaks
Keynotes, Workshops, and Live Events

Harlan is a professional speaker who has visited more than 400 college and high school campuses. Harlan speaks to students, parents, and professionals on a wide range of issues, ranging from college life, parenting, dating, relationships, consent, leadership, alcohol awareness, and risk-taking. His expertise, sharp humor, and ability to connect with audiences has made him a favorite presenter. Harlan's events can be customized to fit your needs and incorporate live music on the guitar (he sings), audience participation, and the latest stats, facts, and trends.

Harlan Can Host Your:
- New Student Event
- Parent Event
- Leadership Training & Development
- Residential Life Training
- Professional Development
- Greek Programs
- Dating/Alcohol Awareness Program
- Conference Keynotes
- Graduation Keynote

Visit www.HarlanCohen.com/Speaking for information regarding Harlan's events, programs, and keynotes. Watch Harlan's TEDx talk: www.HarlanCohen.com/tedx.

Naked Advice

Harlan is like Dear Abby, only younger, hairier, and a man. His syndicated Help Me, Harlan! advice column can be read in local daily and college newspapers around the globe and is distributed by King Features Syndicate.

If you would like to read Harlan's advice column in your local newspaper, please email your newspaper editor and demand that the paper run Help Me, Harlan! (Demand it nicely.) Also, feel free to send a note to syndication@helpmeharlan.com and we'll pass along the word for you. In the meantime, check out Harlan's columns on his websites and in newspapers across the country.

The Naked Author's Music
Listen and Download...

Harlan is proud to announce the release of his album *Fortunate Accidents*. Based on themes addressed in *The Naked Roommate* and in his syndicated Help Me, Harlan! advice column, this musical journey explores the complexities of love, loss, and life in a professional studio recording. *Fortunate Accidents* features such classics as:

- "My Roommate Stu"
- "The Chlamydia Jive"
- "Girl Walks Bye"
- "The Syphilis Song"
- "Open-Toed Sandals"

Sample songs by visiting www.NakedRoommate.com and www.reverbnation.com/HarlanCohen. *Fortunate Accidents* is available on Harlan's website, iTunes, and at CDBaby.com.

About the Naked Author
Once Upon a Time...

Harlan Cohen is a *New York Times* bestselling author of five books, a professional speaker, and syndicated advice columnist.

Harlan's writing career began at Indiana University's school newspaper, the *Indiana Daily Student*. He shifted his path toward advice after interning at *The Tonight Show with Jay Leno* in the summer of 1995. Harlan was inspired to begin writing his column after meeting a writer who had penned a similar column while in college. When he returned to campus, Harlan immediately launched his Help Me, Harlan! advice column. At first, he wrote questions and answers to himself. When he started to help himself, he knew he was good. Then real letters started rolling in. Harlan's balance of honest advice, helpful resources, and sharp humor turned the column into an instant success on and off campus. As the column spread, Harlan began writing books, speaking on college campuses, launching his websites, and creating original music to bring the topics addressed in his writing to life.

Harlan is the bestselling author of the books *The Naked Roommate: And 107 Other Issues You Might Run Into in College* (Sourcebooks), *The Naked Roommate: For Parents Only* (Sourcebooks), *The Naked Roommate's First Year Survival Workbook* (Sourcebooks), *Getting Naked: Five Steps to Finding The Love of Your Life (While Fully Clothed and Totally Sober)* (St. Martin's Press), *Dad's*

Expecting Too! (Sourcebooks), and *Campus Life Exposed: Advice from the Inside* (Peterson's). Harlan's writing has been featured in the *New York Times*, *Wall Street Journal Classroom Edition*, *Real Simple*, *Details* magazine, *Seventeen* magazine, *Psychology Today*, and hundreds of other newspapers and publications. King Features Syndicate distributes Harlan's Help Me, Harlan! advice column worldwide. He has been a guest on hundreds of radio and television programs, including the *Today Show*. Harlan is a professional speaker who has visited over 400 college campuses. He is an expert who addresses teen issues, college life, parenting, pregnancy, dating, relationships, consent, sex, no sex, rejection, risk-taking, leadership, women's issues, and a variety of other topics.

Harlan is the founder of the websites www.Naked Roommate.com and www.HarlanCohen.com. He is the producer and singer/songwriter on his album *Fortunate Accidents*.

He lives in Chicago, Illinois, with his wife (his lifelong naked roommate), three young children, and dog.

In his spare time he thinks about how little spare time he has (and then his spare time is over, leaving him thinking about how he squandered his spare time, eating up more spare time…). Hey, thanks for spending your time (spare or not) reading this book and this bio.

Psssssssssst, there's more. Check out The Naked Suite of products at the end of the book for more Nakedness.

Index

A

Abstinence
    alcohol, 339–341, 349–352
    drugs, 383–389
    sex, 299–301, 321

Abusive relationships, 281–282, 290–291

Academic advisors, 196, 230–233, 484

Academic department resources, 164, 166, 167, 245

Academic organizations, 156–159, 203

Academics. *See* Classes; Grades; Professors

Acid, 399

Active Minds, 467

Activities. *See* Extracurricular activities

Activities fairs, 167

Adderall, 382, 393–394, 402, 462

Addiction, 468–470
    academics and, 196, 372–373, 469–470
    alcohol, 196, 344, 372–377, 468–470, 500
    drugs, 382–383, 396, 398, 405–407, 468–470
    resources, 500
    sex, 303, 304, 337, 468–470, 500
    technology, 48, 56–57

ADHD (Attention Deficit Hyperactivity Disorder), 472–473
    See also Adderall

Advice column, Harlan's, 85, 291, 337, 513

Advisors
    academic, 196, 230–233, 484
    financial aid, 410, 416–419, 444, 491, 496
    Greek, 175, 187

AIDS, 314, 317, 319, 336

Alcohol, 339–377
    abstaining from, 339–341, 349–352
    academics and, 196, 209–210, 341–342, 348, 372–373, 374
    addiction, 120, 196, 344, 372–377, 468–470, 500
    consensual sex, 247, 304–305, 306, 358–362
    dating and, 250, 353–355, 361
    drink, definition of, 343
    drinking, reasons for, 344–345

F

G

I

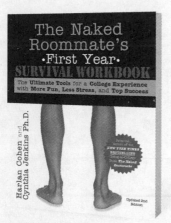

Get Your Hands on The NAKED Suite of Products

- *The Naked Roommate* book
- *The Naked Roommate's First Year Survival Workbook*
- *The Naked Roommate Instructor's Guide*
- *The Naked Roommate* speaking tour
- *The Naked Roommate* professional training (live seminar for instructors using the book as first year experience text)
- *The Naked Roommate* College Boot Camp for Students and Parents (www .NakedRoommateBootCamp.com)

You still reading?

So, I'm done. I've written enough. I have nothing left.

Please, put your shoes back on, button your pants, and get back to what you were doing before you got comfortable and started to read this book. Now, get going to college or to class or to work. I'm here if you need me. And just know that whatever happens or doesn't happen in college, you're never alone.

Have an amazing college experience!

Thanks,
Harlan